CURRENT R[illegible] IN EGYPTOLOGY 2009

Proceedings of the Tenth Annual Symposium

which took place at the

University of Liverpool, 7–9 January 2009

edited by

Judith Corbelli, Daniel Boatright and Claire Malleson

Oxbow Books
Oxford and Oakville

Published by
Oxbow Books, Oxford

ISBN 978-1-84217-412-8

This book is available direct from
Oxbow Books, Oxford

and

The David Brown Book Company
PO Box 511, Oakville, CT 06779, USA
(Phone: 860-945-9329; Fax: 860-945-9468)

or via our website

www.oxbowbooks.com

Cover: Image of Selket on the Coffin of Userhet, E512, Garstang Museum of Archaeology, School of Archaeology, Classics and Egyptology, University of Liverpool. Copyright Steven Snape.

Printed in Great Britain by
Hobbs the Printer, Totton, Hampshire

Contents

Symposium papers not included in this volume

Joanne Backhouse, University of Liverpool "What can Middle Kingdom faience figurines tell us about personal piety?"

Marsia Bealby, University of Birmingham, "Minoan-style Frescoes at Avaris."

Audrey Dégremont, Université Libre de Bruxelles. "Synthesis of the Assessments concerning the Reign of Thutmose IV."

Henning Franzmeier, Free University of Berlin, "Religious vs. material value – implications of the occurrence of some items within New Kingdom tomb equipment."

Amr Gaber, University of Durham, "The Children of Re revisited."

Todd Gillen, Macquarie University, Sydney, Australia, "Narrative texture and style at Medinet Habu."

Kenneth Griffin, University of Swansea, "An Analysis of a Curious Gateway Scene from the Temple of Ramesses II at Abydos."

Meg Gundlach, University of Swansea, "Shabtis of the Chief Lector-Priest Pedamenope."

Maarten Horn, University of Leiden, "Ornaments in Badarian to Early Gerzean Burials of the Qau-Matmar Region."

Joost Kramer, University of Leiden, "Symbolic meaning of the 'separation-scene' of Geb, Nut and Shu."

Steven Larkman, Royal College, "Viewpoint From Thebes During the War of Re-unification in the First Intermediate Period."

Dave Lightbody, University of Glasgow, "Circular symbolism in pharaonic funerary architecture."

Ahmed Mansour, Fayum University, "The Serabit el-Khadim Inscriptions: Formulaic Approach."

Margaret Maitland, University of Oxford, "Representation of social hierarchy in the Middle Kingdom tombs of Middle Egypt."

Claire Malleson, University of Liverpool, "The Medieval Islamic historical landscape of the Fayum (Egypt)."

Richard Mandeville, University of Liverpool, "Wage Accounting in Deir el-Medina"; Ahmed Mansour, Fayum University, "The Serabit el-Khadim Inscriptions: A Formulaic approach."

Massimilano Nuzzolo, University of Naples "L'Orientale", "The sun temples priestly staff: an overview of titles and cult practise through the epigraphic evidence."

Campbell Price, University of Liverpool, "Fishing for Statues": Re-evaluating Late Period Statuary from the Karnak Cachette."

F. Phelan, B. Stern & C.P. Heron, University of Bradford, "An investigation of the use of balsamic resins in ancient Egypt."

Arnaud Quertinmont, Charles de Gaul University Lille, "Chapels' Equipment of the Meroitic Necropolises, new methodological approaches."

Chloé C.D. Ragazzoli, University of Paris-Sorbonne, "Scribal self-fashioning in the New Kingdom : Hand and mouth in the Late Egyptian Miscellanies as emblems of scribal activity."

Gemma Renshaw, University of Swansea, "Third Intermediate Period Coffin Fragments in the Egypt Centre, Swansea."

Kim Ridealgh, University of Swansea, "The Problems in finding a Lost City at Thebes: An Analysis of Papyri BM10068."

Beverley Rogers, University of Swansea, "Collecting Egyptian Antiquities: the Reverend William MacGregor."

Sakura Sanada, University of Liverpool, "Pottery of Lower Egypt during the Neolithic and Early Bronze Age; a view from Sais."

Abeer El Shahawy, University of Montpellier, "The Final Judgement scenes in the Theban tombs of the New Kingdom."

Oli Smith, University of Manchester, "Paleopathology of Cranial Remains from the 'Elliot Smith Collection.'"

Nico Staring, University of Leiden, "Individualizing Old Kingdom tomb decoration: a comparative study of Giza and Saqqara."

Elena Valtorta, University of Basel, "The Ritualised Body: Body Treatment and Ritual Practice in Egyptian Predynastic Burials,"

Lara Weiss, Leiden University and Radboud University Nijmegen, "Practicing piety at Deir el-Medina: Evidence for a religious transformation at village level?"

Cordula Werschkun, University of Liverpool, "How does the Old Kingdom economy fit into economic theory?"

Introduction

The tenth Current Research in Egyptology (CRE) symposium took place at the University of Liverpool between the 7th and 9th January 2009. Bringing together 130 postgraduate and graduate students, lecturers and Egyptological enthusiasts, 45 papers and a number of posters were presented in the usual friendly and relaxed atmosphere that has become typical and unique to CRE.

The conference would not have been possible without the hard work, time and support of so many individuals and institutions. We should firstly like to express our heartfelt thanks to The School of Archaeology, Classics and Egyptology, The University of Liverpool Graduate School, the Higher Education Academy and the Garstang Museum for their financial support and providing the venues for the conference. We thank all those publishers who donated and were represented at the conference, namely Archaeopress, Oxbow Books, Peeters of Leuven, Rutherford Press and Shire Publications. For assistance on sourcing finance, and general advice we should like to thank Prof. Bruce Gibson, Prof. Tom Harrison, Dr Steven Snape and Lyn Hughes of the Higher Education Academy, and special thanks go to Vicky Gashe and Jackie Finch who gave us the benefit of their experience in organising and financing the previous CRE conference in Manchester.

In the organisation of the conference we owe a great debt of gratitude to our colleague, Cordula Werschkun, whose hard work and problem-solving skills were invaluable, and to all those (too numerous to name individually) who gave of their time to ensure the smooth-running of the event. We should also like to say a big thank you to Trillion Attwood for organising the conference meal, and to the Ego Restaurant for providing such fantastic hospitality.

The conference would not have been the success it undoubtedly was without the support of all those who participated, both as speakers and as visitors, and, in this regard, we would like to express our gratitude to the former organisers of the previous nine conferences who chaired sessions or sent words of encouragement. We thank you all sincerely for your presence in making it such an enjoyable and rewarding event.

Prior to the conference a number of ideas and suggestions were put forward regarding the CRE website, resulting in a few changes this year. Peter Robinson has dedicated a number of years to the upkeep of this facility and done a wonderful job and we should like to take this opportunity of thanking him for all his hard work and expertise. The mantle has now passed to Nicholas Wernick, an enthusiastic Egyptologist with a wealth of experience in website design and development.

We should like to express our gratitude to our keynote speaker, Emeritus Professor Kenneth Kitchen, and all those experts who gave of their time to peer-review the papers submitted for this volume and for their ongoing advice and recommendations.

This volume would not have been possible without the staff at Oxbow Books, in particular, Clare Litt and Val Lamb, who have had to cope with an inundation of emails on typesetting, formatting and corrections. Our sincere thanks go to them, and to Esme Hammerle who has coped with the initial Mac versus PC chaos! In the editing of this volume, care has been taken to preserve the individual styles and characteristics of the various authors, whilst at the same time maintaining consistency. The editors would like to thank you all for your co-operation.

Finally, we send our best wishes to the hosts of CREXI in Leiden. It is the first time the conference has moved outside the U.K. and demonstrates the close ties that the conference has forged between the different schools and departments within the Egyptological community at home and abroad. We wish CRE and all those involved the best of luck for the future and for the next successful ten years.

Judith Corbelli, Dan Boatright and Claire Malleson
November 2009

Crossing of the Lake Ritual

Eltayeb Abbas

Introduction

The representations on the walls of private tombs of the Old Kingdom include a ritualised crossing of a lake as a stage in the deceased's funeral procession from his house to the burial place. This crossing was accompanied by recitations of *s3ḫw* texts. The deceased's journey over the Lake of Knives in the New Kingdom Book of the Dead and Sun Hymns was also accompanied by recitations of ritual texts. The Lake of Knives was one of the places which the deceased as the sun god Re had to cross in his journey to the hereafter. Pictorial and textual evidence will be presented to show how the crossing of the lake in the Old Kingdom private tombs and in the Old and Middle Kingdoms texts can be related to the deceased's crossing over the Lake of Knives. This paper also investigates how the crossing of the lake can be compared with the crossing of the sun god Re over the waters of the sky, and how the recitations which accompanied the crossing of the lake mediate the deceased's passage over water.

Pictorial Evidence from Old Kingdom Private Tombs

Pictorial evidence comes from Old Kingdom Mastaba D 62 of the vizier Ptahhotep I at Saqqara. The deceased's funeral procession is depicted on the western wall of the pillared hall (Lepsius 1849–1856, pl. 101). In the middle register on this wall, a boat is depicted with a man designated as *wt* putting his hand on a shrine, while his second hand lies flat on his knee. Behind this man stands a helmsman. Above the two men is a text which reads:

> *m ḥtp m ḥtp ḫr Wsjr*
> In peace in peace before Osiris

In the front of the boat there is a man raising his right hand in recitation, and beneath him there are two men and two women depicted beating their chests. This gesture is called *hnw* and can be used for jubilation and praising of a god and mourning (Dominicus 1994, 61–5). Here it is not a sign of happiness, but a sign of grief for the loss of a deceased (Assmann & Bommas 2002, 14). *hnw* was accompanied by recitations of a lector priest, most probably the priest above the seated women and men as shown in Fig. 1.

The lower register shows on the left hand side, a helmsman, a seated woman, most probably symbolising a kite, and an embalmer. At the prow of a boat a man designated as *ẖrj-ḥbt* is shown putting his hand on his chest in *hnw* gesture. A woman beside him is designated as a kite (*ḏrt*). A label in front of them reads *s3ḫw* 'performing *s3ḫw*'. It is important here to note that the crossing is accompanied by recitations of *s3ḫw.*

Another instance is found in the tomb of In-Snefru-Ishetef at Dahshur (Fig. 2). A scene on

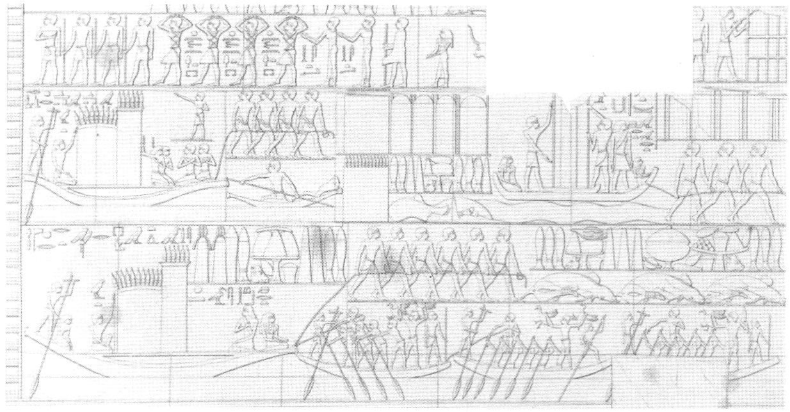

Figure 1. *Crossing the lake from the Mastaba of the vizier Ptahhotep I (After Lepsius 1842–1845, pl. 101).*

the upper register shows a boat with a shrine being towed across water (De Morgan 1903, pl. 22). The shrine most probably houses a statue of the deceased. At the prow of the boat sits a 'kite' or a 'mourner' (*ḏrt*), two undesignated men, and a lector priest with containers holding his equipment. The second *ḏrt* sits at the back of the boat near the helmsman. At the bottom, a boat seems to sail or rest on sand. Above the boat there is a label reading:

> *ḏꜣjt wrt*
> Crossing of the *Wrt*-boat

A 'kite' is represented facing a priest, who stands in a canopy and reads from a papyrus roll. There is also a 'kite' sitting at the back of the boat with a man designated as an embalmer (*wt*). The text accompanying the scene reads:

> *sšm ḥb m mw jn ẖrj-ḥbt jjmḥ*
> Conducting a ritual in water by the lector priest *Iimeh*

The rest of the scene shows three men towing a boat, offerings being presented and figures of men slaughtering an ox (Wilson 1944, 208).

Figure 2. *The funeral procession of In-Snefru-Ishetef at Dahshur (Drawn by Wilson 1944, pl XIV from De Morgan 1903, pl. 22).*

Figure 3. *The funeral procession of Hetepherakhti (After Mohr 1943, pl.1).*

In the second register in the first corridor on the north wall of the tomb chapel of Hetepherakhti, a shrine with a statue of the deceased is shown being transported to the tomb on a papyrus boat (Mohr 1943, 37–38). At the back of the same boat sits a man without designation, and a woman designated as a 'kite' (*ḏrt*) (Fig. 3). At the front of the boat sits a lector priest and an undesignated man. The text above this scene reads:

> *ḫnt sšm ḥb jn ḫrj-ḥbt*
> Sailing and conducting ritual by the lector priest

In all these scenes the physical crossing and the recitations run together and the aim of both is to mediate the deceased's passage to another state, the state of being an *ꜣḫ*.

Textual Evidence from the Old Kingdom Private Tombs

Crossing the lake as a stage in the funeral procession occurs in the tomb of the vizier Ptahhotep I from Saqqara:

> *hꜣjt r pr=f n ḏt m ḥtp nfr wrt*
> Going down to his house of eternity in very great peace,
> *wn jmꜣḫ=f ḫr jnpw ḫntj-ḫrt-nṯr*
> That he might be provisioned before Anubis-Foremost-of-the-Necropolis,
> *m-ḫt pr n=f ḫrw ḥr tp ḳrrt*
> After an invocation offering is brought to him on the top of the tomb,
> *m-ḫt nmi.t(j) š m-ḫt sꜣḫ.t(j)=f in ḫrj-ḥbt*
> After the lake was crossed, after he has been made an *ꜣḫ* by the lector priest
> (Sethe 1933, 189, lines 4–6).

According to the inscriptions on the false doors of Ptahhotep I, Wilson (1944, 209) states that 'it is possible to argue that there were successive acts; crossing the water, landing on the west bank, entering the necropolis and finally the burial'. What is explicit is that during crossing the water, there was a ritual conducted for the deceased.

On the false door of the tomb of Tepemankh at Saqqara, crossing the lake is described as:

> *prt r tp ḏw n jmnt m-ḫt nmj.t(j) š*
> Going out to the top of the mountain of the west after crossing the lake,

js s3ḫ jn ḫrj-hbt
During making into an *3ḫ* by the lector priest,
jrj n=f ḫt jn wt ḫr inpw
And the rite was carried out for him by the embalmer before Anubis
(Sethe 1933, 190, lines 8–9).

The inscription states that the deceased reached the west after he had crossed a lake. The crossing was accompanied by a fully equipped ritual, conducted for him by a lector priest. The inscription maintains the acts of the lector priest by relating that:

sšm r js=f n jmnt
A procession to his tomb of the west,
m-ḫt ḫnt=f m wrt
After rowing him in the *wrt*-boat,
sšm n=f ḥb ʿpr
And a fully equipped ritual had been conducted for him,
ḫft sš n ḥmt ḫrj-ḥbt
According to the writing of the craft of the lector priest (Sethe 1933, 190, lines 12–13).

On the right inner jamb of the false door of the Mastaba of Neferseshemre at Saqqara, crossing a Firmament (*bj3*) and traversing a lake occur.

ḏ3jt bj3 m ḥtp nfr wrt
Crossing the Firmament in very great peace.
prt jr tp ḏw n ḫrt-nṯr
Going out to the top of the mountain of the necropolis.
nḏrt ʿ=f jn jtw=f [...] tp nb jm3ḫ
His hand is grasped by his fathers [and…] Lord of *jm3ḫ*.
prt-ḫrw n=f
An invocation offering (is brought) for him,
ḥr tp ḳrrt m pr=f n ḏt
On the roof of the tomb in his house of eternity,
sk sw j3wt [nfrt wrt ḫr Wsjr]
When he has reached [a very good old age before Osiris].
h3t r pr=f ḏt m ḥtp nfr wrt
Going down to his house of eternity in very great peace,
wn jm3ḫ=f ḫr jnpw ḫnty-ḫrt-nṯr nb-t3-ḏsr
That he might be venerated before Anubis-Foremost- of-the-Necropolis, Lord-of-Sacred Land,
m-ḫt prt-ḫrw [n=f] ḥr tp ḳrrt
After an invocation offering has been brought [for him] on the top of the tomb,
m-ḫt nmj.t(j) š
After traversing the lake,
m-ḫt s3ḫ.t(j)=f jn ḫrj-ḥbt
After he has been made into an *3ḫ* by the lector priest (Kanawati 1998, 35–6, pl. 58).

Crossing the lake takes place while the deceased is made into an *3ḫ*. In other words, a lector priest was reading or reciting texts while the crossing of the water was in process. Wilson (1944) concludes that:

> 'There was a great deal of physical, ritual, and religious activity necessary to make the deceased a blessed and fully effective immortal. Priestly ritual and utterance are involved in this *s3ḫ* beautifying' (Wilson 1944, 210).

sꜣẖw texts included liturgies recited in the night before burial and at the day of funeral, and their aim is to mediate the deceased's passage to become an *ꜣẖ,* and to pass the place of passage safely (Assmann 2008, 26–31).

Pyramid Texts Evidence

Crossing of the Lake occurs in Pyramid Text spell 603 and reads:

> *ṯs ṯw jt=j ṯs n=k tp=k [sꜣḳ] n=k ꜥwt=k*
> Raise yourself my father! Raise for yourself your head, and assemble for yourself your limbs.
> *wṯs ṯw [m] rdwj=k sšm ṯw jb=k*
> Raise yourself with your legs so that your heart will lead you.
> *sẖs jnw=k ntꜣj ḥwwt=k*
> Your messengers have run, your heralds have hastened,
> *jj smj=k n=[k] m ꜣẖt*
> And your report has come for you in the horizon.
> *jj jnpw ẖsf=f [jm=k]*
> Anubis has come to meet you.
> *dj.n n=k ḥtp ꜥ=f*
> The Contented One has given you his hand.
> *nḥn.n nṯrw [j]ẖ[ꜥꜥ] [šmsw-ḥ]r*
> The gods have rejoiced, and Ho[rus's followers] have celebrated.
> *jj ꜣẖ m ꜣẖ=f jn psḏtj*
> 'An *akh* has come in its status of being an *akh,*' says the Dual Ennead,
> *[ḏ]ꜣ.n=f š nmj.n=f d[ꜣ]t*
> When he has crossed the lake and has traversed the *Duat* (Allen 1984, 680).

The spell starts with a call for the deceased to raise himself up, which refers to the common goal of all rituals, aimed at the activation of the deceased from the embalming process to the mortuary offerings. It is a wakeup call intended to awaken the deceased from his unconscious state, and alludes to the fact that he is undergoing the resurrection ritual (Assmann 2005, 332). The deceased will gain his ability of movement, and mediate his passage with the recitation of these texts and crossing the lake which comes at the end.

In the Pyramid Texts raising oneself up and uniting the limbs is often connected with an invitation to receive offerings, especially libation offerings. They consist of a series of interrelated and complicated rituals, and sometimes it is not explicit which ritual comes first. The aim of these rituals is to mediate the deceased's passage to become an *ꜣẖ*, which allows him to escape the realm of death and join the realm of *ꜣẖw* (Assmann 2005, 332).

The evidence discussed above comes from Old Kingdom royal and private tombs, and in both, the crossing of the lake is closely associated with becoming an *ꜣẖ,* mediated by a lector priest who recites liturgies from a papyrus roll. Crossing a lake, whether this lake is given a name or not, lies in a resurrection ritual context in which libation offerings are presented to a deceased.

Finally libation is envisaged as a lake, and the deceased should cross over it. This is reinforced by some Old Kingdom libation basins which were decorated with boats crossing over water. For instance, on one of the offering tables from Abydos, there is a depiction of four boats carved on the narrow step of the offering basin, which indicates that these basins were used as

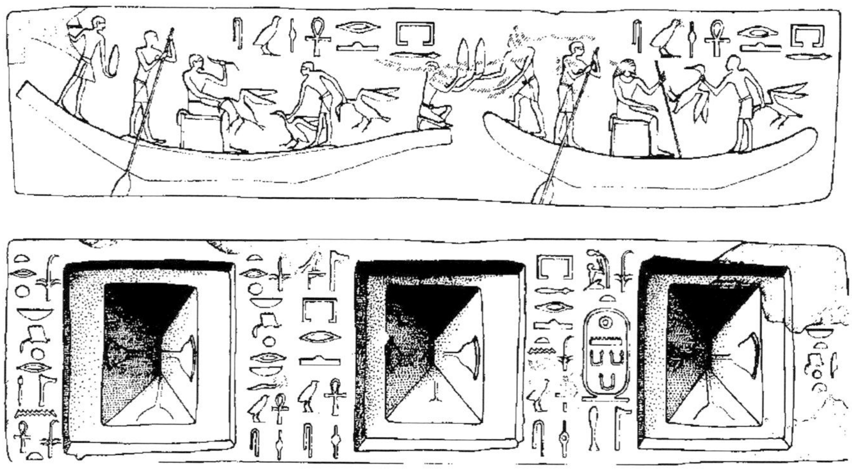

Figure 4. *Offering table Louvre E 25369 (After Mostafa 1982, pl. XXXI).*

replacements for the lakes and rivers over which the deceased can travel to the Netherworld (Hölzl 2002, 67).

Another instance is also found on the offering table of the Ankh Wedjes now in the Louvre Museum (Louvre E 25369) (Fig. 4). This offering table consists of three basins with lotus flowers carved into the stepped inner sides of the basins. The decoration on the longitudinal exteriors shows the deceased sitting in a boat being offered ducks while sailing is in progress (Hölzl 2005, 313–314).

In the Pyramid Texts the lake is called the Great Lake, and the deceased has to avoid its dangers. It is also a passage which leads to the *ꜣḫw*.

> *hꜣ N pw [sꜣ ṯ]w š wr pw jr ꜣḫw*
> O this N beware of this Great Lake which (leads) to the *ꜣḫw,*
> *ḫns pw jr mwt*
> This water course which (leads) to the dead,
> *sꜣ ṯw rmṯ jptf nt pr Bꜣ-pf*
> Beware of those people of the house of *Bꜣ-pf,*
> *ḥrt-ḏꜣt m rn=sn pw n ḏꜣtt*
> Terrible-Opponents in this their name of 'female opponents',
> *jmj=sn nḏrw ꜥ=k jr pr Bꜣ-pf*
> Let them not to take your hand towards the House of *Bꜣ-pf,*
> *sw sw mr sw nh sw jꜣb sw*
> It is dangerous, it is painful, it is nasty (?), and it is foul-smelling
> (Allen, 1984, 691–692; Assmann & Bommas 2002, 339; Assmann 2005, 143).

Middle Kingdom Evidence

Crossing a lake occurs in Coffin Text spell 62, which reads:

> *dj=j jrj=k ḫprw ḥnꜥ ḏwjt*
> I cause that you make manifestations with the *ḏwj.t* bird (?).

dj=j ḏꜣj=k ptrwj ḏꜣj=k š
I cause that you cross the *ptrwj* (?) and cross the lake,
nmj=k wꜣḏ-wr (m) ṯbt
And traverse the sea (in) sandals,
mj jrj.n=k tp tꜣ
As you had done on land.
ḥkꜣ=k jtrw ḥnꜥ bnw
You will rule the river with the heron,
nn rḳw=k r wꜥrt
And no opponent will be against you at the district of water.
dj=j wḏ=k m smꜥ n mḥ 40
I cause that you progress with a sounding-pole of 40 cubits,
m srd n ꜥš n kbn ꜥḥꜥ.tj m wjꜣ n Rꜥ
Of planted wood of cedar of Byblos, as you stand in the Barque of Re,
ḏꜣj.n=k š n rḫjt
And you have crossed the Lake of *rḫjt.*
smꜣꜥ-ḫrw=k hrw wḏꜥ-mdw
You will be vindicated (on) the day of judgment,
m ḏꜣḏꜣt nt nb gmwt
In the tribunal of the Lord of Suffering.
šd n=k ḫbs tꜣ
A liturgy of Hacking up the Earth will be recited for you,
ḫsf n=k sbj jj m grḥ
And the enemy who comes at night will be driven off for you
(De Buck 1935, vol. I, 266h–268).

This spell occurs only on the outer coffin of Amenemhat, nomarch of el-Bersha. The text was recorded five times on the coffin, which was published in de Buck's edition as B10C. Willems dates the coffin to the end of the reign of Sesostris I and the beginning of the reign of Amenemhat II (Willems 1988, 74–75). Coffin Texts spell 62 is a liturgy by itself (Assmann 1996, 18–19; Assmann & Bommas 2002, 39; Assmann 2005, 270). It is a speech by Horus to his father Osiris, containing three mortuary liturgies to be recited in the context of a wake (Assmann & Bommas 2002, 40–41). This long speech of Horus to his deceased father resembles the speech of the goddess Neith to Merenptah as recorded on the lid of his sarcophagus (Assmann 1972, 47–73, 115–139). The spell belongs to the *sꜣḫw* texts and is aimed at the restoration of the deceased's social and physical aspects. It begins with an address of Horus to Osiris describing the ritual acts carried out by the son for his father.

jnḏ ḥr=k jt=j Wsjr
Greetings to you, my father Osiris
mk wj jj.kw jnk ḥr
Behold, I have come, I am Horus.
wpj=j rꜣ=k ḥnꜥ ptḥ
I will open your mouth with Ptah,
sꜣḫ=j ṯw ḥnꜥ ḏḥwtj
I will spiritualize you with Thoth (De Buck 1935, 265a-d).

Horus will carry out the Opening of the Mouth ritual for his father and he will make him an *ꜣḫ* with Thoth. Horus causes his father to make manifestations with the bird, and to cross the lake. After passing safely through the mummification and becoming an *ꜣḫ,* the deceased will have the ability of free movement over water (Assmann 1996, 5–10). By means of crossing the water, the deceased will mediate his passage and escape the realm of death, become an *ꜣḫ,* and steer the barque of Re. The next verses show the roles of the deceased in the sun boat. The deceased will stand at the prow of the sun barque measuring the water level, as he did in his daily life (Assmann 2005, 274).

The lake is also described as the Great Lake, and the deceased has to avoid its dangers. Coffin Text spell 67 reads:

> *jꜣ N pn sꜣ ṯw š wr*
> O this N, beware of the Great Lake
> *jr mwt nh=k sw*
> As for death, you will escape it.
> *ꜣb=k wꜣt r=f*
> And you will avoid the route to him
> *jmj=sn jṯj ṯw r pr Bꜣ-pf*
> They shall not drag you off to the house of *Bꜣ-pf,*
> *jmj=sn jrj ḏꜣjt r=k*
> And they shall not make opposition to you,
> *m rn=sn n ḏꜣjw*
> In their name of Opponents (De Buck 1935, 284e–285a).

The deceased's journey starts with a warning against crossing the Great Lake. Coffin Text spells 62 and 67 form parts of the *jj-ṯhb-wr* Liturgy. In this liturgy, the warning against crossing the Great Lake might refer to the deceased's return into his tomb, while he is already in the world of the dead, to partake of the offerings presented to him in his tomb. The *jj-ṯhb-wr* Liturgy was recited in the morning before sunrise at the conclusion of the night rituals (Assmann & Bommas 2002, 133). The consumption of the deceased's offerings is envisaged as travelling across the sky and joining the barque of Re (Assmann 2005, 336–337).

New Kingdom Evidence

In New Kingdom private tombs, particularly in the Ramesside tombs, the crossing to the west is described as 'the Great Ferry'. For instance, in TT 133 the boat which carries the coffin is equated with the Great Ferry which the deceased uses for the transition from the realm of death to the underworld (Barthelmess 1992, 19). The text in TT 133 reads:

> [*ḏꜣ*] *mḫnt wrt nt jmntt*
> Fare across, Great Ferry of the West.
> *mj ḏꜣ m ḥtp r jmntt*
> Come! Fare in peace across to the West.
> *jw dj (=j) t n ḥḳr mw n jbw dꜣjw n ḥꜥw*
> I gave bread to the hungry, water to the thirsty, and clothing to the naked (Barthelmess 1992, 19).

Here the deceased says that he has given bread to the hungry and water to the thirsty, which are required for his safe passage to the west. The deceased, before giving this food stuff to the hungry, was in the pre-liminal or marginal stage of the rites of passage, as characterised by Van Gennep (Van Gennep 1975, 10) and which separates the marginal and post-liminal stages. By providing the hungry and thirsty with food and drink, the deceased mediates his passage to the west and leaves the marginal state and enters the post-liminal, the state of being an *ꜣḫ* which comes after his crossing to the west (Franke 2006, 106–107).

It seems reasonable to equate a boat carrying a statue of a deceased with the *Neshmet*-Barque of Osiris. In TT 347 the deceased's barque is that of Osiris. The statue of the deceased, priests and mourners are shown on the boat, while Isis and Nephthys are depicted at the foot and the head of the deceased (Barthelmess 1992, 20). This depiction of the boat reminds us of the Old Kingdom tomb representations of a boat crossing a lake mentioned above, where an embalmer, kites, and lector priests are depicted in a boat traversing a lake. So, crossing to the West in the New Kingdom private tombs might be described as a ceremonial or symbolic crossing just as it was in the Old Kingdom. The text describing crossing to the West in TT 347 reads:

> *ḏd n pꜣ ꜥš-ḥꜣt ntj m ḥꜣt n tꜣ nšmt*
> Speech of the pilot at the prow of the *neshmet*-Barque,
> *jmj-wrt jtḥ r jmntt*
> To the west, tow (your boat) to the west,
> *pꜣ dmjt nmꜣꜥtj ḫft-ḥr-nb=s njwt jmn*
> The Town of the Righteous, That-which-in front-of-its-Lord, the city of Amun.
> *wḏ=f sw n NN tꜣ mnj gr=k*
> He (Amun) has given it over to NN, the mourning land of your Silent One,
> *wnf.wj st m ẖnw=s*
> How the place (the tomb) rejoices at it!
> *ḥt-ḥr ḥnwt jmntt tꜣ mḏꜣt n jmj-wrt*
> Hathor, Mistress of the West, the Protector of the Western Side,
> *tꜣ jr...... n mꜣꜥtj nb*
> She [who prepares a place] for every Righteous,
> *šsp=s NN m ḳnw=s*
> May she take NN in her embrace (Barthelmess 1992, 20–21).

Crossing to the West is envisaged as a transition or a passage into a sphere of security and divine presence that is only granted to the righteous. It is not a mere physical transfer of a corpse from one place to another, but rather a ritual procession (Assmann 2005, 304–305). As a result, the crossing over a lake or over a river is not connected with the geographical location of the necropolis as it might be thought, Saqqara in the Old Kingdom and the West of Thebes in the New Kingdom, but with the ritual enacted on the day of traversing the lake.

Crossing the Lake of Knives

When the *mꜥnḏt* barque of the sun god Re crosses the Lake of Knives, it is said that the barque is in *hnw.*

> *mꜥnḏt m hꜣj hnw tꜣ m ḥb*
> The day bark is in jubilation and celebration, and the land is in festival.
> *nṯrw m ḥsfw bꜣ=f ḥrj-ib ṯꜣwj=fj*
> The gods are greeting the one whose soul dwells in his two fledglings.
> *spr=f r imnt nfrt m ḥtp*
> He arrives in peace to the Beautiful West,
> *ḏꜣ.n=f mr nḫꜣwj*
> After he has crossed the Lake of Knives,
> *r hnn=f wꜣw wḏꜣ sp 2*
> According to the movement of its waves safely (completely)
> (Naville 1886, pl. XVIII, lines 3–7).

In the Old Kingdom the family and relatives receive the funeral procession of the deceased in lamentation, and the Book of the Dead Sun Hymn mentioned above alludes to the same situation. Here the gods gather and greet the sun god Re in his barque when he crosses the Lake of Knives. It is the barque that carries the image of Re, with whom the deceased is identified. The aim of the deceased's crossing the lake in the Old Kingdom private tombs was to reach the west, which is the same destination of the barque of Re's journey over the Lake of Knives.

In his journey over the Lake of Knives, Re was threatened by the snake of the primeval waters Apep, who tried hard to stop the solar barque proceeding through the *dwꜣt*. In the Book of the Dead Chapter 15, the journey of the sun god Re over the Lake of Knives is described as:

nnj n ḥr=k
Adoration to your face;
ḥpt ṯw mꜣꜥt r trwj
Maat embraces you at the two times,
nmj=k ḥr pt m ꜣw-ib
When you travel across the sky in joy.
mr nḫꜣwj ḫpr m ḥtpw
The Lake of Knives has become in peace.
njk ḫr ꜥꜣwj=fj ḥsk
The *Nik*-serpent is overthrown and his arms are cut off.
šsp.n sktt mꜣꜥw nfr
The *msktt-barque* has received good wind.
jmj ḳrs=f ib=f nḏm
He who is in his shrine, his heart is pleased (Naville 1886, pl. XVI, lines 10–11).

As the deceased is warned against crossing the lake in the Pyramid and Coffin Texts, the sun god Re is threatened by Apep while crossing the Lake of Knives. Nine books are read aloud while the Apis crosses the Lake of the King, and the Book of Apep should be recited when the sun god Re crosses the Lake of Knives. In one of the New Kingdom composite Sun Hymns, the journey over the Lake of Knives and the Sandbank of Apep is described as follows:

jnḏ ḥr=k Rꜥ m wbn=k Jmn sḫm nṯrw
Hail to you Re, at your rising, Amun, power of the gods.
wbn=k sḥḏ.n=k tꜣwj dꜣj=k ḥrt m ḥtp
You rise when you have illuminated the two lands. You cross the sky in peace.
jb=k ꜣw m mꜥnḏt swꜣ=k ḥr ṯst n mr nḫꜣwj
Your heart is joyful in the *Mꜥnḏt* barque. You pass over the Sandbank of the Lake of Knives.
sḫrw ḫftjw=k jw=k ḫꜥj.tj m ḥwt šw
Your enemies have been felled. You have appeared in the House of Shu,
ḥtp.tj m ꜣḫt jmntt šsp.n ḥm=k jmꜣḫ
And have set in the western horizon. Your majesty has received veneration.
ꜥꜣwj mwt=k m-sꜣ ḥꜣ=k m-ḫrt hrw nt rꜥ nb
The arms of your mother protecting you, daily, every day.
mꜣꜣ=j tw m ḥb=k nfr m ḫnt=k nt ḏsr-ḏsrw
May I see you in your beautiful festival, as in your Deir el-Bahri voyage.
ḫpr jꜣḫw=k ḥr šnbt=j dwꜣ=j tw nfrw=k m ḥr=j
May your radiance be upon my breast. May I worship you, (with) your beauty in my eyes.
dj=k ḥtp=j m ḥwt jrt.n=j m ḥswt nt nṯr nfr

May you allow me to rest in the house I have built, in the favour of the good god.
dj=k wn=j m šmsw=k ḥtp=kw ḫrt nt dd=k
May you allow me to be among your followers, resting in the tomb granted by you,
mj jrrwt n mꜣꜥtj tp tꜣ
As is done for the righteous on earth (Assmann 1969, 281–183; 1983, 24; 1995, 13).

The first stanza in this hymn is adoration to the sun god Re at his rising and setting. The sun god rises and illuminates the two lands, and crosses the sky in a joyful heart. Then, the hymn mentions the crossing of the sun god Re over the Sandbank of the Lake of Knives, in which the enemies of the sun god Re have been felled. The hymn then moves to the description of the movement of the sun in the sky. The sun is protected by the two arms of the sky goddess Nut.

The next stanza deals with the beating of the sun on the chest of the deceased. In a recent article, Bommas argues that the motive of the morning sun beating on the breast of the deceased can be considered as the first sign for the funerary procession. It marks the end of the rituals which have taken place in the embalming place, and the beginning of the deceased's funeral procession to the forecourt of his tomb. It refers also to the deceased's wish to cross the borders from this world to the next by means of rituals. Horus is envisaged as a sun-disk protecting the ways of his father from the embalming chamber until he reaches the open forecourt of his tomb (Bommas 2007, 15–22). This theme is also well known in the Underworld Books of the New Kingdom and is connected with the deceased's wish to go out by day and to take part in the daily solar cycle (Assmann 2005, 317–324).

Although this Sun Hymn may belong to a different text genre, it still retains most of the themes mentioned in the texts connected with the mummy's transition to the tomb. The funeral procession from the place of embalming to the tomb forecourt includes crossing the Lake of Knives. The journey of the deceased is parallel to the journey of the sun god Re from the east to the west. The sun shines in the east and on its way to the west it crosses the Lake of Knives. It is also important to note that the sun's journey from the east to the west in this hymn is envisaged as a procession in the Beautiful Festival. It is plausible here to say that the deceased's procession is also envisaged as a procession in which crossing the Lake of Knives takes place.

The Apis Bull Procession over the Lake of the King

Crossing the lake in the Old Kingdom private tombs goes well with the description of the Apis Bull procession over the Lake of the King in the Ptolemaic Period and with that of Diodorus Siculus (Oldfather 1946, 92). The Lake of the King was a place where a kiosk was put up for the funeral rites of the Apis Bull, which was conveyed by boat before burial. In this ritual, two priests are brought to the place of embalming, and with the help of the rope they pull the coffin containing the mummy of the Apis outside. After the mummy with the coffin is taken outside the embalming house, two *wꜥb* priests pull the rope from the hand of the Great Ones of the House of the Inundation of the Nile. During this process, loud lamentations take place. The coffin is then placed in a boat and the Apis is transported to the Lake of the King accompanied by Isis, Nephthys, Wepwawet of Upper Egypt, Wepwawet of Lower Egypt, Horus and Thoth. When the procession reaches the lake, the Apis is placed on a platform and his face is pointed southwards. After that the Apis mummy sails across the lake, and the priests read aloud the nine sacred books until they reach the purification tent, where the Opening of the Mouth Ritual is carried out for the Apis (Vos 1993, 159–160).

Vos describes the procession across the lake as an episode from the Osiris mysteries and drama, in which the resurrection of Osiris is made manifest. It can also be seen as a symbolic depiction of the journey of the sun god Re. The Osiris resurrection and the solar procession are equated together in the Apis procession over the Lake of the King. The papyrus boat (*wjꜣ*) of the Apis is identical to the sun boat in which Re sails over Nun and it is also equated with the (*nšmt*) barque of Osiris (Vos 1993, 162). Osiris on his bier is equated with the sun god in his bark (Willems 1988, 156–158). The deceased on his bier is threatened by Seth, and the sun god Re in his barque is threatened by Apep. The sun god Re overcomes his primeval enemies, and the Bull's resurrection will be achieved by reciting the nine books which are read aloud while sailing over the Lake of the King (Vos 1993, 166).

The Apis Bull procession was accompanied by Isis and Nephthys, which reminds us of the two kites in the funeral procession in the Old Kingdom mastabas across the lake mentioned above. *sꜣḫw* texts are read while sailing over the lake in the Old Kingdom private tombs, and nine holy books are read aloud while sailing over the Lake of the King. The recitations mediate the passage of the Apis Bull and the deceased while sailing over water.

During the Old Kingdom, the journey of the deceased was apparently across the river or a canal that connects the land of the living with the necropolis. This is made explicit in the tomb of Niankhkhnum and Khnumhotep at Saqqara (Fig. 5). In this tomb the journey to the west in two boats is depicted on the lower register of the eastern section of the northern wall. The boat to the left shows a pilot standing at the prow and is designated as *ḥm kꜣ ḥsj,* and behind him sit the rowers. Two helmsmen stand at the back of the boat. The steersman, who guides the ship's crew as his title indicates *jmj-rꜣ jswt wr-nbḏw,* is depicted at the top of the canopy (Moussa and Altenmüller 1977, 85). In the middle of the boat stands the tomb owner leaning on a staff with his left hand and listens to a report by a man who stands in front of him. The man is designated as *ḥm kꜣ šs Kꜣ(.j)-ḫr-ptḥ*. The way followed by the ship is the Canal of the West (*jrj ḥr jmj-wrt n t[pt-ꜥ]=k r šmw nfrw mr jmnt nfrt*), and the journey's destination is the Beautiful West the place of the Venerated Ones (*sḳdwt r jmnt nfrt m jmꜣḫw*) (Moussa and Altenmüller 1977, 86).

Crossing to the west can also be a symbolic one. Textual evidence describing crossing the lake to reach the west is not only found in Saqqara private tombs but also in the tombs of Harkhuf and Meru at Aswan. It was a symbolic crossing, and the deceased's crossing over the lake might refer to his spiritual crossing of the sky on his way to the netherworld (Wilson 1944, 209; Bolshakov 1991, 37). The evidence that the crossing was a symbolic one is obvious from

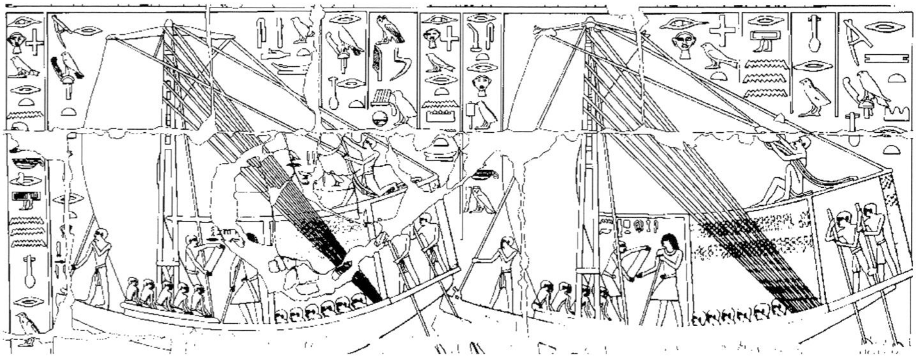

Figure 5. *The journey to the west in the Tomb of the Two Brothers, Fifth Dynasty, Saqqara (After Moussa and Altenmüller 1977, Fig. 10).*

the inscriptions of the Mastaba of Neferseshemre mentioned above. In this text, the crossing of a Lake is compared with the crossing of a firmament. The deceased is said to cross a firmament to the mountain of the necropolis. Then offerings are presented to him at the top of the tomb after he has crossed a lake. It is still not explicit what is meant by crossing a firmament, but it is always compared with the sun god Re crossing the sky. Assmann (2005) states that 'Crossing the firmament is a formally established turn of expression for the sun god's crossing the sky and it is at the same time the basic principle of Egyptian mortuary belief' (p. 291). The funeral procession mentioned above thus might be explained as crossing the sky and not merely crossing a body of water, whether this body was a lake, a river or a firmament (Altenmüller 2004, 31).

Conclusion

It can thus be concluded that crossing the lake is a ritual enacted on the day of the funeral. The funeral procession of the deceased over the lake in the Old Kingdom was accompanied by the recitation of *s3ḫw*, which runs contemporaneously with the crossing over the lake. The Apis Bull procession over the lake was also accompanied by the recitation of nine sacred books, and the title of one of these books is *s3ḫw*. The offering of libation in the Old Kingdom Pyramid Texts was envisaged as crossing over water, and while the ritual was taking place the spells were recited.

Crossing the lake of Knives was also accompanied by the recitation of the Book of Apep. The crossing over the lake as a rite of passage was parallel to the sun god Re's crossing over the waters of the sky, and also to the crossing of the *wrrt* boat of Osiris. The deceased, who is equated with both gods, crosses the lake of Knives, equipped with the recitation of texts which will mediate his passage from the world of the dead to the world of *3ḫw*.

University of Liverpool

Bibliography

Allen, J. P. (1984) *The Inflection of the Verb in the Pyramid Texts*, BAe 2, Malibu, California, Undena Publications.

Altenmüller, H. (2004) 'Der Konvoi der Sonnenschiffe in den Pyramidentexten', *Studien zur altägyptischen Kultur* Vol. 32, 11–33.

Assmann, J. (1969) *Liturgische Lieder an den Sonnengott. Untersuchungen zur ägyptischen Hymnik* I, MÄS 19, Berlin, Hessling.

Assmann, J. (1972) 'Die Inschrift auf dem äuβeren Sarkophagdeckel des Merenptah', *Mitteilungen de Deutschen Archäologischen Instituts* Vol. 28, 47–73.

Assmann, J. (1972) 'Neith spricht als Mutter und Sarg. Interpretation und metrisch Analyse der Sargdecklinschrift des Merenptah', *Mitteilungen des Deutschen Archäologischen Instituts* Vol. 28, 115–139.

Assmann, J. (1983) *Sonnenhymnen in thebanischen Gräbern*, Theben 1, Mainz am Rhein, von Zabern.

Assmann, J. (1995) *Egyptian Solar Religion in the New Kingdom. Re, Amun and the Crisis of Polytheism*, London, Paul.

Assmann, J. (1996) 'Spruch 62 der Sargtexte und die ägyptischen Totenliturgien' in Willems, H. (ed.) *The World of the Coffin Texts. Proceedings of the Symposium held on the Occasion of the 100th Birthday of Adriaan de Buck. Leiden, December 17–19, 1992*, EU 9, Leiden, Nederlands Instituut voor het Nabije Oosten, 17–30.

Assmann, J. (2005) *Death and Salvation in Ancient Egypt*, translated from German by D. Lorton, Ithaca and London, Cornell University Press.

Assmann, J. (2008) *Altägyptische Totenliturgien,* vol. III, *Osirisliturgien in Papyri der Spätzeit*, Supplemente zu den Schriften der Heidelberger Akademie der Wissenschaften, Philosophisch-historische Klasse 20, Heidelberg, Winter.

Assmann, J. and Bommas, M. (2002) *Altägyptische Totenliturgien*, vol. I, *Totenliturgien in den Sargtexten des Mitteleren Reiches*, Supplemente zu den Schriften der Heidelberger Akademie der Wissenschaften, Philosophisch-historische Klasse 14, Heidelberg, Winter.

Barthelmess, P. (1992) *Der Übergang ins Jenseits in den thebanischen Beamtengräbern der Ramessidenzeit*, SAGA 2, Heidelberg, Heidelberger Orientverlag.

Bolshakov, A. O. (1991) 'The Old Kingdom Representations of Funeral Procession', *Göttinger Miszellen* Vol. 121, 31–54.

Bommas, M. (2007) 'Das Motiv der Sonnenstrahlen auf der Brust des Toten. Zur Frage der Stundenwachen im Alten Reich', *Studien zur altägyptischen Kultur* Vol. 36, 15–22.

De Buck, A. (1935) *The Ancient Egyptian Coffin Texts* I. *Texts of Spells 1–75*, Chicago, University Chicago Press.

Dominicus, B. (1994) *Gesten und Gebärden in Darstellungen des Alten und Mittleren Reiches,* SAGA 10, Heidelberg, Heidelberger Orienverlag.

Franke, D. (2006) 'Arme und Geringe im Alten Reich Altägyptens: "Ich gab Speise dem Hungernden, Kleider dem Nackten…"', *Zeitschrift für ägyptische Sprache und Altertumskunde* Vol. 133, 104–120.

Hölzl, R. (2002) *Ägyptische Opfertafeln und Kultbecken. Eine Form-und Funktionsanalyse für das Alte, Mittlere und Neue Reich*, HÄB 45, Hildesheim, Gerstenberg Verlag.

Hölzl, R. (2005) 'Libation Basins from the Old to the New Kingdom: Practical Use and Religious Significance' in Amenta, A. Luiselli, M. M. and Sordi, M. N. (eds) *L'acqua nell'antico Egitto: vita, rigenerazione, incantesimo, medicamenti: Proceedings of the First International Conference for Young Egyptologists*, Rome, L'Erma di Bretschneider, 309–317.

Kanawati, N. and Abdel-Raziq, M. (1998) *The Teti Cemetry at Saqqara* III. *The Tombs of Neferseshemere and Seankhuiptah*, ACE Reports 11, Warminster, Aris and Phillips.

Lepsius, C. R. (1842–1845) *Denkmäler aus Ägypten und Äthiopien*. Zweite Abtheilung: *Denkmaeler des Alten Reichs*, Berlin, Nicolai.

Morgan, J. de (1903) *Fouilles à Dahchour en 1894–1895*, Vienna, Holzhausen.

Mohr, T. H. (1943) *The Mastaba of Hetep-Her-Akhti: Study on an Egyptian Tomb Chapel in the Museum of Antiquities Leiden,* Mededeelingen en Verhandelingen 5, Leiden, Brill.

Mostafa, M. (1982) *Untersuchungen zu Opfertafeln im Alten Reich*, HÄB 17, Hildesheim, Gerstenberg.

Moussa, A. M. and Altenmüller, H. (1977) *Das Grab des Nianchchnum und Chnumhotep*, AV 21, Mainz am Rhein, von Zabern.

Naville, E. (1886) *Das Aegyptische Tötenbuch der XVIII. bis XX. Dynastie aus verschiedenen Urkunden,* Berlin, Asher.

Oldfather, C. H. (1946) *Diodorus of Sicily* I, London and Cambridge MA, Heinemann.

Sethe, K. (1933) *Urkunden des Alten Reichs*, Leipzig, Hinrichs.

Van Gennep, A. (1975) The Rites of Passage. Translated from French by Vizedom, B. and Caffee, L., Chicago, University of Chicago Press.

Vos, R. L. (1993) *The Apis Embalming Ritual. P. Vindob. 3873*, OLA 50, Leuven, Peeters.

Willems, H. (1988) *Chests of Life*, Leiden, Ex Oriente Lux.

Wilson, J. A. (1944) 'Funeral Services of the Egyptian Old Kingdom', *Journal of Near Eastern Studies* Vol. 3, 201–218.

Is Selket 'The Lady of Chemmis and Wife of Horus'?

Hebatallah Abdou

Introduction

This study examines the title 'Lady of Chemmis, Wife of Horus,' which appears in many magical and medical papyri, but without a clear indication of the holder. Primary attention is focused upon the texts in which this title appears in relation to the scorpion goddess Selket and the possibility that she is the one addressed. Selket's curative abilities in the textual material are also discussed in the context of medical and magical practice in ancient Egypt.

Sources

The title appears in a magical incantation in the Turin Papyrus 1993[5] (Pleyte, and Rossi 1899, pls. 31+77, 12; Gardiner 1917, 40–41), with a parallel in Papyrus Chester Beatty XI, recto 4, 8 (Gardiner 1935, pl. 65) in relation to the name of Selket. Gardiner's translation of the text is as follows:

> 'They are in the hand of the *ḫrp* Selket, everywhere, the Lady of Chemmis and the Wife of Horus.' (Gardiner 1917, 41).

The *ḫrp* Selket is a person who deals with medical spells, especially with regard to bites and stings. In the text, the word 'everywhere' separates 'Selket' from the title 'Lady of Chemmis', which induces an element of doubt as to whether this title belongs to Selket or not. Gardiner, in his analysis of the text, assumes that the title does belong to Selket, and explains this separation either as a type of 'dittography' (Gardiner 1917, 40–41), or that the verse-points are misplaced, as the same separation is found between the words *ḫrp* and Selket. Gardiner confirms his theory by adding that the following spell also starts with the same title:

> 'Another spell: The Lady of Chemmis, Wife of Horus.' (Pleyte and Rossi 1899, pls. 31+77, 13; Gardiner 1917, 41).

However, an alternative translation of the Chester Beatty passage may be:

> 'Which (*wnnw*) are in the hand of the *ḫrp* Selket, in respect of every place (of?) the Lady of Chemmis and the Wife of Horus.'

This possible translation assumes a connection between Selket and the title and would indicate that the healing skills of the priests of Selket are in the places of the Lady of Chemmis and Wife of Horus.

The title appears again in relation to the name of Selket in British Museum Papyrus 10309, incantation 2, in a spell against scorpions and snakes. This spell has a parallel on the Leiden Magical Statue Base, but this ends just before the relevant part here. The final part of the spell, which explains magical or medical practice, instructs that the spell has to be recited over the patient with images of specific deities. The relevant text reads:

> 'An image of Selket, Lady of Life, an image of the Lady of Chemmis, Wife of Horus.' (Leitz 2000, 28, pl. 10).

The repetition of the words 'an image of' might either indicate that the two goddesses have different images, or that the scribe omitted the word Selket from the second part of the sentence to abbreviate the phrase, or to avoid further repetition of the name of Selket. The phrase 'an image of' may have been deliberately repeated for effect, or it may reiterate that the spell has to be recited over two images of Selket, one as the Lady of Life and the other as the Lady of Chemmis and Wife of Horus.

The Leiden Magical Statue Base (Leiden F 1950, 8.2), bears texts which are spells against the bites of venomous reptiles, (Klasens 1952, 1) with a parallel in the British Museum Papyrus 10309. Spell VIII contains the passage:

> 'His behind is the Mistress of Chemmis, the Wife of Horus.' (h 13–14) (Klasens 1952, 41, 60, 105).
> 'Return, poison fall down... at the words of the Lord of Life, the Lord of Protection, at the words of the Mistress of Chemmis, the Wife of Horus.' (h 20–21) (Klasens 1952, 42, 107).

Selket does not appear in these texts, but Klasens associates them with her, in particular for her connection with the rear of the body. He justifies this identification by referring to Coffin Text III, spell 74 a.

> '*NN* discharges with his behind like Selket' (CT III, 74 a).

Klasens, however, disregards the appearance of the same relationship between Selket and the rear part of the body which appears in the Pyramid Texts, utterance 493.

> 'N relieves in her rear parts, like Selket.' (PT§ 1061).

This repetition of the association between Selket and the rear part of the body would suggest that she is the one addressed by these texts. It also seems sensible to assume that the rear part relates to the sting of the scorpion. However, the exact relationship between Selket, Chemmis, and Wife of Horus needs further investigation.

Selket, Lady of Chemmis

With regard to the first part of the title, Chemmis (*ꜣḫ bit*) is the city in which Horus the child was concealed and grew up. Gardiner states that Chemmis is located in the north of the Delta, close to Buto (Gardiner 1944, 52–62) in the Khasou nome. Selket is strongly connected with the Khasou nome, and this relationship is clearly represented on the statuette of Penhoutbit, now in possession of Andrea de Beaumont Bonelli. It dates to the reign of Psammatik I, and was found in Sais (de Meulenaere 1960, 117–129). It is inscribed with a text referring to Selket as 'The Lady of Qedem'. The place Qedem took the determinative sign of the sixth nome of Lower Egypt, Khasou (the mountain bull), known as Xois in Greek, and Sakha in Arabic (Gardiner 1947, 181–187). This representation indicates that a cult of Selket existed in the Khasou nome, where the city of Chemmis was located.

Selket is also related to Chemmis in British Museum Papyrus 9997, incantation 6 (Leitz 2000, 20). The translation of the text is as follows:

> '"X, born of Y. [...] Lady of Chemmis", so says Selket.' (Leitz 2000, 20).

Here Selket is promising some resolution for the person, under the authority of the Lady of Chemmis, and the sentence implies a connection between the Lady of Chemmis and Selket. The title 'Lady of Chemmis' also appears on a Cippus of Horus (A1053) from the Leiden Museum, dating to the New Kingdom; a female figure standing in the same position as the protective goddesses, she is standing behind Selket (Sternberg-El Hotabi 1999, 145, 305).

Selket, Wife of Horus

With regard to the second part of the title, many names are known for the Wives of Horus. They appear in Chester Beatty Papyrus VII, recto 1, 4–2, 5 (Gardiner 1935, 56–57, pl. 33). Gardiner's translation reads:

> 'Another (spell). Flow forth, thou scorpion.....thou of the long back and the many joints, (1, 5)...... of Speret–...[Come hither at my utterance(?) according as] I say. I am the god who came into being of himself.....Isis. The poison....Rēa, which(?) Nut, who bare [the gods?] said....... [N, born of] M.
>
> Come, [issue forth. So saith...wife of] Horus. [Behold, I am] Horus, the physician soothing the god. [Flow forth from the limbs.]
>
> Come, [issue forth. So saith ... wife of] Horus. Behold, [I am Horus, the physician soothing the god]. Flow [forth from the limbs].
>
> Come, issue forth. So saith ... (2, 1)–ifdet [wife of Horus]. Behold, I am Horus, the physician [soothing the god. Flow] forth from the limbs.
>
> Come, issue forth. So saith Wep-sepu, wife of Horus. Behold, I am Horus, [the physician soothing the god]. Flow forth [from the limbs.]
>
> [Come, issue forth. So] saith Sefed-sepu, wife of Horus. Behold, I am Horus, the physician [soothing] the god. [Flow forth from the limbs.]
>
> [Come], issue forth. [So saith Metemet?] Nofret-iyes, wife of Horus. Behold, I am Horus, the physician [soothing] the god. Flow forth from the limbs.
>
> Come, issue [forth. So saith ... wife of Horus]. Behold, I am Horus, the physician soothing the god. Flow forth from the limbs.
>
> .....Horus.....Semy.... Flow forth from the limbs.' (Gardiner 1935, 56–57, pl. 33).

Gardiner argues that all these names of the Wives of Horus are likely to be epithets of Selket (Gardiner 1935, 56), and the idea is supported by Griffiths, who says: 'various names of Selket are used and they are Wives of Horus' (Griffiths 1960, 49). Also Ritner, in his detailed study of the Wives of Horus, remarks on the fact that scorpions in general can be referred to as 'Wives of Horus', and suggests that this title is a way of referring to scorpions, 'who are perhaps included within the figure of Selket' (Ritner 1998, 1032).

The association between Horus and the scorpion appears in many texts, in a sequence of events, which begins when Horus marries a scorpion, but at the commencement of intercourse she stings him between his shoulders. This incident is inscribed on the statue of Ramesses III from the Cairo Museum (JE69771) (Drioton 1939, 65–67). Borghouts's translation reads:

> '[Spell]s for conjuring (Sni) a scorpion (Dl) ......Do recite for my Horus, the little one, that he may go and be healed for his mother – by the blood of *ṯꜣ-biṯ.t* when Horus deflowered her in the evening. Close the mouth of any reptile, oh *ṯꜣ-biṯ.t, ṯḥn-ḥr, Mn.t,* wife of Horus! May Horus live and be healed!' (Borghouts 1978, 73, no. 101).

ṯꜣ-biṯ.t, is a scorpion goddess, who is related to the loss of virginity. A similar text is inscribed in Papyrus Turin 1993 [16] (Pleyte and Rossi 1899, pls. 136, 12–137, 4). Borghouts's translation reads:

> 'As for the night when the wife of Horus was bitten – I will not let the Inundation to surge flow along the bank, I will not let Shu illuminate the soil .... The protection (*sꜣw*) is a protection of Horus.' (Borghouts 1978, 80, no. 115).

Over a period, the wife reveals to Horus her powerful name and heals him, so that he acquires medical skills and becomes 'Horus the Doctor', and returns, cured, to his mother Isis (Ritner 1998, 1032). The text occurs in the Chester Beatty Papyrus VII, recto 4, 2–4, 4 Gardiner's translation reads:

> 'Come...; so saith Sepertu-eros Sep-nas-to, the first body of Prēa. She tells her name to Horus every (?) three years, the hidden blood being on her thighs since Horus opened her. Come to me, and draw forth these malignant <humours> which are in the limbs of N, born of M, even as Horus went to his mother Isis on the night when he was bitten.' (Gardiner, 1935, 58, Pl. 34).

This scenario comes from a series of texts, establishing a relationship between Horus marrying a scorpion and becoming Horus the Doctor, in which the mythology seems well established.

Selket is also connected to the title 'Wife of Horus' in the hieratic ostracon Deir el-Medineh 1227 (Posener 1972, pl. 56). The author's translation reads:

> '*ḫrp* Selket is the name of the Wife of Horus.'

Horus the Doctor also appears in the Geographical Papyrus of Tanis, beside the title of *ḫrp* Selket (Petrie 1889, pl. XI; von Känel 1984, 213, 288) and Horus the Doctor appears as *ḫrp* Selket on the statue of Djedher the Saviour, in the Cairo Museum (JE 46341).

> 'I am Horus, justified, the *ḫrp* Selket. I come to Shednu....... I am Horus the great, the doctor who calms the god.' (Jelínková-Reymond 1956, 7, 15–16; von Känel 1984, 205).

Selket therefore has a strong connection with the title 'Lady of Chemmis' and all the authors cited above are agreed that she is the one addressed by the title 'Wife of Horus'.

On the whole I lean towards the hypothesis that Selket is the 'Lady of Chemmis, Wife of Horus'. Confirmatory evidence is to be found in Turin Papyrus 1993[5] (Pleyte, and Rossi 1899, pls. 31+77, 12; Gardiner 1917, 40–41) with a parallel in Papyrus Chester Beatty XI, recto 4, 8–10 (BM 10691: Gardiner 1935, 116–121, pl. 65), which represents the power of the Lady of Chemmis, and Wife of Horus in protecting Horus, and controlling all venomous reptiles. Gardiner's translation reads:

> 'Another spell. The Lady of Chemmis, Wife of Horus, the beneficent, efficient in words, who protects her Horus everyday, to whom the great god has given power (?), knowing her excellence, to close the mouth of all worms, in the sky and earth, and in the water. She is named when serpents are called upon, when scorpions are caught by the tail (?).' (Gardiner 1935, 116–121, pl. 65).

This text probably refers to Selket, as suggested by Gardiner in his analysis of the text (Gardiner 1935, 116–121) because of her principal role in controlling poison. The magical and medical texts presented here invite investigation upon the medical and curative abilities of Selket.

Selket, a Curative Goddess

Selket's abilities to heal scorpion bites and control poison appear in many papyri, ostraca, and healing statues. The best scenario is presented in British Museum Papyrus 10309, incantation 3, in a spell against snake poison. The text is badly damaged, but it emerges that Selket is empowered to treat snake bites. The translation of Leitz (2000, 28–29) reads:

> 'There comes Selket the great, whose arms are on her head, [….] her [ta]il is with whom? ……. as Selket said to Isis, My son [...] many wounds …..[…] *ḳr<r>ty*-snake, …… Have no fear! Have no fear! (My) sister Isis [….]. It is my [son] Horus who lives. The arms […] poison. The living fall, those who are in [their] mounds. Have spat out the poison […] without (you) moving round in any limb of Horus, without […], without slaying the vessels which are [….]. Turn back! […] I am the one who commands theft and the one who commands weakness. I am the mighty one who commands repulsion. I am who commands your arising. I am […] who commands your lament.'

This text represents Selket as a scorpion, and clearly shows her power in controlling and driving out the poison, as well as her role in curing Horus from the bite of the snake. In the same papyrus, incantation 2, Selket appears as 'the Lady of Life' (Leitz 2000, 28). This expresses her ability to cure fatal stings. The same title 'Lady of Life' is also held by Selket on the magical stela of Horus, from Mit-Rahineh, in the Cairo Museum. (JE 33264, CG 9402) (Daressy 1903, 3).

Selket's ability to control poisonous bites of venomous reptiles is also well presented in Chester Beatty Papyrus VII, recto 4, 8. Gardiner's translation reads:

> 'O poison(s) come to me. I am Selket.' (Gardiner 1935, 58, pl. 34).

And again, in Chester Beatty VII, verso 5, 6, the text instructs the poison not to occupy different parts of the body because they are under the protection of a long list of gods, of which Selket is the last. The author's translation reads:

> 'You shall not take your stand in a bite; Selket is against you, Lady of the Bite.'
> (Gardiner 1935, pl. 37).

The name of Selket significantly appears in the title of a long spell in Turin Papyrus 1993[5], (Pleyte, and Rossi 1899, pls. 131, 3; 77+31); parallel to Chester Beatty Papyrus XI, recto 1, 3–4–2. The spell is for knowing the name of the primeval god Re. It relates to the story of the god, who was bitten by a snake, or a scorpion, and expresses his suffering and the pain caused by the poison. Borghouts's translation of the relevant part reads:

> 'Spells for warding off poison (*mtw.t*), from the primeval period (*sp tpy*), when beings came into existence against it who knew its nature (*ḳmꜣ*). Powerful is the god out of whom it originated. Words spoken by Selket:……' (Borghouts 1978, 51, no. 84).

Isis cured the god by means of her magic, and in a later part of the spell, there is a clear indication of the practice of magic in warding off the poison. Borghouts's translation reads:

> ‘Words to be said over an image of Atum-Horus-Hekenu, a woman’s figure of Isis and an image of Horus. To be drawn on the hand of the sufferer. To be licked off by the man. To be done in the same manner on a piece of fine linen, to be applied to the sufferer’s throat. The herb is the ‘scorpion’s herb’. To be ground with beer or wine. To be drunk by one who suffers from a scorpion’s sting. It is an excellent means to kill (the effects of) poison, proven an infinite number of times.’ (Borghouts 1978, 55, no. 84).

The Medicinal Herb

The above texts indicate the use of a ‘scorpion herb’ (*smw wḥˁt*), to cure the stings of scorpions. Although this plant cannot be identified, it is known that a considerable number of herbs are associated with scorpions in Egyptian and later traditions. Some studies have been devoted to the analysis of ancient Egyptian herbs, but without any satisfactory conclusion as to the nature of the scorpion herb. Manniche assumes that Birthwort (Arabic Zarâwind) was used in the treatment of the bites of reptiles, and identifies its use with the Snakeroot, which was used in treating snake bites and infectious diseases, quoting the Italian Physician, Prospero Alpini, who mentions both. He says that it was the ‘round’ one, presumably *Aristolochia rotunda*, that was used to treat scorpion bites, ‘mixed with caper root in aromatic wine’ (Manniche 1989, 84–85). This does not however, establish that the scorpion herb is the Birthwort.

Basil (*Ocymum basilium*) is also known for its association with the scorpion. Grieve, in her study of the Modern Herbal, quoted Parkinson (English herbalist): ‘being gently handled it [basil] gave a pleasant smell, but being hardly wrung and bruised would breed scorpions. It is also observed that scorpions do much rest and abide under these pots and vessels wherein basil is planted.’ She added that ‘It was generally believed that if a sprig of basil were left under a pot, it would in time turn into a scorpion…’ (Grieve 1931, 97).

The Scorpion Senna herb (*Coronilla Scorpioides*), named after the scorpion, is used for regulating the flow of urine, curing heart problems, and as a laxative. Senna is also widespread in Egypt (Grieve 1931, 727). The curing of scorpion poison is recounted in many magical texts, among which is Turin Papyrus 1993 [12] (Pleyte and Rossi 1899, pls. 135, 10–136, 1) which refers to a drink called ‘Hedeb-drink’ used in the curing of scorpion bites. Borghouts’s translation reads:

> ‘Hi you scorpion (*ḏl*) who came forth from under the tree with its sting (*ˁb*) erect, the one who has stung the herdsman in the night when <he> was lying down! Was no reciting done (*šdi*) for him? Reciting was done for him? Reciting was done for him over *ḥdb*-drink and beer, as (for) any strong fighter.’ (Borghouts 1978, 77–78, no. 108).

This text concurs with that quoted above, the spell being recited over a curative drink mixed with beer, to control the poison. Other practices are mentioned in Chester Beatty Papyrus VII recto 5, 5–6, 2 (Gardiner 1935, 59, pl. 34). Borghouts’s translation reads:

> ‘This spell is to be said over a node (?) of reed, soaked in fermented mucus. To be twisted leftwise. To be fitted with 7 knots, to be applied to the mouth of the stinging wound. This spell is to be said every [… ...].’ (Borghouts 1978, 56, no. 86).

Here a similar method is used, with the variation that the spell is recited over a reed or herb, then added to fermented liquid and applied directly to the wound.

Garlic is also connected to protection against scorpion stings. A long spell on Stela Ny Carlsberg A 764 (Mogensen 1930, II, pl. 116) represents the power of garlic in killing and repelling venomous reptiles, and protecting the household. The spell is entitled 'Garlic will protect Wennofer's dwelling'. Borghouts's translation reads:

> '[....] That One (*pfy*) for the garlic (*ḥḏw*), when you enter this house (*pr*) where Osiris, the god's father and servant of Min........., is – to close the mouth of any male snake (*ḥfꜣw*), any female snake, any scorpion (*ḏl*), any reptile (*ḏdf.t*) that bites (*psḥ*) with its mouth, that stings (*ḏdb*) with its tail. You will kill them.' (Borghouts 1978, 82, no. 121).

The spell then names the deities helping in the protection against enemies, and ends with the practice of the spell. Borghouts's translation reads:

> 'Words to be said over garlic, ground and pulverized together with beer. To sprinkle the house with it in the night, before daybreak. No male snake, female snake, scorpion (*ḏl*), reptile, male dead (*mt*) or female dead will enter this house.' (Borghouts 1978, 83, no. 121).

Conclusions

The collection of magical and medical texts presented here provides a considerable body of information about the title of 'The Lady of Chemmis and Wife of Horus'. Despite the absence of an incontrovertible identification of the holder of the title, it is obvious that there is a strong connection to Selket and her role in magic. These texts also illuminate magical practice in ancient Egypt in connection with scorpion stings, and add to the picture of the curative abilities of Selket, as a fundamental aspect of her nature.

School of Archaeology, Classics and Egyptology
University of Liverpool

Bibliography

Allen, J. P. (2005) *The Ancient Egyptian Pyramid Texts,* Atlanta, Society of Biblical Literature.

Borghouts, F. J. (1978) *Ancient Egyptian Magical Texts*, Leiden, Brill.

de Buck, A. and Gardiner A. H. (1935) *The Egyptian Coffin Texts*, 8 vols, Chicago, University of Chicago Press.

Daressy, G. (1903) *Catalogue Général des Antiquités Égyptiennes du Musée du Caire: Textes et Dessins Magiques*, Le Caire, Service des Antiquités de l'Égypte.

Drioton, E. (1939) 'Une Statue Prophylactique de Ramsès III', *Annales du Service des Antiquités de l'Égypte* 39, 57–87.

Faulkner, R. O. (1973) *The Ancient Egyptian Coffin Texts*, Warminster, Aris & Phillips.

Faulkner, R. O. (1985) *The Ancient Egyptian Pyramid Texts*, Warminster, Aris & Phillips.

Gardiner, A. H. (1917) 'Professional Magicians in Ancient Egypt', *Proceedings of the Society of Biblical Archaeology,* 39, 34–41.

Gardiner, A. H. (1935) *Hieratic Papyri in the British Museum*, Third Series: Chester Beatty Gift, Two Volumes, London, British Museum Press.

Gardiner, A. H. (1944) 'Horus the Behdetite', *Journal of Egyptian Archaeology* 30, 24–62.

Gardiner, A. H. (1947) *Ancient Egyptian Onomastica*, II, Oxford, Oxford University Press.

Grieve, M. (1931) *A Modern Herbal: the Medicinal, Culinary, Cosmetic and Economic Properties, Cultivation and Folklore of Herbs, Grasses, Fungi, Shrubs and Trees with all their Modern Scientific Uses*, London, Cape.

Griffiths, J. G. (1960) *The Conflict of Horus and Seth, from Egyptian and Classical Sources: a Study in Ancient Mythology*, Liverpool, Liverpool University Press.
Jelínková-Reymond, E. (1956) *Les Inscriptions de la Statue Guérisseuse de Djedher-le-sauveur*, Le Caire, Institut Français d'Archéologie Orientale.
von Känel, F. (1984) *Les Prêtres-Ouâb de Sekhmet et les conjurateurs de Serket*, Paris, Presses Universitaires de France.
Klasens, A. (1952) *A Magical Statue Base (Socle Béhague) in the Museum of Antiquities at Leiden*, Leiden, Brill.
Leitz, C. (2000) *Hieratic Papyri in the British Museum, Seventh Series: Magical and Medical Papyri of the New Kingdom*, London, British Museum Press.
Manniche, L. (2006) *An Ancient Egyptian Herbal*, London, British Museum Press.
de Meulenaere, H. (1960) 'Une Statuette Égyptienne à Naples', *Le Bulletin de l'Institut Français d'Archéologie Orientale* 60, 117–129.
Mogensen, M. (1930), *La Glyptothèque Ny Carlsberg: la Collection Égyptienne*, 2 vols, Copenhague, Levin & Munksgaard.
Petrie, W. M. F. and Griffith, F. Ll. (1889) *Two Hieroglyphic Papyri from Tanis*, London, Egypt Exploration Fund.
Pleyte, W. M. F. & Rossi F. (1899) *Les Papyrus de Turin [del] Museo Egizio*, 2 vols, Leiden, Brill.
Posener, G. (1972) Catalogue des *Ostraca Hiératiques Littéraires de Deir el-Medineh*, Tome II, Le Caire, Institut Français d'Archéologie Orientale.
Ritner, R. K. (1998) 'The Wives of Horus and the Philinna Papyrus (PGM XX)', in Clarysse, W., Schoors, A. and Willems, H. (eds.) *Egyptian Religion: The Last Thousand Years* II, Leuven, Peeters, 1027–1041.
Sethe, K. (1935–1962) *Übersetzung und Kommentar zur den Altägyptischen Pyramidentexten*, 6 vols, Gluckstadt, Augustin.
Sternberg-El Hotabi, H. (1999) *Untersuchungen zur Überlieferungsgeschichte der Horusstelen*, 2 vols, Weisbaden, Harrassowitz.
Szpakowska, K. (2008) *Daily Life in Ancient Egypt: Recreating Lahun*, Oxford, Blackwell.

Dwarves at Amarna; Social Acceptance or Amusement for the Royal Family?

Trillion Attwood

Introduction

The depictions of dwarves within Amarna tombs mark an important change in Egyptian artistic traditions. Dwarves had been a regular feature of tomb decoration during the late Old Kingdom. However, depictions dramatically ceased at the end of this period. This abundance of Old Kingdom material has resulted in substantial modern research (Dasen 1988; 1993; Weeks 1970) and, although additional information is available from other periods, this is where the focus has remained. The Amarna period marks an important point in Egyptian artistic form and it is here that dwarves are again depicted in tomb decoration. These scenes are especially important as they are the only dwarves depicted in close proximity to the royal family.

The depictions of dwarves from the Old Kingdom are relatively formulaic and although not identical, they do represent similar ideas. Essentially, dwarves are depicted in relatively unskilled occupations that draw attention to their height, and, in some instances, great efforts are made to highlight their height and condition through juxtaposition with other adults or animals (see the tombs of Kaemnefert (Dasen 1993, fig. 9.6) and Mereruka (Dasen 1993, fig. 9.11)). These scenes imply little respect for dwarves, who are included as a point of amusement within the scene. This is especially seen in dancing scenes where the nature of the condition can be further highlighted through movement (see the tomb of Nunetjer (Dasen 1993, fig. 9.17)). The attitudes portrayed indicate actual attitudes towards dwarves at this time, most likely not intended maliciously, but neither fully accepting of them.

After the Old Kingdom dwarves are no longer represented in tomb decoration, and there are very few images of them in other media, with the only examples of ordinary dwarves being servant statues, which offer no context in which to understand their relative position. The only further alternative is the Bes image, although this image undergoes considerable transformations and should not necessarily be compared to mortals. It is for this reason that the Amarna images are important, as they offer a tangible context in which to understand the position of dwarves during the New Kingdom, and thereby offer the most solid impression of how society's opinion of these individuals developed over time.

Throughout this paper the term dwarf will be used to refer to all individuals of short stature, both human and mythical. This term is not used condescendingly but rather as a convenient generic term (Dasen 1988, 253) and it shall cover all forms of dwarfism rather than distinguishing different conditions.

Definitions

There are a wide variety of different forms of dwarfism. However the only condition identified and depicted during the Old Kingdom and in the Amarna period is Achondroplasia. This form of dwarfism displays short limbs, feet and hands, large heads with prominent forehead and chin, and a depressed nasal bridge. The condition also displays marked lumbar lordosis and a protuberant abdomen (Marshall 1977, 140). This creates a striking image and gives a substantial number of diagnostic features that the Egyptian craftsmen could represent.

The possible alternative form of dwarfism depicted is Hypochondroplasia which presents with similar symptoms, though with lesser marked limb shortening, and no facial disfigurement (Marshall 1977, 140). The two conditions are easily confused and some scholars have chosen to interpret these images as showing Hypochondroplasia. However key features of Achondroplasia are often present in these images, such as the lumbar lordosis, not seen in Hypochondroplasia. Other key diagnostic features, such as hand shape, are rarely visible enough within Egyptian depictions to be diagnostic, thus Achondroplasia seems the most probable condition.

The reason such a specific condition was selected for depiction was to ensure effective communication; depictions of alternative forms of dwarfism could be misunderstood as representing an individual of lesser status, due purely to his height. For example, another form of dwarfism presents with normal proportions, though far smaller than is normal, and thus would not be suitable for the Egyptian cannon. In addition, dwarves were often depicted naked, a state often reserved for children (Aldred 1980, 17). Furthermore there are examples of dwarves being depicted with the forefinger to the mouth or a side lock of youth, again indicating childhood, and therefore potentially very misleading. In these examples it is the highly distinctive nature of the condition that allows the audience to understand the scene as intended.

The dwarves

The dwarves depicted within the Amarna tombs are two specific females. They are portrayed repeatedly in the tombs of Panehesy (Fig. 1) and Ay, and once in the tombs of May and Tutu. The two individuals are always seen together and generally close to, if not immediately beside, Berenmut, believed to be Nefertiti's sister (Davies 14, 1905). They are also almost always given the titles 'The vizier of the queen, Ernheh ('To Eternity')' and 'The vizier of his mother, Para ('The Sun') (Davies 1908, 18). The names have also been put more simply as *Hemet-niswetrneheh* and *Mutef-Pre* (Murnane 1995, 116). Davies (1905, 14) has gone some way to attempt to explain the names, suggesting 'his mother' refers to Tiye, Akhenaten's mother and that 'the queen' may also refer to Tiye, or alternatively another Queen of Amenhotep III. The former suggestion seems most probable with both dwarves belonging to the same individual. How they came to be with Berenmut is not clear. Davies (1905, 14) suggests that the three may have come from Thebes for an extended visit from the Theban court.

***Figure 1**. Dwarves in the Tomb of Panehesy (Davies, 1905, Plate V (Detail).*

It would appear that the names were never intended to be taken literally. They are not the type of names that would be given to attendants, and based on the information available, these individuals did not serve in the position of vizier. Rather, these names could possibly indicate that these individuals were not taken seriously. There is no indication of their original names, though the change to alternative names may indicate foreign origins. This suggestion is based upon the interpretation that Berenmut is in fact Tadukhipa (Davies 1908, 21), although there is no solid basis for this theory. One should not expect to see the original names at Amarna; if they were visiting from Thebes they would not be well known within the area and so leave little in the record. It is also for this reason that these dwarves can be seen in very few tombs, reflecting their limited visit.

On the supposition that the dwarves were on a visit from the Theban court, the nature of the given names makes sense and may indicate the position of these individuals within their immediate surroundings. It seems that these dwarves may have had, on a primitive level, some form of entertainer status, possibly even in the manner of jester. The concept of court jester is a modern idea; however, the association of dwarfism with humour is very visible throughout both the ancient and modern world, and while not considered politically correct today, possibly even taboo, it is impossible to assess such a disability in Egyptian culture without addressing these less liberal ideas.

The two dwarves under discussion are probably also in the position of close personal attendants to Berenmut. During the Old Kingdom, dwarves were commonly depicted in the position of attendant (see tombs of Khentkaus (Dasen 1993, fig. 9.7) and Kaemnefert (Dasen 1993, fig. 9.6)) and thus the Amarna scenes may display an element of continuity. Suggestions as to why dwarves were suitable for this position vary; possibly they were perceived as attendants and entertainers. Alternatively they may have been suited to this position as they were not considered as fully adult and did not, therefore, carry some of the traditional threats. This idea is conveyed by the depiction of male dwarves in the position of women's attendants in the Old Kingdom (as in the tombs of Wehemka (Dasen 1993, fig. 9.3) and Queen Meresankh at Giza (Dasen 1993, fig. 9.2)). It is also possible that, as the position of attendant was one of the few available to women (Bryan 1996, 40), dwarves filled this position as a lack of other suitable alternatives.

There is little additional evidence available about the dwarves themselves; the type of dwarfism depicted, for instance, is for artistic convenience. It is not possible to establish their approximate height as they are shown in scenes where comparison to Akhenaton would make them a few centimetres tall. In other scenes they are shown with no point of comparison making it impossible to estimate their height.

What is unusual about the depictions of the dwarves is that they are always shown with their feet turned inwards. This is not a feature necessarily indicative of any condition pertaining to dwarfism, and it is highly unlikely that two individuals would both have such a unique additional medical condition. Perhaps only one of the individuals had an additional complication, but the artist felt compelled to illustrate the feature on both. It is also possible that the artist was unaware of the differences between the two, or that artistic symmetry became a factor. It also seems probable that this relates to the idea of highlighting the condition, possibly for clarity.

The dwarves' positions in the scenes shows a certain level of importance, as they are almost always shown in close proximity to Berenmut, and in turn close to the entire royal family. This close proximity, combined with the names, suggests that they held a unique position within the upper echelons of society. Prior to this period of Egyptian history the depictions of dwarves were never named or portrayed within this type of context, and while the names do not appear to be real, the fact that they have them at all implies a certain level of significance within the scene and the royal court. Given the developments in art at this time, the dwarves' repeated presence in tomb decoration is at the request of the ruling class.

There is also a lack of information regarding various aspects of these individuals. Notably, it is not possible to establish age, with the only possible indicator being the complete lack of hair, possibly indicating relatively old age, which combined with the associations with Tiye, may represent an element of reality. Unfortunately, given the general life expectancy at this time, combined with the added complications of the medical conditions of these individuals, it seems highly unlikely that they would reach such an age. It is probable that the dwarves are, in part, depicted bald for artistic convenience. The princesses are also depicted bald and so depicting the dwarves likewise offers better artistic effect and displays the association between the dwarves and children as a whole (as discussed below).

What the images reveal

All the images of these two dwarves are remarkably similar. Beyond the basic representation of their condition, there are a number of additional elements that may be indicative of social understanding. Their dress is interesting, both being shown wearing knee length dresses that project sharply from around the naval. The dresses have narrow straps and are of a simple tubular shape. The sharp angle makes them appear heavy, especially when compared to the other women's light and almost sheer garments. This type of garment is, however, relatively similar to that which was worn by attendants in earlier images (see Dasen 1993, 113).

The women are also depicted wearing simple headbands which consist of a disk placed centrally on the head from which a long, wide flap extends to cover the ear. In the case of the dwarves, these flaps extend to the jaw line. In contrast, on the princesses wearing the same garment, the flaps reach shoulder height. That the dwarves are shown wearing the same garment as the princesses is significant, possibly indicating a level of acceptance or, more likely, to preserve symmetry within the scene. This latter element is of course significant, but the depiction of these dwarves wearing the same garment in all probability does represent some level of status.

A key issue that emerges when examining these images is the striking resemblance between these dwarves and children. They appear to have been stripped of all femininity, wearing heavy garments, few accessories, no hair and have none of the womanly grace distinctive of this period. This was a period when femininity was to be represented to almost a characteristic level, and so the complete absence of any real femininity, and even greater absence of sexuality, is of relevance.

Certainly it should be kept in mind, as a result of the medical condition of these dwarves, that childbirth would pose an exceptionally perilous experience. Childbirth was already dangerous enough in healthy individuals with the limited medical knowledge of the time, and would have been an even greater risk for an individual who suffered from existing complaints. It seems that, as a result of these major challenges, perhaps combined with their height, female dwarves were not seen as complete women. This concept of not being a complete adult was an idea that has been explored using the representations of male dwarves as attendants to women during the Old Kingdom (Dasen 1993, 114), being represented in this position as they were not considered to pose the traditional hazard to women posed by an ordinary male. It is possible this idea extended to females suffering from similar conditions.

Although the overall dress may be adult in form, the headband would support this childlike element. Robins (1999, 57) states that the key features that identify a female child within

Egyptian art are nakedness and a bald head, with the transition into womanhood being shown though the presence of hair and dress. As such, it seems that these images under discussion clearly indicate that these individuals are trapped somewhere between childhood and womanhood which is not understood by Egyptian society and so is expressed in this manner. This is further highlighted by their presence beside the children within scenes of the royal family. Clearly a major consideration in the composition of this scene was artistic effect, and conformity to specific artistic conventions. This association with children is possibly the most important element when attempting to understand the position of dwarves within Egyptian society.

These representations are in marked contrast to scenes from the ancient Greek and Roman worlds (Dasen 1988). There are a number of images of predominantly male dwarves from both societies, although it is interesting to note clear differences. Dwarves are depicted as distinctly male, shown as balding and with a beard. They, too, are often shown naked with their genitals clearly visible. This emphasis upon sexuality and adulthood is in marked contrast to that which was seen in Egypt. There is a lack of representations of female dwarfs from Ancient Greek and Roman contexts, and so direct comparison is impossible. Nevertheless, there is clearly a striking difference between the imagery of the different societies.

It could be argued that there was more respect towards dwarves in Egypt during the later periods of Pharaonic Egypt and that here they were regarded as highly valuable, possibly in part or as a direct result of the strong divine associations. Bes was emerging as a distinct character from the Middle Kingdom and came to prominence during the New Kingdom (Dasen 1993, 55). This divine association would certainly have helped the position of dwarves within society, and has led to some interpretations of dwarves having magical qualities. Based upon this association it seems surprising that, in the Amarna period specifically, dwarves remain popular, although this may indicate that their magical or divine associations are not as strong as may be expected within Egyptian culture as a whole. The close association between Bes and fertility may have made it a preferred choice to have a dwarf as an attendant, especially for a member of the royal family.

The issue of disability and the understanding of such issues in Egypt is a key subject that emerges in the production of these scenes. Clearly these individuals are afflicted with a very specific condition and, if we are to believe the representations, a relatively severe form with disfigured feet. Previously there had been significant emphasis on the nature of the condition, representing individuals undertaking activities that would highlight this. In contrast, the individuals are depicted in a static position, with little specific involvement in the scene. This could possibly lead to the conclusion that the issue of disability is no longer such a priority; however, the representation of the feet contradicts this. This is further corroborated by the scene arrangements where the dwarves' height can be highlighted through the juxtaposition of other healthy adults and children, thus emphasising the contrast.

The disability remains central to the identity of these individuals from society's perspective. It is due to their disability alone that they are represented within these scenes and this is further highlighted by various techniques used by the artist. They may also have gained some respect as a result of having lived and survived with such a condition, and possibly attained an almost magical perspective as a result. Regardless of the reasons, the disability remains central to their presentation.

Conclusion

The evidence of dwarves depicted at the Amarna royal court is rather surprising compared to the general Egyptian attitude to the depiction of the human form. The brief appearance, and then dramatic decline of such images after the Old Kingdom had set a standard of absence that was then reversed for such a brief period that these images are rarely noted. For this reason the depictions of these two dwarves are of a particular and unique relevance. It is also surprising to find two individuals repeated on such a regular basis within a number of tombs of some of the key members of society. As to what all of this means remains confusing. Clearly the individuals are particularly associated with Berenmut, and it is through this that they have gained such a level of popularity. It seems that the lack of respect that was depicted in the Old Kingdom images is not seen within these and so perhaps dwarves receive a higher level of respect than had been seen earlier.

In contrast, the names given to these individuals indicate that the issues of being points of amusement remains. There is a reduction, however, of this element of amusement from these images, for example ungainly dancing, as seen in the Old Kingdom, and this indicates some progression. In addition, there is still clearly an emphasis on the issue of disability, with the reason for depiction remaining the condition and not the individual. This is seen most simply in the variety of different diagnostic features visible, as well as the fact that no other attendants are regularly named.

The potential for interpretation of the role these two individuals possessed is relatively complex in many ways but there is an overall simplicity to the reason they were included. They hold the position of close personal attendant and/or entertainer to Berenmut, which suggests they were guaranteed a period of comfort during their lifespan. Whether they would have been faced with so many of the problems that would have existed for ordinary dwarves remains to be seen. It is quite possible they may have received the additional medical attention needed for certain specific elements of their condition that could have been offered by medical practitioners at this time.

The nationality of these individuals remains an issue; although they are depicted as Egyptian, the names could indicate non-Egyptian origins. It is probable that, as the more important element in their depiction was their condition rather than their ethnicity, it may have been overlooked entirely. It is also relevant that they do have some similar elements in dress to the other Egyptian women depicted, both royal and non-royal, but they do not match either group closely, possibly indicating their non-Egyptian roots.

The idea of royalty bringing dwarves for their personal entertainment was most clearly seen in the letters of Harkuf, who is sent to a foreign land, possibly Punt, to collect a dwarf for Pepi II (Lichtheim 1973, 26–27). Although there is a considerable time difference, this is a clear example of bringing an individual with a specific medical condition a considerable distance for royal entertainment. This may indicate the way in which dwarves were perceived by the elite, possibly as commodities rather than individuals. As to the significance of these representations in regard to the position of dwarves as a whole, this is difficult to ascertain, but one can develop a reasonable level of understanding. It seems clear that there has been some development since the Old Kingdom. Previously there had been much attention paid to humour through depictions of dwarves and this does not seem to have gone completely. They have, in part, been depicted as a point of interest and the focus is no longer quite so heavily upon amusement.

It is possible that by the Amarna period there had been some acceptance of male dwarves as men. Previously, male dwarves had been seen depicted regularly as attendants to both men and women, but here clearly two females are depicted. This may suggest some progression within society at this time; it is possible that the Bes associations helped to establish more masculinity for male dwarves. It is difficult to develop this idea, however, due to the lack of evidence.

The material examined in this paper has offered an important insight into the position of dwarves in Ancient Egypt. It appears essentially that the position of dwarves had not greatly improved; they still served in similar positions and their condition was paramount to any possible achievements. It seems that although dwarves were no longer perceived in quite the same negative manner, they were still predominantly viewed as points of interest. Essentially with time, more of a balance had been achieved; however some of the same issues did remain. As to whether this was the case for the whole of society or simply the ruling class is still impossible to know. Possibly additional information will offer further clarity on this subject; however given the relative rarity of suitable evidence, it is necessary to draw all possible conclusions from the available data. There are also a number of statues of dwarves from the period (Dasen 1993, 148) but, given the lack of context, they are not relevant to this study. What is certain is that at this time these two particular dwarves represent the exception, and, though possibly not accepted fully by modern standards, they did encounter the best that could be expected within the society and time that they lived.

University of Leicester

Bibliography

Aldred, C. (1980) *Egyptian Art*, London, Thames and Hudson.

Bryan, B. M. (1996) In Woman good and bad fortune are on earth: Status and roles of women in Egyptian culture in Capel, A. K. and Markoe, G. E. (eds), *Mistress of the house, Mistress of heaven: women in ancient Egypt*, New York, Hudson Hills Press.

Dasen, V. (1988) 'Dwarfism in Egypt and classical antiquity: Iconography and medical history', *Medical History 32*, 253–276.

Dasen, V. (1993) *Dwarfs in Ancient Egypt and Greece*, Oxford, Claredon Press.

Davies, N de G. (1905) *The Rock Tombs of el-Amarna, part II*, London, Egypt Exploration Society.

Davies, N de G. (1908) *The Rock Tombs of el-Amarna, part VI*, London, Egypt Exploration Society.

Lichtheim, M. (1973) *Ancient Egyptian literature: A book of Readings vol. 1 The Old and Middle Kingdoms*, Berkeley, University of California Press.

Marshall, W. A. (1977) *Human Growth and its Disorders,* London, Academic Press Inc.

Murnane, W. J. (1995) *Texts from the Amarna Period in Egypt*, Georgia, Scholars Press.

Robins, G. (1999) 'Hair and the construction of identity in Ancient Egypt', *Journal of the American Research Center in Egypt 36*, 55–69.

Weeks, K. R. (1970) *Anatomical Knowledge of the Ancient Egyptians*, New Haven, Yale University Press.

The Use of Scientific Techniques and the Study of Ancient Egyptian and Near Eastern Weaponry from the Garstang Museum, School of Archaeology, Classics and Egyptology, University of Liverpool

Dan Boatright

Introduction

The museums of the UK hold significant amounts of ancient Egyptian and Near Eastern weaponry, yet the degree to which these artefacts are considered useful can vary from one scholar to another. A lack of provenance, largely resulting from museum collections amassed from donations by wealthy philanthropists or purchased on the antiquities market, has been a major problem encountered when studying these artefacts. This has been exacerbated by the ad hoc system deployed by exploration societies who donated many artefacts to museums but did not keep adequate records, as well as poor records being kept within museums. Those weapons that were recorded in detail are few and far between, and rare in British museums. Philip (1989, 2006) makes it very clear that any study should only ever include this small corpus of recorded material so that the work does not suffer from bias or dating errors. This approach, however, requires either a large travel fund or an over reliance on photographic material, leaving a large body of data unaccounted for and, whilst they may never be adequately dated, these objects can still provide information on production techniques, weapon design and military practices.

In this paper the analysis of these weapons from the Garstang Museum will be discussed and put into the wider context of the author's research. The use of scientific techniques will be evaluated along with the evidence they provide, not only from an academic point of view but also with the objectives and aims of the museums and institutions housing these weapons in mind. This latter consideration is of vital importance as the techniques used to obtain a chemical and structural analysis are destructive to the weapon and, while this can be conserved, it is important to consider the requirements of the many stakeholders in British museum collections, not only the researchers, curators and conservators who work with the objects, but also the general public who visit them.

The Objects, Objectives and Techniques

The fourteen Garstang weapons are part of a wider corpus being studied, for a Ph.D. thesis, to analyse the technological and production techniques used to manufacture Bronze Age Egyptian and Near Eastern swords, daggers, axes and spears. Arrowheads were initially omitted as their large number require a work of their own; however, a small number were later added. Spearheads from Manchester Museum appear to fall into two different groups, one of a smaller size that closely resembles large arrowheads with a distinct chemical composition, whereas the second group are larger, usually have a socket for attaching to the shaft and have a 'cleaner' composition with a higher tin content. By adding arrowheads from the Garstang collection it was hoped that a clearer understanding of whether two variants existed, possibly on the basis of whether smaller spear and arrowheads designed for throwing (and therefore disposable) were made using inferior technologies. Of course regional variation and other possible issues will also be addressed. Overall this thesis aims to answer such questions as: Why were these objects made? Could they be used to fight? How were they made? Why those particular designs? Were they ever used? Is it possible to deduce where these objects were made and by whom? When attempting to answer these questions, how the Egyptian weapons fitted into the technological and production framework of the Near East will also be considered; a topic often discussed by such authors as Shaw (2001) and Philip (2006). With so many questions in mind, and the large amount of data involved, only objects that were chemically and/or metallographically analysed have been included in the study. While many more weapons exist, it was determined that including them in the work would provide an unmanageable corpus and restrict development of the objectives beyond producing an extensive catalogue.

The Garstang weapons constitute about ten percent of the overall number of objects being chemically analysed, but almost one third of the objects being metallographically sampled. The latter can prove difficult, not only as it is preferable to take samples from already damaged weapons, (which limits the number of objects) but also as transporting the objects for sampling can be problematical. While the chemical sampling only requires a hand-held drill with a 0.6, 0.8 or 1 mm drill bit, which is portable and can be taken to the museum, the saw used requires the objects to be brought to the University of Liverpool, where all the sampling and analyses are carried out by the author (as demonstrated in Fig. 1). Other collections included in this thesis

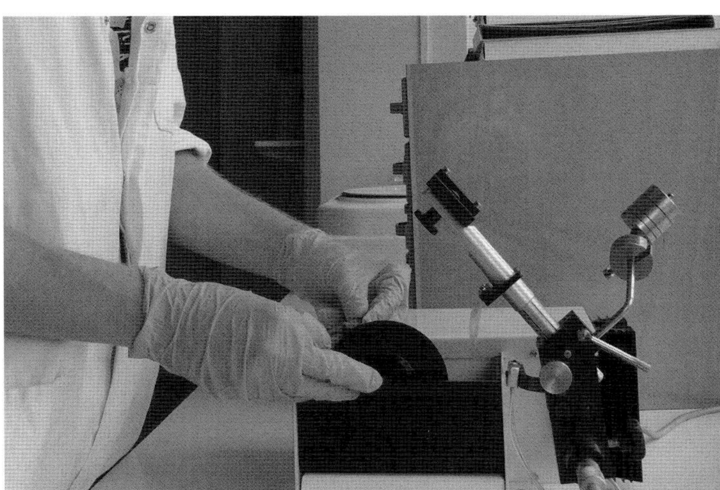

Figure 1. *The saw being used to cut a sample. This can either be done by putting a small object in the vice and cutting the object using the automated system, or larger objects can be done by hand (author's own).*

are from Manchester, Bolton, Birmingham and Bristol Museums, the World Museum, Liverpool and the Institute Collection and Petrie Museum at University College London.

No attempt to provenance the objects was made and, unless there is a justifiable date, this was not included in the thesis. It is for this reason that such a wide timeframe was used. With so many objects believed to be of Bronze Age context, but little known about their origins, it is logical to start with all objects available, determine their worth in scientific examinations and decide whether it is valid to use them in future research. This is not normally attempted by scholars, with Philip (1989, 9) noting that uncontexted objects have little evidential worth, and stating that the approach used here leads to a concentration too focused on the objects, rather than the context. Yadin (1963) takes a very different stance and visually analyses weaponry from the viewpoint of function-efficiency and this has become increasingly popular in the study of British, Irish and Minoan Bronze Age weaponry (Bridgford 1997a; 1997b; Molloy 2007; Peatfield 2007), where swords especially have been analysed in detail and replicas produced to determine fighting techniques and capabilities. This work aims to study weapons using an approach somewhere in between, with a visual analysis being conducted alongside the technical studies, and it is hoped that this analysis will lead to the production of as full an account of technological techniques and production practices as possible.

The Garstang collection includes one sword (E1530, Fig. 2), eleven axes, and three dagger blades, two of the latter being from Jericho. Five of the axes were originally metallographically sampled by Simpson (1993) as part of a project to study corrosion in ancient Egyptian artefacts, and these samples have been reused in this project. This has been problematical as the samples were taken from the butt or tang of the weapon, rather than the blade edge (which is far more useful in determining technological and production techniques). The samples taken from the other objects have been from the blade, to ensure that maximum information could be extracted from the material, and were typically 3–4mm wide. Samples for chemical analysis were taken from inconspicuous parts of the objects, such as the tang of the dagger, along the thickest part of the axe body or, wherever it is possible to drill into an existing damaged area (such as the site of a previously extracted metallographic sample).

Chemical analysis was conducted by atomic absorption spectrometry, a method which allows the researcher to test for all of the major and minor elements, and most of the important trace elements in an ancient copper alloy. The sampling and analytical techniques are detailed in Hughes *et al.* (1976). The metallographic examination was conducted after the samples were mounted in resin, ground and polished using progressively finer papers and pads, down to one quarter of a micron. The samples were analysed under the microscope, unetched and etched, in

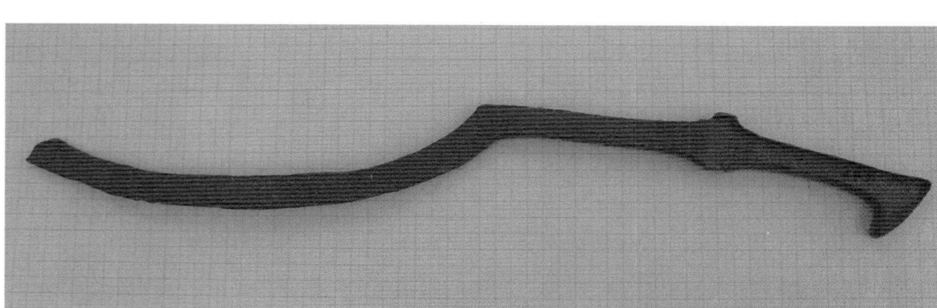

Figure 2. *The sword from the Garstang Museum, photographed on 1mm squared paper to show scale.*

alcoholic ferric chloride and aqueous ammonium persulfate to determine what structures were present. The sampling and analytical techniques are discussed in Scott (1991).

The Results

As the aim of this paper is to discuss the presentation of scientific data in museums and the interpretation of the information itself, rather than to publish the full results, only the information required for this paper will be presented. A full account of the data, the methodology used and analysis of the results can be found in Boatright (2010). A general overview is of course required and the data presented in Figs 4 and 5 is the chemical analysis of the Garstang weapons. These results show that these weapons are all copper or copper alloys with varying levels of arsenic, tin and other minor and trace elements expected for Bronze Age metals of this period. The exception is E1401, shown in Fig. 3. The high zinc level in this axe would not have been possible in Bronze Age Egypt, nor is it likely to have come from another civilisation in the region. Craddock (1978, 1) notes that it is not until the First Millennium BC that brasses with particularly high zinc contents emerge. Such an artefact could have been purchased on the antiquities market or could have been found in a tomb of Bronze Age provenance but re-used in later antiquity.

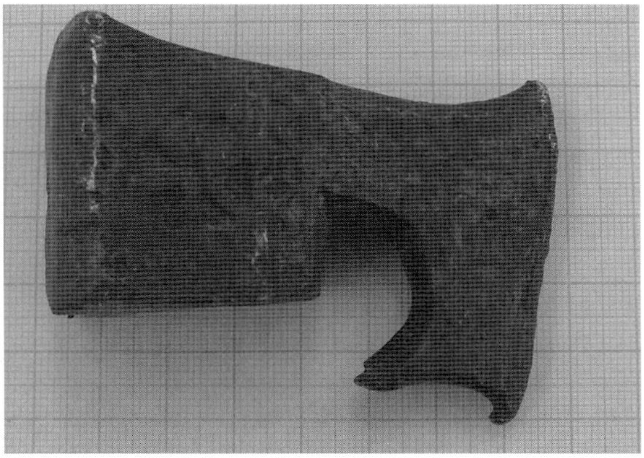

Figure 3. *Axe E1401 (author's own).*

It is difficult to perform a detailed statistical analysis of such a small group of weapons but a simple scatter diagram (Fig. 4) revealed that a small group, with two axes and the sword, contained high amounts of tin and low arsenic levels, consistent with what Craddock (1976, 100) notes as being the optimum for bronze weaponry with a mechanically hardened edge. A similarly sized group, in this case just axes, appear unalloyed, while another group contain a varying amount of arsenic, from 1 to 5%, but no tin. Two objects have a measurable amount of both. Both arsenic and tin are known for their strengthening properties and it would, therefore, be expected that any weapon produced may have had at least a measurable amount of one or the other. The varying levels of tin and arsenic have also been discussed, namely by Cowell (1987), Budd *et al.* (1991) and Northover (2001), and a general consensus is that anything over 1% arsenic and 2% tin can be considered a deliberate alloy to some degree, whether an additive in the melt or the choice of ore with the alloy being naturally produced.

It is also potentially possible to analyse the composition in order to characterise the different types of ores that may have been used to produce the metals for these weapons, or what types of processes were used to produce them. For instance iron ore was used as a flux in ancient Egypt and the Near East, as it aids the smelting process (Cowell 1987, 98–9) and was extensively used at such smelting sites as Timna, where high iron levels are characteristic of these production centres (Hauptmann and Wagner 2007, 67, 73; Roman 1990, 81). This iron can be removed through subsequent processes and can also be an indicator of how well refined the metal is. As shown

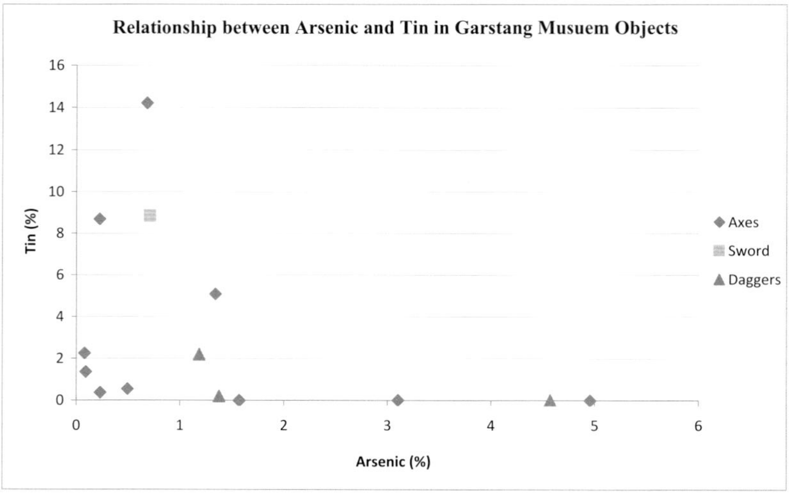

Figure 4. *Scatter diagram showing the levels of arsenic relative to the levels of tin in the analysed weapons.*

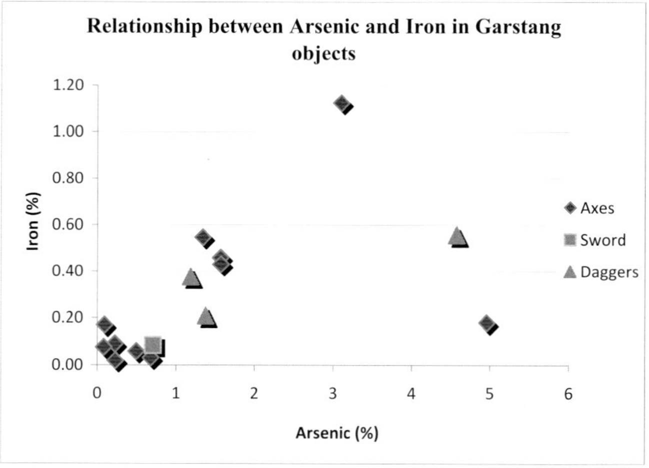

Figure 5. *Scatter diagram showing the levels of arsenic relative to the levels of iron in the analysed weapons.*

in Fig. 5 several of these weapons had been produced from alloys made from copper produced from iron-flux processes, and this is particularly evident with the daggers, but axes E1504 and E1498 are especially high in content. There are possible suggestions that this iron content is linked to the arsenic. However, this is too small a dataset to establish firm conclusions. It is also difficult to establish whether these objects are from Timna ores specifically as so few metal processing regions have been excavated so extensively, but they were certainly manufactured from a copper produced in a manner consistent with ancient smelting sites.

Many of the other elements, such as silver, gold and cobalt are analysed to determine the levels of trace elements within the composition. These minute amounts can indicate which ores may have been used to produce these artefacts. For instance, silver and arsenic together can indicate ores often found in the Near East (Hauptmann and Wagner 2007), whereas gold can indicate Egyptian Eastern Desert extractions (El Gayar and Jones 1987). Zinc is often found as a trace element within ancient metalwork but the levels found in the axes E1506, E1516 and E1533 are unexpectedly higher, being over 2%. The exact cause of this is unknown but Vatandoust (1999, 136) noted sixteen objects from Iran with higher levels of zinc, between 1 and 3%. Two objects from Booken (Iran), a copper knife (1.13%) and a pin (2.59%) had notable levels but there does not appear to be a definite regional variation and so no correlations can be made. Additionally it has been suggested that zinc ores are found alongside copper ores in Egypt (Said 1962) and so it is becoming increasingly likely that this was an infrequent, but accidental, addition to copper alloys throughout the Near East.

Metallographic analysis can also provide a wealth of information, not only about the structure of the object, but the corrosion products present can reveal the conditions of deposition and areas of weakness within the object. A sample was taken from E1506, a curved thin axe, with a sharp blade that has the potential to be an effective fighting weapon. The sample was taken from the end marked A on Fig. 6 and, once etched in alcoholic ferric chloride, revealed some very interesting features. As seen in Fig. 7, the weapon has re-crystallised, equi-axed, hexagonal

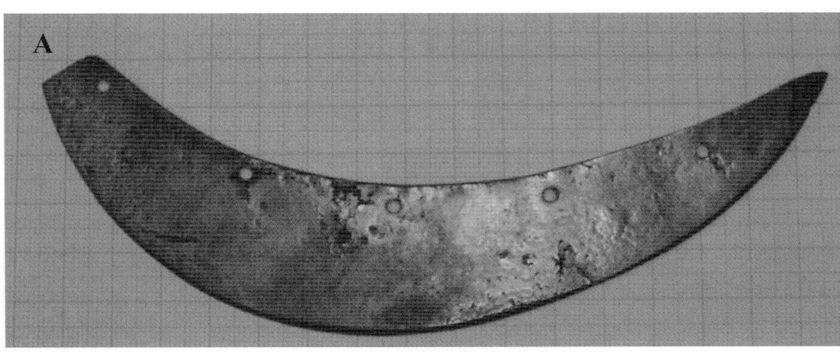

Figure 6. *Axe E1506 (author's own).*

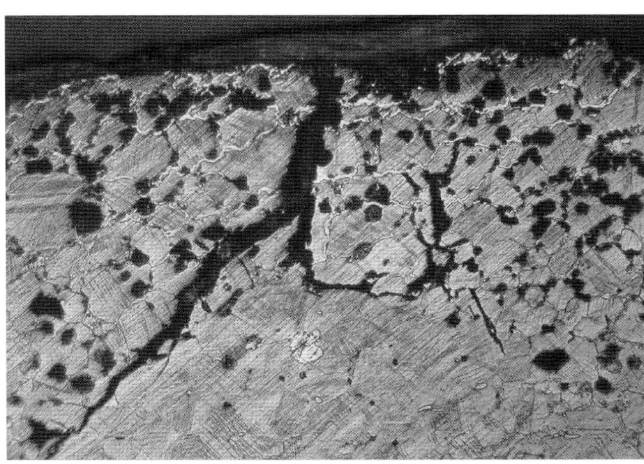

Figure 7. *A micrograph of E1506, showing an area of the blade edge. The structure has clearly visible slip lines on equi-axed hexagonal grains and a large vein of inter-granular corrosion running through the area. Along the surface a layer of leached material has formed in between the grains. Etched in alcoholic ferric chloride, field of view 1.5mm. (Author's own).*

grains, with all grains showing strain with slip lines clearly visible, and it is now suffering from severe inter-granular corrosion. Such a structure is interpreted by Scott (1991, 92) as showing that the weapon has been heavily hotworked, as indicated by the straightness of the slip lines and is unlikely to have undergone many annealing cycles. As a result of this working, the arsenic in the melt would have risen to the surface, creating this silvery layer on the surface of the object, known as inverse segregation. This would have altered the appearance of the object significantly, which today is rather dull and brown in colour, but in antiquity would have been very shiny and silver in colour. This may have been a deliberate technique to make the object appear more valuable, and while not often seen on Egyptian weaponry previously, has been observed on Bronze Age axes of the UK (Close-Brooks and Coles 1980) and Spain (Meeks 1993).

In contrast to E1506, the sample taken from E1533 reveals a totally different structure. E1533 is a large, thick and blunt axe with green corrosion product on the surface and three rivet holes down the tang side. The sample was taken from the tang, as shown on Fig. 8, by Simpson (1993) for a project analysing the role of lead in ancient Egyptian metalwork, but it has subsequently provided vast amounts of information about the structure of the weapon. The metallographic examination indicated that the weapon was cast, with long dendrites visible across the surface and coring visible at the end of the dendrites (Fig. 9). Dendritic structures result from different phases of the melt cooling at different temperatures and creating branch-like formations with the cores as a result of the contraction of the melt during cooling and air pockets remaining (Scott 1991, 12–15). The silver material interspersed within the structure is lead, which is not

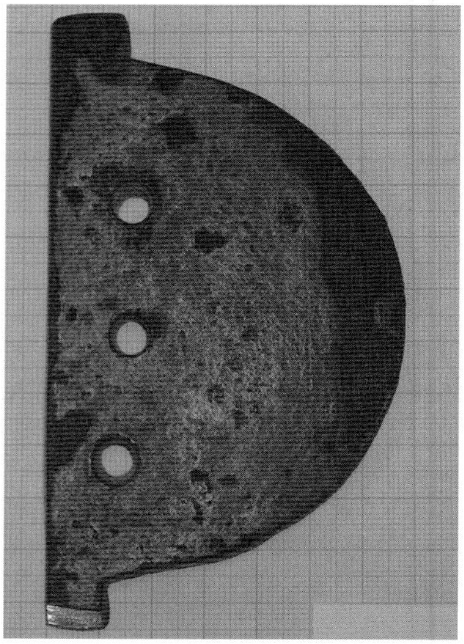

Figure 8. *Axe E1533 (author's own).*

Figure 9. *Micrograph of an area of E1533 (author's own).*

soluble within copper and also demonstrates that no working has taken place, the globules being randomly aligned and in varying shapes and sizes. This axe would certainly be very different to manipulate, compared to E1506, but both are equally effective for their intended purpose, E1506 being a sharp axe ideal for cutting and slashing, E1533 being more suited to striking heavy blows with maximum impact. While the production of E1533 could certainly be considered simpler it would have been of very different usage to E1506 and whether they reflect a change of styles over different periods, or a reflection of changes in warfare or individual preference is not clear but they do demonstrate some of the production techniques being used in Bronze Age Egypt.

This variation in design has been a feature of many avenues of research by scholars in recent years, with Philip (1989; 2003; 2006), Bridgford (1997a; 1997b; 2002), Molloy (2007) and Peatfield (2007) all discussing various facets of functionality, ritual symbolism, religion and the design of Bronze Age weaponry across Europe and the Mediterranean. Various opinions exist regarding the importance and validity of individual theories discussing the causes and effects of technological change on weaponry production, and the methodology for research into the purpose of weaponry in Bronze Age cultures has become very diverse, ranging from typological analysis (Philip 1989; 2006) and statistical analysis (Bridgford 1997a; 2002) to reproductions of ancient weapons used in reconstructed battle conditions (Molloy 2007; Peatfield 2007). Scientific analysis is rarely seen in this area of study, with only Craddock (1976; 1978), Cowell (1987) and Lang (1987) producing large studies and this has largely declined in recent years. This has resulted in many technical discussions lacking the full picture of production practices and technological development in the Bronze Age. This is not necessarily the result of a lack of interest but, rather, a reservation on the part of museum curators, scholars and the general public to see aesthetically pleasing objects being sampled for academic study with the resultant damage being very visible to all but the results being very much aimed at a particularly small group, the academic community, where reports on the sampling and resultant findings are filed away, but not utilised for educational purposes or for the benefit of the general public.

The Use of these results at the Garstang Museum

It should be stressed that the scientific study of ancient materials is by no means a new phenomenon. Allen *et al.* (1970) conducted a metallurgical study of objects in the Pitt Rivers Museum, and, for Davies' (1987) catalogue of Egyptian axes housed in the British Museum, detailed chemical (conducted by Cowell 1987) and metallurgical (by Lang 1987) examinations of the objects was conducted. Considering the frequency with which PhD research at least utilises some facet of scientific analysis, it is startling how little reaches the public domain (Craddock 1976; 1978; Khalil 1980; Mei 2000). This is very much in conflict with the more traditional sciences, where, for example, the Science Museum in London is specifically aimed at engaging the public with science and engineering, and the Pitt Rivers has incorporated microscopes and large screens into their exhibitions so that the public can investigate botanical and faunal remains (as shown in Fig. 10). This is particularly important in the current climate,

Figure 10. *Microscopic examination being utilised as part of an exhibit at the Pitt Rivers Museum. Photograph courtesy of J. Cromwell, March 2008.*

with interest in scientific subjects in schools, colleges and universities declining in recent years (Osbourne 2003, 1049).

Archaeology is in a very unique position, having the material to inspire the general public, with popular television shows, such as Time Team and Timewatch drawing large audiences, and films and books dedicated to history and archaeology (both fiction and non-fiction) being multi-million pound industries. Many of these media draw on scientific analyses and reconstructions, the use of laboratory and scientific practices, and CSI-style investigations, yet museums have been slower to actively engage with the public in this manner. It is, however, entirely possible to use such scientific examinations in this manner. The use of a weapon in battle, how it was used to attack, what damage it could inflict on a foe, how it was held and where it was used, are all questions posed by museum visitors when confronted by ancient weapons. The technology used to produce the objects, as well as the production facilities, are also ideas that cross the mind of visitors. The weapons can also often be supported by the evidence from mummified remains, such as the soldiers of Neb-hepet-rē' Mentu-hotpe whose bodies are riddled with brutal injuries inflicted in battle (Winlock 1945). This type of exhibition has briefly been tackled by small exhibits in such museums as Manchester Museum, where a video of the manufcture of a traditional Medieval English longbow was shown, alongside a number of the actual artefacts from the collection.

The exhibit at the Garstang Museum is aimed at bridging this gap; by putting a facet of academic research into the wider context of Bronze Age Egypt, and showing what practical science can reveal about the production and technology of this period to both interested academics and the general public alike. As part of a wider scheme to promote the Garstang collection, and produce a series of temporary cases, using the material alongside current research, the exhibit (shown in Figs 11 and 12) is focused very much on the objects, the samples taken from them, the results shown and how these results can be placed into the wider context of the cultures of Egypt and the Near East. This has become a common theme when attempting to obtain samples from museums: how can any proposed research be utilised beyond academia? This is a question rightly asked.

Museums, as institutions, now find that accountability is a reality of modern expectations. As Falk *et al.* (2006, 335–6) note, trustees, funding bodies and the public all expect an institution to provide evidence of accomplishment and to maximise the quality of the learning experience of visitors. Additionally, museums are increasingly under pressure to demonstrate how taxpayers' money is utilised. If an academic wishes to use an object from a museum the various stakeholders involved have to be considered, even if any damage caused by sampling is to be conserved. A common problem is that samples have been taken in the past without the analytical information being reported back to the relevant museums, or only cursorily submitted without contact details. This has been combatted by museums imposing conditions on any sampling requests, requiring reports of results within a set time limit and the return of any remaining sample for future use.

Simons (2006, 114) notes four criteria that need to be addressed when requests for destructive sampling are submitted;

1) Will the sampling compromise the future utility of the object?
2) Are there alternative means of obtaining the data?
3) Does the expected information gain justify the damage caused?
4) Is the researcher making the request competent to carry out the tests?

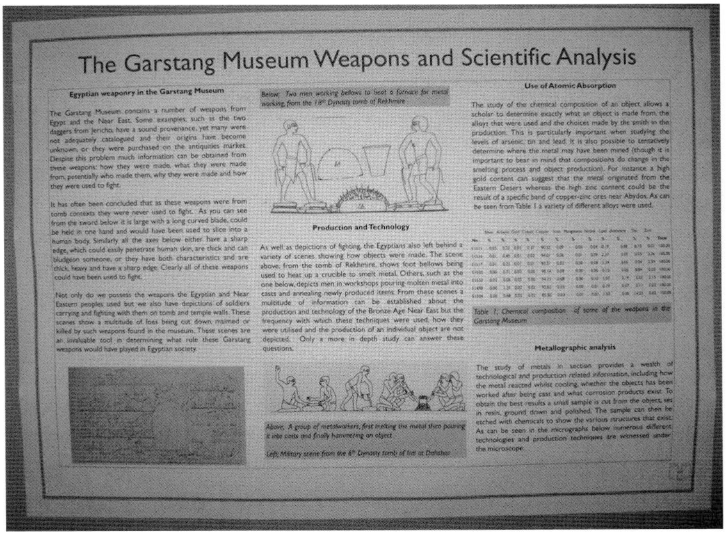

Figure 11. *The poster accompanying the objects and sample photographs in the Garstang Museum (author's own).*

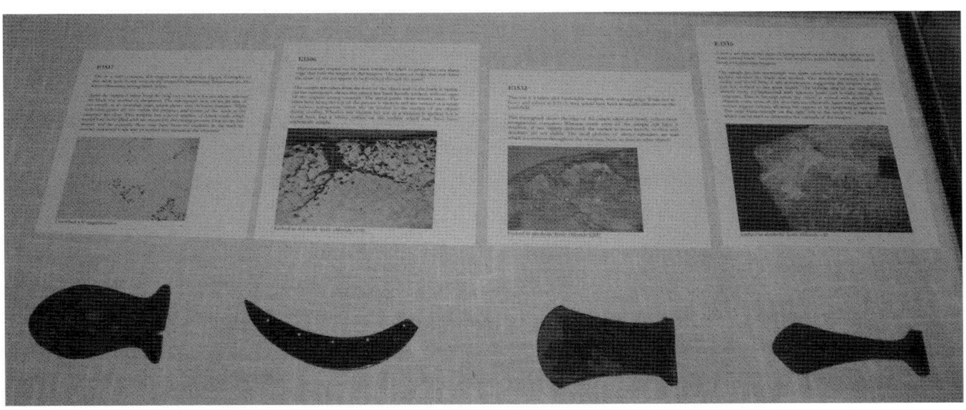

Figure 12. *The objects sampled, and micrographs of the structures found after analysing the samples displayed in the Garstang Museum. The descriptions detail the object and its potential use in antiquity (author's own).*

The first three points are very much inter-linked, with the need for conservation of the objects being at the forefront of any analyses request. It should be stressed, however, that while destructive analyses cause permanent damage to an object, if the sample is taken correctly the information produced is invaluable and, in the case of this research, no known alternative exists for a metallographic sample. The alternative to AAS is using the non-destructive EDXRF but, as the results of Philip *et al.* (2003) show, the surface analysis of a tin bronze is very different to the centre, and so at best produces semi-quantitative results. Of course the researcher must be competent and have the relevant experience, though it must be noted that such experience can only be gained through practice. It is also important for researchers to achieve the maximum benefit from sampling museum objects, and this requires a solid research agenda which identifies a specific research problem and aims to build on existing knowledge.

By developing a proposal with these concerns in mind, all the stakeholders involved should be able to access academic research undertaken in museums. While the weapons held at the Garstang Museum belong to a university they are visited by a number of academics, interested individuals, as well as large parties, including schools and colleges, and are very much a part of a teaching collection, being used by the lecturers and students of the School of Archaeology, Classics and Egyptology, and within the archaeology modules of the Continuing Education Department at the University of Liverpool. Therefore any destructive sampling is very quickly noticed. Despite this, many objects have, in the past, been sampled with little of the research being communicated to visitors and students. This is now being remedied by having a small exhibit explaining what has been done to these objects publicising what research is being carried out and how it is being used to develop our understanding of Ancient Egypt. It can also be used to demonstrate the multitude of scientific techniques now being deployed in Egyptology and how this research has developed over time.

The use of scientific analysis in the future

The exhibiting of these results within the Garstang Museum has clearly shown that scientific, academic research can have a place in an archaeological museum, and demonstrates one of the many ways in which this can be achieved. The use of science within archaeology has been very much established since the beginning of archaeological practice in the nineteenth century. In fact Lucas and Harris (1962) pioneered many different avenues of scientific analysis in Egyptology specifically, yet museum exhibitions have been more centred on art history and the displaying of the objects, rather than attempting any practical interpretation. It has long been established that museums play a pivotal role in the education of children and the general public, but only more recently has the concept of 'active learning' been employed in the design of new exhibitions. Hooper-Greenhill (2007, 170–1) states that speaking, reading and listening are not enough to engender true learning and it is bodily action that promotes a fuller understanding. Therefore it makes sense to add practical exhibits, such as that mentioned above, at the Pitt-Rivers Museum, where the visitor can actively engage with the material. Similarly the Conservation Centre in Liverpool promotes active demonstrations by academics of their sampling and research activities, allowing the public to see for themselves the work being conducted.

The consideration of learning and 'stakeholders' has become an important facet of Museology and this has become visible in recent exhibitions in the UK, with some concentrating on personal experience (such as the Lindow Man exhibition at Manchester Museum) while others have considered the development of interest in a particular field (such as the Egyptomania exhibit at Bolton Museum). The development of scientific research certainly has its place within this movement. Interesting work has emerged on DNA, and other biological analyses (the various articles in Renfrew and Boyle 2000), faience and glass has become a massive area of scientific study (including Nicholson 2007, Tite and Shortland 2008, Hammerle, this volume) and Pyrotechnology in general continues to develop as a field within scientific archaeology (Rehder 2000). All of these areas would certainly intrigue the average museum visitor, while making use of the mass of material often found lying idle in the stores of a museum.

School of Archaeology, Classics and Egyptology
University of Liverpool

Acknowledgments

I would like to thank all those who have prompted me to think about the topics discussed in this paper, especially the museum curators and conservators who have dealt with my sampling applications, in particular Bryan Sitch, Karen Exell and Irit Narkiss at Manchester Museum and Tom Hardwick, formerly of Bolton Museum. I would also like to thank Steven Snape at the University of Liverpool for allowing me to contribute to the Garstang Museum, and Pat Winker for her help in achieving this. Finally I would like to thank Jenny Cromwell for her photographic mastery, and Ian Shaw and Matthew Ponting for reading various versions of this paper.

Bibliography

Allen, I. M., Britton, D. and Coghlan, H. H. (eds) (1970) *Metallurgical Reports on British and Irish Bronze Age Implements and Weapons in the Pitt-Rivers Museum,* Oxford, Pitt Rivers Museum.

Boatright, D. (2010) *Weapons Technology and Production in Bronze Age Egypt in the context of the Eastern Mediterranean*, Liverpool, Unpublished PhD Thesis.

Bridgford, S. D. (1997a) 'Mightier than the Pen? (An Edgewise look at Irish Bronze Swords)' in Carman, J. (ed.), *Material Harm, Archaeological Studies of War and Violence*, Glasgow, Cruithne Press, 95–115.

Bridgford, S. (1997b) 'The First Weapons devised only for War', *British Archaeology* 22 March 1997, 7.

Bridgford, S. D. (2002) 'Bronze and the First Arms Race – Cause, Effect or Coincidence?' in Ottoway, B. S. and Wager, E. C. (eds) *Metals and Society. Papers from a session held at the European Association of Archaeologists Sixth Annual Meeting in Lisbon 2000,* Oxford, BAR International Series, 123–132.

Budd, P. and Ottaway, B. S. (1991) 'The Properties of Arsenical Copper Alloys: Implications for the Development of Eneolithic Metallurgy' in Budd, P., Chapman, B., Jackson, C., Janaway, R. and Ottoway, B. (eds), *Archaeological Sciences 1989. Proceedings of a conference on the application of scientific techniques to archaeology*, Bradford September 1989, Oxford, Oxbow, 132–142.

Close-Brooks, J. and Coles, J. M. (1980) 'Tinned Axes' in *Antiquity,* Vol. LIV, 228–229.

Cowell, M. R. (1987) 'Chemical Analysis' in Davies, W. V. (ed.), *Catalogue of Egyptian Antiquities in the British Museum VII, Tools and Weapons I; Axes*, London, British Museum Publications.

Craddock, P. T. (1976) 'The Composition of the Copper Alloys used by the Greek, Etruscan and Roman Civilisations. 1. The Greeks before the Archaic Period', *Journal of Archaeological Science* Vol. 3. No. 2, 93–113.

Craddock, P. T. (1978) 'The Composition of the Copper Alloys used by the Greek, Etruscan and Roman Civilisations 3. The Origins and Early Use of Brass', *Journal of Archaeological Science* Vol. 5, 1–16.

El Gayar, S. and Jones, M. P. (1989) 'Old Kingdom Copper Smelting Artefacts from Buhen in Upper Egypt', in *The Journal of the Historical Metallurgy Society.* Vol. 23, Number 1, 16–24.

Falk, J. H., Dierking, L. D and Adams, M. (2006) 'Living in a Learning Society: Museums and Free–choice Learning' in Macdonald, S. (ed.), *A Companion to Museum Studies*, Oxford, Blackwell Publishing, 323–339.

Hauptmann, A., and Wagner, I. (2007) 'Prehistoric Copper Production at Timna: Thermoluminescence (TL) Dating and Evidence from the East' in La Niece, S., Hook, D. and Craddock, P. T. (eds), *Metals and Mines. Studies in Archaeometallurgy*, London, British Museum, 67–75.

Hooper-Greenhill, E. (2007) *Museums and Education. Purpose, Pedagogy, Performance*, London, Routledge.

Hughes, M. J., Cowell, M. R. and Craddock, P. T. (1976) 'Atomic Absorption Techniques in Archaeology', *Archaeometry* Volume 18 No. 1, 19–37.

Khalil, L. (1980) *The Composition and Technology of Ancient Copper Alloy Artefacts from Jericho and Related Sites.* UCL, unpublished thesis.

Lang, J. R. S. (1987) 'Metallurgical Examination' in Davies, W. V. (ed.) *Catalogue of Egyptian Antiquities in the British Museum VII: Tools and Weapons I: Axes.* London, British Museum Publications, 119–124.

Lucas, A and Harris, J. R. (1962) *Ancient Egyptian Materials and Industries*, New York, Dover Publications Inc.

Meeks, N. D. (1993) 'Surface Characterisation of Tinned Bronze, High Tin Bronze, Tinned Iron & Arsenical Bronze' in La Niece, S and Craddock, P. (eds) *Metal Plating and Patination: Cultural, Technical and Historical Developments,* Oxford, Butterworth-Heinemann, 247–275.

Mei, J. (2000) *Copper and Bronze Metallurgy in Late Prehistoric Xinjiang: Its Cultural Context and Relationship with Neighbouring Regions.* Oxford, BAR International Series.

Molloy, B. (2007) 'What's the bloody point?: Bronze Age swordsmanship in Ireland and Britain' in Molloy, B. (ed.), *The Cutting Edge: archaeological studies in combat and weaponry*, Stroud, Tempus, 90–111.

Nicholson, P. T. (2007) *Brilliant Things for Akhenaten: the Production of Glass, Vitreous Materials and Pottery at Amarna Site O45.1*, London, Egypt Exploration Society.

Northover, J. P. (2001) 'Analysis of the Metalwork from Tell Brak' in Oates, D., Oates J. and McDonald, H. (eds), *Excavations at Tell Brak. Volume 2, Nagar in the Third Millenium BC*, Cambridge, British School of Archaeology in Iraq, 254–6.

Osbourne, J. (2003) 'Attitudes Towards Science: a review of the literature and its implications', *International Journal of Science Education* Vol. 25, No. 9, 1049–1079.

Peatfield, A. (2007) 'Reliving Greek personal combat-Boxing and Pankration' in Molloy, B (ed.), *The Cutting Edge: archaeological studies in combat and weaponry*, Stroud, Tempus, 20–33.

Philip, G. (1989) *Metal Weapons of the Early and Middle Bronze Ages in Syria-Palestine Parts I and II*, Oxford, BAR International Series.

Philip, G. (2006) *Tell el-Dab'a XV: metalwork and metalworking evidence of the late Middle Kingdom and Second Intermediate period*, Wein, Verlag der Österreichen Akademie der Wissenschaften.

Rehder, J. E. (2000) *The Mastery and Uses of Fire: a sourcebook on ancient pyrotechnology,* Montreal, McGill-Queens University Press.

Renfrew, C and Boyle, K. V. (eds). (2000) *Archaeogenetics: DNA and the Population Prehistory of Europe*, Cambridge, McDonald Institute for Archaeological Research.

Roman, I. (1990) 'Copper Ingots' in Rothenburg, B (ed.), *The Ancient Metallurgy of Copper. Archaeology-Experiment-Theory*, London, Institute for Archaeo-Metallurgical Studies, 176–181.

Said, R. (1962) *Geology of Egypt*, Amsterdam, Elsevier Science Ltd.

Scott, D. A. (1991) *Metallography and Microstructure of ancient and historic metal*, California, The Getty Conservation Institute.

Shaw, I. M. (2001) 'Egyptians, Hyksos and Military hardware: causes, effects or catalysts?' in Shortland, A. J. (ed.), *The Social Context of Technological Change: Egypt and the Near East 1650–1550BC*, Oxford, Oxbow, 59–71.

Simmons, J. E. (2006) *Things Great and Small. Collection Management Policies,* Washington DC, American Association of Museums.

Simpson, G. M. (1993) *Analysis of Ancient Egyptian Copper and Bronze Artefacts by using Scanning Electron Microscope and Metallographic Techniques*, Two Volumes, Liverpool, Unpublished MA Dissertation.

Tite, M. S. and Shortland, A. J. (2008) *Production Technology of Faience and Related Early Vitreous Materials,* Oxford, Oxford University School of Archaeology.

Vatandoust, A. (1999) 'A view on Prehistoric Iranian Metalworking' in Hauptmann, A., Pernicka, E., Rehren, T. and Yalcin, U. (1995) *Proceeds of the International Conference "The Beginnings of Metallurgy", Bochum, 1995,* Bochum, Bergbau Museum, 121–140.

Winlock, H. E. (1945) *The Slain Soldiers of Neb-hepet-Re Mentuhotpe*, New York Metropolitan Museum of Art.

Yadin, Y. (1963) *The Art of Warfare in Biblical Lands in the Light of Archaeological Discovery*, London, Weidenfeld and Nicolson.

Egypt's Encounter with the West: Race, Culture and Identity

William A.Cooney

This paper investigates how the history of the 'Libyans' has been written. It is an historiographic and not historical examination and will focus, specifically, on the development of 'Libyan' identity over the century from AD 1837 to 1937. It will attempt to emphasize how much of what we know – or think we know – about this population is inherently linked to interpretations developed about this group during this formative period. It will critically re-examine the sources which were key in the creation of 'Libyan' identity and will explore how nineteenth Century ideas of race (such as skin and eye colour) and culture (such as dress accessories) have variously impacted on current perceptions of how 'Libyans' are defined.

Introduction

The identity of the 'Libyans', as they are understood currently, relies on two convergent historiographic events: On the one hand, it relies heavily on the anachronistic association which was made between the Egyptian term *Rebu,* which first appears in the thirteenth Century BC, and much later references to *Libues* in Greek sources which do not antedate the First Millennium BC. The identity of the Rebu as 'Libyan', in the first instance, rests on the close phonetic similarity between it and the Greek λιβυες, bearing in mind the fact that ancient Egyptian did not make a clear distinction between the phonemes *r* and *l*. As such, it is possible, as Frédéric Colin has suggested, that the equation is the product of a mere coincidence (1996, 13). On the other hand, the identity of 'Libyans' from the ancient Egyptian records relies on an underlying assumption of the 'African' identity of this group that has been derived, largely, from early interpretations of images of the group labelled Rebu.

In its current usage, the name 'Libyan' is an umbrella term used to refer principally to four different groups found in Egyptian texts: the Tjehenu, Tjemehu, Rebu and Meshwesh (Ma) and their various orthographic variations. The identity of all of these groups as 'Libyan,' however, rests largely on their association, often iconographic, with images of Rebu.

A brief history of the Rebu

Of all of the so-called 'Libyan' groups, the Rebu are one of the least understood, and the least well documented in Egyptian records. Moreover, they are the very last to appear in the records. Contrary to the statement of earlier scholars, such as Bates, who claims that Senwosret I (c. 1974–1929 BC) campaigned against the Rebu (1914, 212), the earliest mention of a group called Rebu dates to the reign of Ramesses II. Bates' confusion is due to the fact that he was using Breasted's translation of the Story of Sinuhe and not the original text. Where Breasted translated the term 'Libyan' (BAR I, sec. 492), Bates understood this to mean 'Rebu.' In actual fact the terms used in Sinuhe are Tjehenu and Tjemehu. The Rebu play no part in the story.

The Rebu do not come to prominence, however, until Merneptah's reign (c. 1212–1201 BC) where they are the principal antagonists in his campaign of Year 5 (c. 1208 BC). From this period onwards they are closely associated with various groups of Sea Peoples. The earliest illustrations of this group (as well as the only pictorial evidence of them from the New Kingdom) appear on Ramesses III's (c. 1185–1153 BC) mortuary temple at Medinet Habu, where they are again often associated with Sea People, specifically the group called the Tjekker, as well as the Amorites, Meshwesh and Tjemehu (Medinet Habu Epigraphic Survey, Vol. I, Pls. 18 and 43, and Vol. V, Pl. 317, and KRI V, 65). By Year 11 of Ramesses III's reign, the Rebu, along with the Meshwesh, had been deported from Egypt as is recorded in the Papyrus Harris (BAR IV, sec. 405) and the stela of Ramesses III dedicated to Mert Seger at Deir el-Medina, Chapel C (KRI V, 91: 5–7). At the end of the Ramesside Period, they are mentioned in the accounts from the workmen's village at Deir el-Medineh (KRI VI, 564:14–15), where they apparently bartered goods with the workmen, and where their presence, often during festival days, resulted in the cessation of work (Haring 1992, 75ff.).

Following the collapse of the New Kingdom state (c. 1070 BC), the Rebu created a petty chiefdom in the western Delta during the so-called 'Libyan period.' Somewhat confusingly, the name of this period has nothing to do with the Rebu themselves and there is no evidence that the kings of this period were related in any way to the 'Chiefs of the Rebu' in the western Delta, nor is there any evidence to suggest that the kings of this period were, necessarily, of 'Libyan' origin. This is generally assumed in the literature on the subject of the 'Libyan Period' and is based on 1) the 'Libyan' identity of the Tjehenu-people and the association of this latter group with an ancestor of Sheshonq I (first king of Dynasty 22) whose name is enumerated on the Pasenhor Stela as Tjehenu-Buyuwawa and has, since the days of Breasted, been translated as 'Buyuwawa, the Libyan' (for the only significant objection to this translation, see Le Page Renouf, 1891, 599–603); and 2) on the assumption that Sheshonq I's title 'Chief of the Ma' is an abbreviation of a similar title "Chief of the Meshwesh." This assumption has been current in the literature on this subject since it was first suggested by Vicomte de Rougé (1873, 87). Significantly, the identity of both the Tjehenu and Meshwesh as 'Libyan' is based largely on the explicit use of the penis-sheath by these two groups as depicted in Egyptian art. As the present article will propose, the association between the penis-sheath and 'Libyan' identity is founded on a false representation of a Rebu wearing such a garment. Indeed, the first and only recorded 'Rebu King' in Egypt does not appear until the very end of this period when Tefnakht, the last known 'Great Chief of the Rebu and Great Chief of the Ma' proclaimed himself king in the aftermath of Piye's invasion of Egypt in the last half of the eighth century BC.

It is undoubtedly on account of this paucity of evidence, combined with the fact that, like the Sea-peoples, the Rebu suddenly appear in the Egyptian records, that various theories have been proposed to account for their elusive origins. Unlike the 'Sea-peoples,' whose origins have been debated for the better part of the last century (see most recently Cline and O'Connor 2003, 112), the origin of the Rebu as coming from 'Libya' has remained largely unquestioned and is based almost entirely on the anachronistic connection between later references to *Libues* in Greek with earlier references to Rebu in Egyptian texts.

The following, therefore, will briefly survey the early historiography of the 'Libyans,' it will examine how many of the current theories regarding the 'Libyans' are based on a flawed – indeed falsified – dataset and it will suggest that only by correcting this dataset will we be able to write a proper history of Egypt's encounter with her western neighbours.

Wilkinson's Rebu

One of the earliest scholars to write extensively on the Rebu was Sir John Gardner Wilkinson who in 1837 published his *Manners and Customs of the Ancient Egyptians.* In it, he described the Rebu as:

> 'One of the most formidable Asiatic enemies encountered by the Egyptians' (1841, 371), which 'from the style of their costume, and the lightness of their complexion, it is evident that they inhabited a northern as well as Asiatic country, very distant from Egypt, and of a far more temperate climate' (1841, 372f.).

Wilkinson later identifies these Rebu as similar to 'Persians' or 'Parthians' (1841, 373).

Indeed, the identification of the Rebu as an eastern, or a northern population was not uncommon during the nineteenth century, and even at the end of the century, Maspero in his *The Struggle of the Nations* (1896), wrote of the Rebu (or as he called them, the 'Labu'):

> 'They were men of tall stature and large of limb with fair skins, light hair, and blue eyes; everything, in fact indicating their northern origin' (1896, 430).

Returning briefly to Wilkinson, there are two curious phenomena which are associated with his publication. First is the fact that many of his original words were changed or omitted in the second reprinting of this work by Samuel Birch in 1878. In Birch's edition, some of the mentions of 'Asiatic' Rebu are deleted altogether, whilst others are amended with the footnote that the 'The Rebu are the Libyes or Libyans' (Wilkinson 1878, 250 n. 3). Such an amendment is completely contradictory to Wilkinson's original words, yet completely in-line with the burgeoning theory at the time that the Rebu were indigenous North Africans, directly ancestral to the Greek λιβυες.

The second curiosity associated with Wilkinson's publication is the identity of the people depicted in Wilkinson's accompanying woodcut (no. 62 fig. 4 in 1838 ed; and no. 76 fig. 4 in 1878 ed.) under the caption 'Rebu' (Fig. 1).

This particular image of four 'Rebu' standing together is unique and in many ways peculiar in Egyptian art, not least because so few examples of captioned-images of 'Rebu' actually exist. Whilst the term is commonly used as both an ethnonym and toponym in historical texts from the beginning of Dynasty 19, the only images of 'Rebu' which can be dated prior to the Third Intermediate Period (and the rise of the 'Chiefs of the Rebu' in the western Delta; for these see Yoyotte 1961, 142ff.) are found exclusively at Ramesses III's mortuary temple at Medinet Habu. Because of this restricted dataset, it is possible to question the authenticity of Wilkinson's plate, which, on closer examination, is clearly not a true 'historic' monument at all.

Figure 1. *'Wilkinson's Rebu' (from Wilkinson 1878, woodcut 76 fig. 4).*

In fact, none of the figures on this plate

can be positively identified as assembled together in like manner under a caption of 'Rebu' on any Egyptian monument – from any period! Despite this 'forgery,' earlier scholars, such as Bates, believed this to be an authentic depiction of Rebu-'Libyans' and described Wilkinson's plate in the following manner:

> 'A Libyan (Rebu) chief is shown, followed by a sword-bearer, an archer, and a tribesman who bears no arms, and who is, except for a single plume and the *penistasche*, unclad. It is important to note that in this instance only the chief himself, whose decorations are very similar to those of the Temehu of the tomb of Seti I, is tattooed' (Bates 1914, 138).

When placed next to the image of the Tjemehu from Seti I's tomb, it is all but certain that this figure was copied from Seti I's tomb in the Valley of the Kings (KV 17) (Lepsius III, 136). Furthermore, a clue to this particular identification is provided by Wilkinson himself, who, though not stating directly, implies that at least some of the figures in the wood-cut are from 'Belzoni's tomb.' As such, the leading figure in Wilkinson's plate should not be captioned as 'Rebu' but as 'Tjemehu.'

Whilst the authenticity of this image as a fabrication was previously pointed out by Wainwright (1962, 92 n. 5), it is clear that the belief in the veracity of this image had more than a minor role in the creation of a 'Libyan' identity. Particularly, this image influenced opinions regarding ancient 'Libyan' styles of dress during the late nineteenth and early twentieth centuries. However, it was the publication of a Rebu in Lepsius' *Denkmaeler* in 1848 which has had arguably the greatest impact on the modern identification of the iconography of the so-called 'Libyans' and, in particular, the use of the penis-sheath as a feature of 'Libyan' dress.

Lepsius' 'Libyans'

Within ten years of Wilkinson's original publication, claiming the Rebu to be Asiatic or Northern, a rival theory regarding the origin of the Rebu was developed. This theory, originally developed by Brugsch (and his contemporaries; see Brugsch 1858, 79f.) claimed that the Rebu, far from being Asiatic or Northern, were indigenous inhabitants of North Africa.

Yet, despite the clear phonetic similarities between the terms Rebu and Libya, the evidence in support of this theory is fairly sparse. In fact, like Wilkinson's northern theory which rested largely on the figures illustrated in his wood-cut, the indigenous-theory rests almost entirely on a single image of a Rebu published in Karl Richard Lepsius' *Denkmaeler aus Aegypten und Aethiopien* and reproduced a decade later by Brugsch in his *Die Geographie der Nachbarländer Ägyptens* (1858) (Fig. 2).

Unlike Wilkinson's image which had been manufactured, Lepsius' image is quite clearly from the Eastern High Gate at Medinet Habu and is from the section known as the 'Southern Chiefs List.' It illustrates a person identified

Figure 2. *'Lepsius' Libyan' (from Lepsius, Denkmäler III 199.a; reproduced in Brugsch 1858, fig. 20).*

as 'The Chief of the Rebu' in the accompanying hieroglyphic caption and depicts him with a long-cloak, a side-lock and most importantly a penis-sheath. This image is important in the historiography of the 'Libyans' because to the nineteenth century observer, it all but proved the 'African' origin of the Rebu, based on the presence of that singular article of clothing, the penis-sheath.

Naville and the Naissance of 'Libyan' Identity

The equation between penis-sheaths, Africans and the idea of indigenous 'Libyans' is best illustrated in a brief article written by Edouard Naville in 1899–1900 entitled *Les figurines égyptiennes de l'époque Archaïque*. In it he states without any evidence to back up his claim that:

> 'Les peuples qui portent ce fourreau sont toujours des populations appartenant au groupe africain' (1900, 70).

He then cites Lepsius' image of the Rebu from Medinet Habu, specifically, as one such African group. From this single example, Naville drew a rather broad conclusion that:

> 'Ce fourreau, ce cornet, est donc, une tradition, un trait charactéristique de ce groupe Libyen, qui sous la XIXe dynastie, s'allie aux peuples de la Méditerranée pour marcher sur l'Égypte' (1900, 70).

The Libyan group to which Naville must be referring are undoubtedly the Rebu who, in Merneptah's inscription, and under the leadership of Meryey son of Dydy, allied themselves with other 'Sea Peoples' against Egypt (see, for instance the Merneptah's Karnak inscription; Manassa 2003). Unfortunately, there is no pictorial evidence which survives from this reign to clarify whether they were actually wearing penis-sheaths at *that* time.

Significantly, Naville's sample size and his entire thesis was based on a representation of a single individual 'Rebu.' This would not be problematic were it not for the fact that Lepsius' representation of this individual is completely at odds with all other representations which are captioned as Rebu at Medinet Habu (Table 1). There are 83 additional individuals who, from the associated captions can be positively identified as 'Rebu.' Although the dress of one of them is obscured by the Amorite in the fore-ground, not one of the remaining 82 is represented wearing a penis-sheath.

The reason why Naville over-emphasized the importance of penis-sheaths as an identifying feature of Rebu-'Libyans,' is not entirely clear; though it does fit well with the trend in early twentieth century scholarship to identify penis-sheath wearers and the Rebu-population with 'Africans' generally, and 'Libyans' specifically. Though a brief ten pages, Naville's article was hugely influential during the first decade of the twentieth century in the creation of 'Libyan' identity. Whilst he was certainly not the first to suggest the indigenous origins of the Rebu (an honour which might best be bestowed on Brugsch), or even the equation of the Rebu with Libya (Brugsch again), his article is important in the historiography of the Rebu and 'Libyans' because it set the benchmark of the early twentieth century.

Following Naville, F. Legge identified many of the penis-sheathed figures on pre-dynastic slate palettes as 'Libyans' (1900, 129). Whilst he cites Naville's work, his main corroborating evidence for a 'Libyan' identification for these penis-sheath-clad individuals is the resemblance

Location	Caption	No. Indiv.	Kilt	Penis-Sheath	Cloak	Belt	Feather	Beard	Side-	REF.
North exterior wall, west end	"The fallen ones of the Rebu in front of the fortress 'Ramesses III-repels-the-Tjemehu'"	28	Y	N	Y	N	N	Y	Y	MH I, pl. 22
Interior Second Court, South wall, east end	Counting hands and phalli of the "fallen ones of Rebu"	35	Y	N	Y	N	N	Y	Y	MH I, pl. 23
Interior Second Court, East wall, south of doorway	Presenting "Rebu" to Mut and Amun	15	Y	N	Y	N	N	Y	Y	MH I, pl. 26
North exterior wall, west of 2nd Pylon	"words spoken by the fallen Rebu"	4	25%	N	75%	N	N	Y	Y	MH I, pl. 43
"Treasury scene" Pillared Hall, South wall.	Rebu	1	?	?	?	?	Y	Y	?	MH V, pl. 317

Table 1. *Details of the depicted Libyans in the Merenptah Inscriptions.*

of their attire with modern sub-Saharan African populations. He cites, for instance, the prisoner being smitten by Narmer on the Narmer Palette (discovered at Hierakonpolis in 1898) as wearing 'a moocha, or small bark apron like that worn by the Nyam-Nyam and other races of Central Africa' (Legge 1900, 129).

Elsewhere, Legge identifies the costumes on these palettes as being reminiscent of 'the Bantu sheath,' and 'of German East Africa [modern Tanzania]' (Legge 1900, 137; 1904, 300). Yet despite the ethno-archaeological association which Legge makes with *sub*-Saharan Africa, he ultimately concludes:

> 'The enemies over whom Narmer is here shown triumphing appear to be *Libyans*, as are the slave slipper bearer and the attendants on the two-tailed monsters' (1900, 137; emphasis mine).

It is not entirely clear how the use of modern sub-Saharan African penis-sheaths results in a parallel with ancient North African Libyans, except to reinforce the inherent 'African' nature of this dress, nor is the Egyptian, Aegean or other possible origin of such costume even considered.

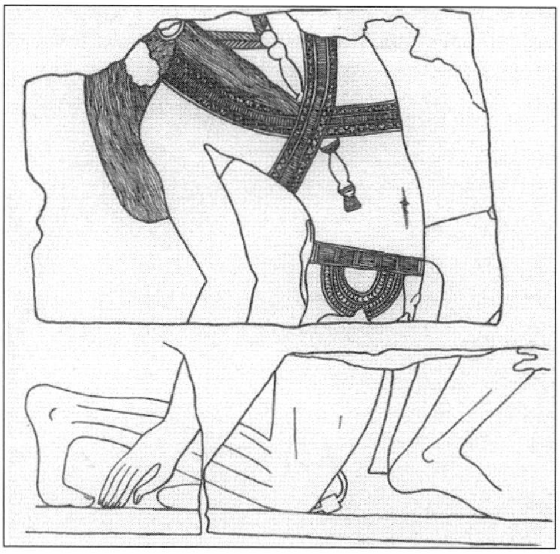

Figure 3. *Borchardt's "Libyan" in the mortuary temple of Neuserre. (Borchardt 1907, fig. 31).*

Throughout the first decade of the twentieth century, discoveries of depictions of penis-sheath wearers on Egyptian monuments became more numerous. When Borchardt uncovered the first Old Kingdom example of a penis-sheath-wearing individual in the mortuary temple of Neuserre (1907, 47), he published the figure as a 'Libyan' (Fig. 3). This was in spite of the fact that none of the names/ethnonyms associated with this individual survived, and was based solely on the remains of a depiction of a penis-sheath ('Vorn hängt daran die 'Penistasche,' die sogar einige ägyptische Gottheiten von den Libyern übernommen haben'; 1907, 47). He based this identification on Naville's earlier work (Borchardt 1907, note), but in the process, set a mine-field for all succeeding scholars. Suddenly, penis-sheaths everywhere became associated with 'Libyans.'

By the next year, the penis-sheath had inherited the title of 'national dress' of the 'Libyans,' as defined by Gustave Jéquier, 'l'étui phallique en usage en Égypte à la period la plus ancienne, le [qarnati] que les Libyens seuls conservèrent presque comme insigne national' (1908, 43). Again, Jéquier cites Naville's article in support of this claim (Jéquier 1908, note 6).

By the end of the first decade of the twentieth century, Naville had proposed a definition of an 'African' costume which he outlined in his article on the *Anu* [*Iwntiw*]. Whilst he does not explicitly mention the 'Libyans,' he is implicit in describing them as quintessentially 'African':

> 'Le costume des Africains est plus ou moins complet. L'un des traits les plus charactéristiques, c'est la plume d'autruche. Ils en ont une ou plusieurs. Dans les inscriptions de la XXe dynastie, la plume est l'ornement propre aux Africains et qui distingue même les Nègres. Ces Africains peuvent être imberbes ou avoir une barbe pointue. La chevelure est plus ou moins longue. Elle se prolonge sur le côté en une boucle mince ou en une tresse large et épaisse. Ils ont l'étui phallique ou quelquefois comme lorsqu'il s'agit des porteurs du trône de Horemheb, une sorte de tablier qui leur couvre le ventre et le haut des jambs' (Naville 1910, 56).

Within this definition of 'African,' the Egyptians are quite clearly left out. The only 'true' African peoples are the Nubians to the south of Egypt and the penis-sheath wearing 'Libyans' to the west. Yet, certain aspects of the above definition clearly do not refer to 'Nubian' groups. The Nubians, for instance, are never depicted in Egyptian monuments with a side-lock ('une tresse large et épaisse'); whilst the penis-sheath, in this definition is almost certainly referring, exclusively, to 'Libyans.'

The use of the penis-sheath as a marker of 'African-ness' was still current in the literature on the 'Libyans' as late as 1955, when Wilhelm Hölscher published his PhD thesis (1937) under the title *Libyer und Ägypter* (1955, 37). It was only once Peter Ucko published his anthropological study on penis-sheaths (1969), that the question of the penis-sheath as a purely 'Libyan' garment was questioned. Ucko observed quite rightly that:

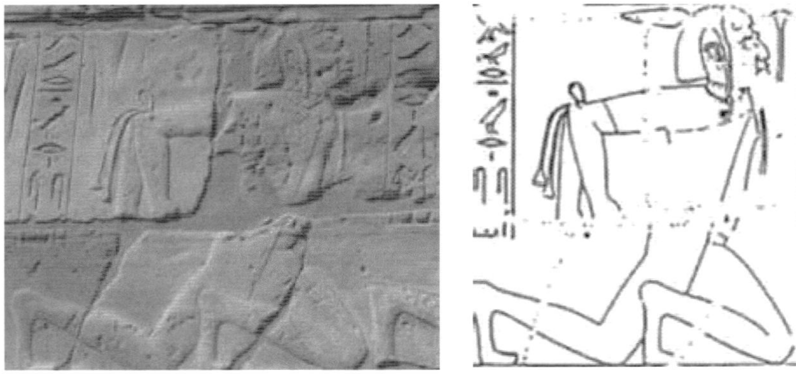

Figures 4 and 5. *Rebu on "Southern Chiefs List" clearly illustrating him with a short kilt and not a penis-sheath (photograph by author, line drawing from Medinet Habu epigraphic Survey, pl. 600).*

> 'Most peoples' attitude has changed little since (Naville's time) and interpretations of any Egyptian representation with a sheath still automatically orientate towards Libya!' [sic] (1969, 352).

Ucko's argument was not meant to question the African nature of the 'Libyans,' or the use of the penis-sheath as a marker of ethnic or African identity. Instead, the main purpose of his argument was to promote the idea that the 'other' African group in North East Africa, the ancient Egyptians, also wore penis-sheaths. The penis-sheath remained, however, a means of identifying the 'African' identity of the individuals depicted. At the extreme end of the argument, as Ucko stated, the belief in the inherent 'African' nature of the penis-sheath has been used as 'evidence of the diffusion of a negro trait not only across Africa from the Western Sudan but also from Africa to Melanesia, New Guinea and South America' (Ucko 1969, 36).

Ultimately, the identity of foreigners depicted with penis-sheaths on ancient Egyptian monuments as 'Libyans' can be traced back almost entirely to Lepsius' publication of a Rebu-man wearing a penis-sheath. This image provided the fundamental link between the nomenclature of 'Libyans' (associated with Rebu) and the major iconographic feature associated with this group (the penis-sheath). Yet, herein lies the rub: On re-examining the evidence, from Medinet Habu, it is clear that Lepsius' original publication of the 'Rebu man,' on which so much of the later scholarly work is based, and which has provided a fundamental contribution to the ethnic identity of the eponymous 'Libyans,' is flawed in one small detail. Contrary to many of the earlier publications, as well as to Naville's thesis on the identity of the 'Libyans,' there is absolutely no evidence that the 'Rebu man' was ever depicted with a penis-sheath.

Far from being anomalous, therefore, the Rebu depicted bound with papyrus-rope (symbol of the 'North') on the so-called 'Southern chiefs List' is similar to all other captioned images of the penis-sheath-less Rebu at Medinet Habu (Figs 4 & 5). The fact that the Rebu are never depicted wearing penis-sheaths was originally pointed out by Hölscher (1937, 44; see also Edwards 1938, 252), and has therefore been known for almost 70 years. Yet, the attribution of the epithet 'Libyan' to all those individuals who wear the penis-sheath has been retained in the underlying dogma associated with other penis-sheath-wearing populations, particularly the Tjehenu and Meshwesh, and is based almost entirely on the historiographic associations which have been derived from Lepsius' original image. It is necessary, therefore, to dismiss the generally accepted view that the depictions which the ancient Egyptians left us of penis-sheath-wearers were, in some way, connected with the Rebu, and as such, penis-sheath-wearers on Egyptian monuments are *ipso facto* 'Libyans.'

Conclusion

The identity of the people or peoples living to the west of Egypt hinges as much on the images which the Egyptians left of them, as on the interpretations which have been made of these images over the last hundred and seventy years. For over a century the identity of people wearing penis-sheaths in Egyptian art as 'Libyans' has been linked with an unfounded assumption that the 'Libyans' wore penis-sheaths. This fundamental association can be traced directly back to an image from Lepsius' Denkmaeler, copied by Brugsch, and propagated by Naville, which erroneously depicts a Rebu figure with a penis-sheath and anachronistically associated the Rebu with Libya. These associations produced a false syllogism:

> The Rebu wear penis-sheaths (a falsification)
> The Rebu are Libyans (an anachronism)
> 'Libyans' wear penis-sheaths

By unhooking the yoke which has tied all of these images of penis-sheath wearers to the Rebu, however, we are perhaps now at liberty to formulate a more nuanced understanding of how the Egyptians might have interpreted the various peoples which they depicted in art without having to resort to the anachronistic assumption that they are, on account of their penis-sheaths, 'Libyans.' Indeed, whilst this article has only dealt with a single aspect of the historiography associated with the 'Libyans' it has hopefully highlighted the way in which 'Libyan' identity was formulated and propagated from the end of the nineteenth century and, in many cases, the need to return to many of the documents referring to so-called 'Libyans' in order to test the nature of their identity in the contemporary world.

University of Durham

Bibliography

Bates, O. (1914; 1970 reprint) *The Eastern Libyans, an essay*, London, Frank Cass & Co.

Borchardt, L. (1907) *Das Grabdenkmal des Königs Ne-user-re'*, Leipzig, J.C. Hinrichs.

Breasted, J. H. (1906; 2001 reprint) *Ancient Records of Egypt* (5 vols.), Chicago, University of Illinois Press.

Brugsch, H. (1858) *Die geographie der nachbarländer Ägyptens nach den altägyptischen denkmälern*, Leipzig, J. C. Hinrichs.

Cline, E. H. and O'Connor, D. (2003). 'The Mystery of the 'Sea Peoples'' in O'Connor, D and Quirke, S. (eds) *Mysterious Lands*, London, UCL Press, 107–138.

Colin, F. (1996) *Les Libyens en Égypte (XVe siècle a.C. – IIe siècle p.C.). Onomastique et Histoire* (2 vols.), Université Libre de Bruxelles, unpublished PhD thesis.

De Rougé, le V. (1873) "étude sur quelque monuments du règne de Tahraka", *Mélanges d'archéologie Égyptienne et Assyrienne* Vol. 1, 85–93.

Edwards, I. E. S. (1938) 'Review of Hölscher's Libyer und Ägypter', *Journal of Egyptian Archaeology* Vol. 24, 251–252.

Epigraphic Survey. (1930–1970) *Medinet Habu* (8 vols.), Chicago, University of Chicago Press.

Haring, B. (1992) 'Libyans in the late Twentieth Dynasty' in Demarée, R. J. and Egberts, A. (eds), *Village Voices: proceedings of the symposium "Texts from Deir el-Medina and their interpretation" Leiden, May 31 – June 1, 1991*, Leiden, Centre of Non-Western Studies.

Hölscher, W. (1955) *Libyer und Ägypter, beitrage zur Ethnologie und Geschichte libysche völkerschaften nach den altägyptischen Quellen*, Glückstadt, J.J. Augustin.

Jéquier, G. (1908) Notes et Remarques IX – Origine du dieu Tanen, *Recueil de travaux relatifs à la philologie et à l'archéologie égyptiennes et assyriennes* Vol. 30, 42–43.

Legge, F. (1900) 'The carved slates from Hieraconpolis and elsewhere', *Proceedings of the Society of Biblical Archaeology* Vol. 22, 125–139.

Legge, F. (1909) 'The carved slates and this season's discoveries', *Proceedings of the Society of Biblical Archaeology* Vol. 31, 204–211 & 297–310.

Kitchen, K. (1969–2008) *Ramesside Inscriptions, Translated and Annotated* (14 vols), Oxford, Blackwell Publishing, Ltd.

Lepsius, C. R. (1842–1845) *Denkmaeler aus Aegypten und Aethiopien*. [Photographic Reproduction], Geneva, Centre de documentation du monde oriental, Éditions de Belles-lettres.

Manassa, C. (2003) *The Great Karnak Inscription of Merneptah: Grand Strategy in the 13th Century BC* [Yale Egyptological Studies 5], New Haven, The Yale Egyptological Seminar.

Maspero, G. (1896) *The Struggle of the Nations*, London, Society for Promoting Christian Knowledge.

Möller, G. (1924) Die ägypter und ihre libysche Nachbarn, *Zeitschrift der Deutschen Morgenländischen Gesellschaf* Vol. 78 (NF 3), 36–60 & tafeln. 2–8.

Naville, É. (1899) 'Figurines Égyptiennes de l'Époque archaïque', *Recueil de travaux relatifs à la philologie et à l'archéologie égyptiennes et assyriennes* Vol. 21, 212–216.

Naville, É. (1900) 'Figurines Égyptiennes de l'Époque archaïque (suite)', *Recueil de travaux relatifs à la philologie et à l'archéologie égyptiennes et assyriennes* Vol. 22, 65–71.

Naville, É. (1910) 'Les Anu', *Recueil de travaux relatifs à la philologie et à l'archéologie égyptiennes et assyriennes* Vol. 32, 52–61.

Renouf, P. Le P. (1891) 'Who were the Libyans?', *Proceedings of the Society of Biblical Archaeology* Vol. 13, 599–603.

Ucko, P. J. (1969) 'Penis Sheaths: a comparative study', *Proceedings of the Royal Anthropological Institute* no. 1969, 24A–67.

Wainwright, G. A. (1962) 'The Meshwesh' *Journal of Egyptian Archaeology* Vol. 48, 89–99.

Wilkinson, J. G. (1841) *The manners and customs of the ancient Egyptians* (2nd Series), London, John Murray.

Wilkinson, J. G. (1878) *The manners and customs of the ancient Egyptians*, Revised and corrected by Samuel Birch (ed), London, John Murray.

Yoyotte, J. (1961) 'Les Principautés du Delta au temps de l'anarchie Libyenne (études d'histoire politique), *Mélanges Maspero* I.4, Cairo, Institut Français d'Archéologie Orientale.

'*The Like of Which Never Existed*': The Memphite Building Programme of Amenhotep III

Anna Garnett

'A history of ancient Egypt which omitted Memphis would be like a history of ancient Italy which omitted Rome' (Smith & Jeffreys 1986: 88).

Introduction

Throughout Pharaonic history, the city of Memphis remained vital in the development of the Egyptian state, when the city's administration, defence, commerce and communications flourished as a direct result of its advantageous geographical location, while the gradual eastward movement of the Nile at Memphis in antiquity led to the exploitation of the newly-reclaimed waterfront for agriculture and new building projects (Jeffreys & Tavares 1994, 155; Smith & Jeffreys 1986, 88). The great wealth and power of the reign of Nebma'atre Amenhotep III (c.1382–1344 BC), founded upon years of military peace and the steady acquisition of gold from Nubia and the Eastern Deserts, allowed the king to launch an unprecedented transformation of the Nile Valley landscape into a monument to '*immortalize his own eternal fame*' (Kozloff & Bryan 1992, 1).

The value of a detailed study of the material partly lies in the very nature of the material itself: while the key Theban foci of Amenhotep III continue to promote stimulating discussion through excavation, the Memphite data remains comparatively under-represented in the archaeological record; a trend predominantly due to the physical and human conditions imposed on the site since antiquity. Extensive quarrying and reuse of elements of the great Memphite Ptah temple precinct during both the Pharaonic and Medieval Periods (for example, the small temple of Ramesses II discussed in association with the Ptah-Sokar shrine below (Johnson 1996a, 5)), together with the rising level of the groundwater at the site, have negatively affected the level of preservation of the surviving monuments and their reliefs. One could argue that Amenhotep III's presence in Memphis equalled, and may even have exceeded, the Theban programme of works; however, such an assertion can be easily challenged when the highly fragmentary assemblage of contemporary Memphite material is taken into account. At this point it is necessary to consider the offices of High Priest of Ptah and High Steward, and the individuals who were appointed to those posts under Amenhotep III.

Memphis, Thebes, and the High Priest Tuthmosis

Though Amenhotep III patronized the cult of Amun on a grand scale, most obviously through the creation of Luxor Temple, the extension and embellishment of the temple of Amun at Karnak, and the creation of his temple at Soleb, his Memphite building programme represents a deliberate

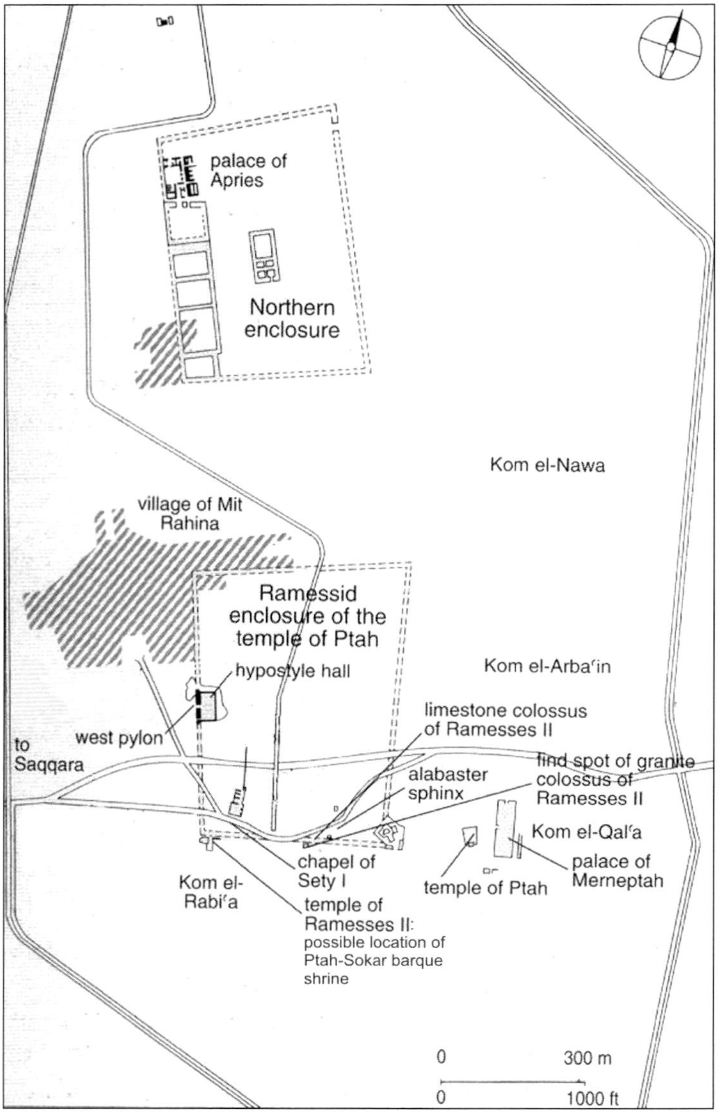

Figure 1. *Plan of the Ptah temple complex (adapted from Baines and Malek 1980: 136).*

emphasis of the Egyptian administration and religion towards the north, in order to create a balance between Memphis and the contemporary growing influence of the Amun cult and its priesthood (Gaballa & Kitchen 1969, 29; Kees 1977, 175). The legitimacy of this hypothesis is yet to be fully established; although it is clear that the most significant development in the growth of the Memphite administration during the reign of Amenhotep III was the installation of the crown prince (*s3-nsw smsw*) and royal heir Tuthmosis as the High Priest of Ptah; an individual who also possessed the titles of '*Sem*-Priest of Ptah', 'Overseer of the Prophets of Upper and Lower Egypt' and who has been described as '*perhaps the best attested non-regnant prince of his line*' (Kozloff & Bryan 1992, 56; Dodson 1990, 87).

The interest of Amenhotep III in Memphis is exemplified by his association with the first known burial of the Apis bull in the Serapeum at Saqqara, the 'Tomb of Apis I', (PM III^2: 780, 782) through the agency of his son Tuthmosis (Dodson 1990, 75; Malek 1992, 65). When the chapel was excavated by Auguste Mariette in 1852, the basic decoration of Tomb I was still partially intact: '*On y voit Aménophis III, accompagné de son fils Djehutimose… faisant l'offrande de l'encens au taureau de Memphis…*' (Mariette 1882, 125). An unpublished stela depicting Amenhotep and Tuthmosis before the divine bull and an alabaster vase preserving the restored name of Prince Tuthmosis were the most notable objects excavated from the burial chamber (PM III 780, 782). The involvement of the king and his Crown Prince in the embellishment and expansion of a key Memphite cult appears to confirm the importance of the Memphite building programme of Amenhotep III, and how it was utilised to create deliberate cultic associations between himself and powerful members of the Egyptian pantheon.

Figure 2. *Scribal statue of Amenhotep-Huy (Ash. Mus. 1913.163; adapted from Kozloff & Bryan 1992, 237).*

The Temple of Amenhotep III Named nb-mꜣʿt-rʿ ẖnmt-Ptḥ, 'Nebma'atre United with Ptah'

A scribe statue bearing the 'autobiographical' inscription of Amenhotep-Huy son of Heby from the great Memphite Ptah temple is the principal source of information for the form and function of the 'Nebma'atre United with Ptah' temple (Urk. IV 1793–1801, Fig. 2). The appointment of this individual as '*Director of the Works*' (line 13) in this temple formed the most significant point in his official career; the text initially describes the royal appointment of Amenhotep-Huy as High Steward of Memphis:

> *dhn=f –wi r imy-r pr wr mdw=i ḥr tpw rḫyt*
>
> '[the king] appointed me to [be] high steward; my staff [was] upon the heads of the common folk' (line 9), and
>
> *dhn=f –wi r ḫrp kꜣ(w)t m ḥwt=f nt ḥḥw m rnpwt*
>
> '[the king] appointed me to direct the works in his 'Mansion of Millions of Years' (line 13);

thus permitting Amenhotep-Huy to feature significantly in the planning and execution of the Memphite building programme of Amenhotep III.

Location of the 'Nebma'atre United with Ptah' Temple

The *bʿḥ* land is identified as the area within which Amenhotep III '*made* [his 'Mansion of Millions of Years'] *anew*' (lines 13–14); in the *bꜥḥ n imntt ḥwt-kꜣ-Ptḥ ḥr idb n ꜥnḫ-tꜣwy*

'[*bꜥḥ*] to the west of the temple for the ka of Ptah, upon the region of Ankh-Tawy' (line 14).

The particular stretch of land west of *ḥwt-kꜣ-Ptḥ* cited by Amenhotep-Huy is referred to by the term '*Ankh-tawy*' (*ꜥnḫ-tꜣwy*, line 14). A section of the Berlin 'Trauerrelief' (No. 12411), the provenance of which has been assigned to the Memphite region on stylistic grounds, appears to suggest that the toponym 'Ankh-tawy' referred to the region between the Ptah enclosure in central Memphis and the Saqqara plateau proper, in the locality of the necropolis: [....] *tn –wi m iw n mꜣꜥ ḫrt n ꜥnḫ-tꜣwy*, literally 'receive me in the island of truth, the necropolis of Ankh-Tawy' (Badawi 1948, 64). The level of contextual bias in this late 18th Dynasty tomb inscription means that this account remains questionable as a descriptive source for the precise location of 'Ankh-tawy'; however, it appears to support Amenhotep-Huy's statement that the temple of Amenhotep III was built to the west of *ḥwt-Kꜣ-Ptḥ* in a very specific region of the much broader entity Ankh-tawy, between the Ptah temple and the Saqqara plateau.

Faulkner (1962, 81) translates *bꜥḥ* as '*abundance*', '*inundated land*', and a '*basin for irrigation*', and Gardiner (Petrie *et al.* 1913, 33) as a '*ground liable to be inundated*'. This phrase is vital for the study of the meaning of the temple location as it appears to designate a natural environment of indeterminate extent as opposed to the environs of a temple or a necropolis. Wild (1979, 312–315) favours a translation of *bꜥḥ* as '*vineyard*' as opposed to '*inundated land*' as Memphite vineyards, together with palm and tree plantations, were in operation during the late 18th Dynasty, note Hayes' (1951) wine jar label 58 from the palace of Amenhotep III at Malkata which documents the Memphite vineyards in production during the third decade of the reign of this king: *rnpt-sp 37 irp n tꜣ ḥwt* (....) *mn-nfr pt kꜣmw* – '*regnal year 37, wine of the land of the temple* [....] *the vineyard [in] Men-nefer*'. For examples of trees and irrigation tracts from the reign of Ramesses II, see K*RI* II, 514, 16 & III, 298,14. However, such estates could not physically function in '*inundated land*' as the roots and shoots of the grapevines would rot and become irreparably damaged by the uncontrolled flooding of the Nile.

Eyre (1994, 70) has argued that if a link existed between the *bꜥḥ* lands in the Nile Valley and the fruit plantations in antiquity, the water entering the *bꜥḥ* would have been controlled to prevent the ground becoming inundated, thus preventing the destruction of the crop and facilitating irrigation channels during the flood season. This would have permitted the large-scale growth of vines and other fruit-producing crops, whilst also generating a series of theological and symbolic implications for the cultic structure through the existence of overland flow. The standard New Kingdom temple plan physically replicated the universe upon earth, with the great pylon as the horizon (*ꜣḫt*) and the entrance to the axial temple pathway, the hypostyle hall with its papyrus and lotus-topped columns symbolic of the dark, chaotic primeval swamp of Nun, and the rising temple floor level towards the sanctuary as an evocation of the primeval mound (Schafer 2005, 6; Kemp 2006, 274).

The link between the *bꜥḥ* land and the growth of vines and fruit trees, together with the idea of abundance, suggests that the walled temple precinct was situated in the cultivable land around the city, in an area which received the yearly flood waters but could control them in order to prevent widespread flooding, thus appearing as an island in the middle of the water during the inundation (C. Eyre, Pers. Comm.). If, according to Amenhotep-Huy, the 'United with Ptah' temple was located in the Memphite *bꜥḥ* land, the controlled waters entering the *bꜥḥ* would have passed over the land around the temple precinct and subsequently receded. The same phenomenon must have taken place at the temple of Amenhotep III at Kom el-Heitan before the collapse of the temple in antiquity, judging from images of the Colossi of Memnon surrounded by water before the construction of the Aswan high dam and the associated loss of the annual Nile flood (Musée du Louvre, Cabinet des Estampes, Vh 176, Réserve, Folio, pl. 199). As a result, one could argue that the *bꜥḥ* land was conceived as one of the vital locational elements for the construction of royal '*Mansions of Millions of Years*' during the reign of Amenhotep III, as a direct association with the divine rebirth and rejuvenation of the king.

Who, or What was 'United with Ptah?'

The inscription of Amenhotep-Huy preserves the name of the Memphite temple of Amenhotep III in full: '*Nebma'atre United with Ptah*' (*nb-mꜣꜥt-rꜥ ẖnmt-Ptḥ*, lines 1 and 31), prompting the question of who, or what, was 'United with Ptah?' If it were the king who was 'united', then he was apparently proclaiming that he existed as the hypostasis of the god Ptah. Morkot (1990, 326) argues in favour of this theory, based on the evidence of Amun 'United with Eternity'; a god solely associated with the temple of Ramesses III at Medinet Habu (Nelson 1942, 128, Pl. IV). Throughout the Amenhotep-Huy text (lines 1, 22 and 45) the name of Amenhotep III appears as a rebus-spelling by omitting the cartouche as opposed to the full writing of the royal name within the cartouche in line 7, where it is used in an explicitly historical context (Morkot 1990, 328; Urk. IV 1793–1801; note Fig. 3). This phenomenon is attested elsewhere during this reign (for example, the extensive collection of wine jar sealings from the palace at Malkata (Hayes 1951, Figs. 25 & 30), and a contemporary inscription at Aswan which preserves the name of the king as a single sign (Varille 1936, 175), thus promoting the hypothesis that the rebus name incorporated into the Amenhotep-Huy inscription refers to a statue or the temple itself, rather than the king (Morkot 1990, 327). Consequently, one may also argue that it was not the king who was the hypostasis of Ptah, but that the ka of a divine form of Amenhotep III – 'Nebma'atre United with Ptah' – may have physically resided within the medium of a statue, set up in the sacred temple space.

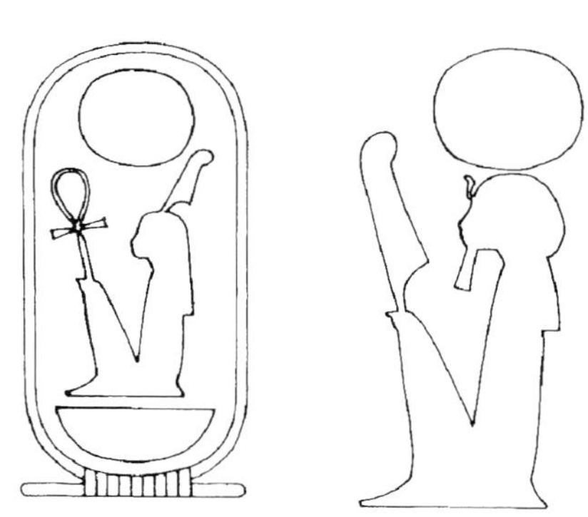

Figure 3. *Normal and rebus (single-sign) spelling of Nebma'atre (adapted from O'Connor and Cline 1998, Fig. 3.34).*

Yet, a careful reading appears to contradict this possibility. Besides showing gender agreement with the word *ḥwt*, the feminine ending of -t in *ẖnmt*, 'United with', may also imply that rather than referring to the king as a masculine entity, the title embodies the physicality of the temple precinct as opposed to the human nature of the pharaoh (Morkot 1990, 327). Therefore, 'Nebma'atre United with Ptah' could instead refer to the relationship between this temple and the great domain of Ptah in central Memphis, and consequently how the king became both physically and symbolically 'United with' the Ptah temple by positioning his own cultic enclosure within the vicinity of the great Ptah temple. In support of this theory, Morkot (1990, 326) argued that the Amenhotep III temple may have been envisaged in antiquity as both an '*administrative and spiritual appendage of the ancient sanctuary*', and that this link existed as a result of the flow of offerings from the small temple to the main precinct. Indeed, any link between the 'United with Ptah' temple and the great Ptah precinct would have presented advantages to both temples through this idea of *'circulating benefits'* (Nelson 1942, 127); however this is a discussion which lies beyond the scope of this paper.

The Exterior Façade and Furnishings of the Temple

Amenhotep-Huy describes the building in hyperbolic and conventional terms:

> *sbꜣ=s nbw m ꜥš n ḫnty-š m stp(w) n gꜣw bꜣk(w) m nbw mꜣꜥ ḥr ḫꜣs(w)t ḏꜥmw ꜥꜣt i͗nr(w) nbt špst šꜣdw š swd(i͗)w m mnw*
>
> '…all its doors [were out] of cedar-wood of Lebanon and from the choicest of Gau, worked with true gold from the deserts, fine gold, and every costly and valuable stone…..the lake was dug and planted with trees' (lines 15–17).

Amenhotep-Huy also describes that his king made the temple,

> *m mnw n i͗tf Ptḥ m kꜣ(w)t mnḫt nt ḏt m i͗nr ḥd n ꜥ(i͗)nw*
>
> 'as a monument to his father Ptah as a splendid work of eternity, in the white stone of 'Ainu' (line 15). 'Ainu' is described by Faulkner (2002, 43) simply as a '*source for limestone*' without giving any further clue to a precise location, yet it is likely that *'Ainu* was another reference to the region of the Tura limestone quarries.

which appears to indicate that limestone was the predominant building material for this temple (O'Connor 1998, 70). However, evidence to contradict this theory exists in the form of two quartzite blocks attributable to the reign of Amenhotep III, excavated from the small temple of Ramesses II at Memphis, illustrating Amenhotep III offering to Sekhmet in delicate sunken relief (MFA 10.650 and AE.I.N 1152) These blocks are significant not only as primary documentation of a possible subsidiary cult of Sekhmet at the site of the temple, but also as an indication of the physical form of the temple in antiquity.

P. Harris I: 45 preserves a statement of Ramesses III concerning the construction of a temple within the Memphite Ptah precinct, of which no evidence currently exists in the archaeological record (Grandet 1994, 102). In the typically formulaic style of royal temple inscriptions, Ramesses states that, together with gold doors and stone pylons, his temple was made from granite covered in limestone (Sandman Holmberg 1942, 209). Despite the highly biased nature of this inscription, it appears to support the theory illustrated by the scant archaeological material from the site and the inscription of Amenhotep-Huy that the 'United with Ptah' temple was constructed largely of limestone, i.e. the local stone, and that quartzite blocks – which were evidently not burnt at a later stage like the limestone – may have been employed to create the outer 'casing' of the temple. One might also deduce that the temple was predominantly constructed from limestone, but that certain architectural elements such as architraves and door jambs, and also possibly the inner sanctuary, were formed from the more valuable quartzite blocks (K. Kitchen, Pers. Comm.). Based on the surviving data, both theories appear equally likely at this point, and may not have been mutually exclusive.

Another equally legitimate hypothesis is that the 'Nebma'atre United with Ptah' precinct was filled with both royal and divine statuary in commemoration of the royal jubilees, as was also the situation at Kom el-Heitan; Note the hundreds of seated and standing Sekhmet statues holding papyrus sceptres excavated from the 'Mansion of Millions of Years' of Amenhotep III at Kom el-Heitan and the temple of Mut at Karnak, together with the various statues of guardian sphinxes, rams, jackals and royal colossi (Sourouzian 2007, Sourouzian *et al* 2004; Kozloff &

Bryan 1992). The presence of large-scale Ptah imagery within the 'United with Ptah' temple precinct may be illustrated by two colossal quartzite Ptah statues produced for Amenhotep III and subsequently recarved during the reign of Ramesses II (Cairo, JE 38430-31 (Kozloff & Bryan 1992, 75)). which imply that the use of quartzite may not have ended with the relief blocks cited above. However, the precise location of these figures in antiquity cannot be fully ascertained, despite a secure Memphite provenance, as they may have been erected either in the main Ptah precinct or in the environs of the 'United with Ptah' temple. A kneeling figure (Fitzwilliam Museum E.82.1913) preserves an image of the king with an offering table and a usurped cartouche, and is suggestive that the figure, and thus perhaps also the temple, were still standing at Memphis during the Amarna period, during which time it was defaced by devotees of the Aten (Bourriau 1982, 56). A quartzite head depicting a youthful, vigorous Amenhotep III was also arguably sourced from the Memphite precinct where the depth of the break at the right side of head implies that the figure originally held a standard against his left side (Kozloff & Bryan 1992, 163).

The date of the 'Nebma'atre United with Ptah' Temple

A wine jar label from the site of the palace of Amenhotep III at Malkata states: *rnpt-sp 26 ỉrp n* [.....] *ʿnḫ-wḏꜣ-snb m mn-nfr*, '*Regnal year 26, wine of (.....)* [presumably Amenhotep III] *LPH in Men-nefer*' (i.e. Memphis, Hayes 1951; Fig. 4, No. 3). This does not prove that the temple proper was fully operational by year 26; however it appears to imply that the Memphite foundation, located on *bʿḥ* land, was producing wine and perhaps other consumable commodities by this time (Morkot 1990, 330). Thus, the temple of 'Nebma'atre United with Ptah' was almost certainly designed and constructed during this great building phase of Amenhotep III, in association with his first sed-festival in year 30. The longevity and significance of this installation is reflected in the evidence that elements of the temple 'Nebma'atre United with Ptah', if not the temple proper, almost certainly remained intact during the Amarna period; a theory best illustrated by the kneeling figure discussed above.

The Memphite Barque-Shrine of Ptah-Sokar in the Reign of Amenhotep III

'Nebma'atre United with Ptah' may have incorporated one or more subsidiary chapels, in order to directly associate the king with specific cults within the sacred space of his 'Mansion of Millions of Years'. Since 1995, the epigraphic work of the Egypt Exploration Society (Malek & Quirke 1992; Wilson *et al* 2001; Smith & Jeffreys 1985, and Jeffreys & Bunbury 2005), at Kôm Rabi'a and the site of the Memphite temple of Ramesses II in the vicinity of the south-west corner of the great Ptah temple enclosure (note Fig. 1) has recovered over thirty relief blocks and reused architectural elements indicative of a shrine dedicated to the Memphite god Ptah-Sokar at the site, dating to the reign of Amenhotep III and designed to house the divine barque of this god.

Ptah-Sokar carried the epithet *Ptḥ-Skr nb Štyt*: *'Ptah-Sokar, Lord of Shetyt' a*s documented in the 19th / 20th Dynasty tomb of Nakhtmin in Lower Nubia, and a New Kingdom tomb at Deir el-Medina (Sandman Holmberg 1946, 134; Bruyère 1927, 17) which referred to the great gilded barque-shrine specific to the cult of this deity at Memphis (Johnson 1996a, 5; Kitchen 1991, 93). It remains inconclusive as to whether this structure existed either within the main Ptah precinct at Memphis, or within a separate domain of Sokar/Ptah-Sokar at Giza or Saqqara; however a

***Figure 4**. Line drawing of a raised relief block depicting the ḥnw -barque of Ptah-Sokar (after Johnson 1996a: 5).*

study of the Festival of Sokar suggests that it may have been located in proximity to the '*White Walls*' of the original Memphite temple precinct, in a region identified as '*Ro-Setau*' (Gaballa & Kitchen 1969, 46; Edwards 1986, 36). This toponym remains geographically enigmatic; though Edwards' (1986, 35) suggestion that Ptah-Sokar's *šṯyt*-shrine for his *ḥnw*-barque was erected in the Delta site of Abusir el-Bana – known as *whyt r3-sṯ3w* – rather than Memphis, may well be legitimated during future studies in the region. However, secure contextual evidence to suggest that this structure existed alongside a smaller Memphite Ptah-Sokar shrine of Amenhotep III has been exposed by the EES excavations in the vicinity of the small temple of Ramesses II, which as a *Shetyt*-shrine (*šṯyt*) would almost certainly have housed a *ḥnw*-barque of Ptah-Sokar (Johnson 1996a, 4).

Two relief blocks from this structure, one executed in sunken and the other in raised relief, preserve images of this '*primeval-looking*' *ḥnw*-barque of Ptah-Sokar (Johnson 1996a, 4). The sunken relief block exhibits a comparatively simple section of a *ḥnw*-barque with three oars which served to steer the boat, together with an atypical representation of Sokar which omits his characteristic shroud and an inscription referring to *Ptḥ* and *nṯr*(*w*) *inb-ḥḏ*, the '*god(s) of the White Walls*' (Johnson 1996a, 4; Sandman Holmberg 1946, 132). The boat fashioned in raised relief exhibits the head of a gazelle at the prow together with largely unfinished images of fish and falcons, as a stark contrast to the highly-detailed representation of the Sokar falcon upon the cabin of the barque (Johnson 1996a, 4, note Fig. 4). A further raised relief block recorded from the Ramesses II temple that appears to join the block in Fig. 4 indicates that this group preserves imagery for the ritual dragging of the *ḥnw* -barque of Ptah-Sokar during his festival around the walls of Memphis by Amenhotep III, who is wearing the *šbyw*-collar, and his priests, as an integral feature of the festival of Sokar/Ptah-Sokar (Johnson 1996a, 4; Raymond Johnson, Pers. Comm.).

The Date of the Shrine

The relief discussed above preserving an image of Amenhotep III associated with the *ḥnw*-barque wearing the *shebyu*- (*šbyw*) collar may provide some evidence of the date of this structure. Based on an analysis of the reliefs of Amenhotep III at Luxor Temple, Johnson (1990, 34; 1996b, 34; 1996c, 2) identified a controversial 'fourth-decade style' iconographical scheme of this king, which incorporated such innovative items of solar and funerary iconography into the elaborate royal costume as floral *wah*-collars, broad elaborate armbands and wristlets, *rishi*-feather patterns on the kilt reminiscent of a falcon's tail and the *shebyu*-collar. This new iconography was initiated by the jubilee celebrations of Amenhotep III from his thirtieth regnal year, when he was physically and symbolically rejuvenated and subsequently '*reborn in a revitalized and timeless form*' to became assimilated with the sun-god Re (Johnson 1990, 49). This information serves to date the Ptah-Sokar shrine to this period either during or after the jubilees of Amenhotep III in his fourth decade; therefore being contemporary with the construction of the 'United with Ptah' temple.

Despite the serious deterioration of the structure and its reliefs since its excavation by its year-round immersion in salt-laden ground water, the unfinished raised relief block described above was almost certainly deliberately left unfinished in a '*hastily executed*' manner by the temple draughtsmen (Johnson 1996a, 5). Therefore, one may tentatively infer that the creation of the Ptah-Sokar shrine was cut short by the death of Amenhotep III in his regnal year 38, and as a result, its decorative scheme stood unfinished until the dismantling of the structure by Ramesses II when the blocks experienced a renewal of life through the identification with the name of the living pharaoh. All of the blocks examined to date are of limestone, which suggests that it formed the fundamental building material for the shrine (Johnson 1996a, 4). However, the possibility that granite and/or quartzite was utilised together with limestone for the shrine, as well as in the creation of the 'United with Ptah' temple, should not be discounted until the epigraphic work of the EES is completed.

Was there a Palace Associated with the 'Nebma'atre United with Ptah' Temple?

Kemp (2006, 272) states: '*By the mid-18th Dynasty kings were no longer residing in Thebes. They lived for the most part in the North of Egypt, particularly in the palaces at Memphis*'; a theory supported by van Dijk (1988, 38), '*the more or less permanent residence of the king was Memphis, which the king left for Thebes only on important religious occasions such as the celebration of the Opet Feast*'. These observations are predominantly based upon fragmentary evidence of both a Memphite palatial complex of Tuthmosis I (Urk. IV, 2028, 7; 2031, 15; van Dijk 1988, 37; Helck 1958, 97) as a new base for his military campaigns, and of the great royal palace at Memphis associated with the temple of Ptah, which despite the presence of a substantial, and apparently primarily residential, palace structure associated with the temple of

Amun at Karnak (O'Connor 1991, 279) apparently point towards a more permanent Memphite royal residence during the 18th Dynasty (Jeffreys & Smith 1988, 64; Kemp 2006, 289). As the head of the Egyptian administration, the king would almost certainly have resided for extended periods in both Thebes and Memphis, in order to govern the country effectively and thus maintain cosmic order within an appropriate royal palatial setting alongside his vizier (van Dijk 1988, 38).

It may be reasonably argued that if a palace were constructed to be physically and symbolically associated with the 'United with Ptah' temple, then it would have exhibited aspects of both ceremonial and ritualistic activity associated with the temple cult(s), as opposed to its construction as a predominantly residential building. If, as Kitchen (1991, 96) argues, the Memphite palace of Amenhotep III is to be located east of the main Ptah precinct – a considerable distance from the supposed western position of the 'Nebma'atre United with Ptah' temple – then it may in effect have acted as a northern royal residence to parallel the Malkata complex, though evidently on a less significant scale and with a lesser ritual component. Such '*Tempelpalast*' are evident from Thebes and possibly also Amarna, and have been described as '*a palace attached to a temple and used occasionally by the pharaoh when taking part in festivals*', most notably the Sed-Festival celebrations at Malkata which required an extensive space for the many participants of the feast (Stadelmann 1973, 235).

O'Connor (1991, 178) argues that the Memphite palace of Merenptah, together with the evidence for the Theban palatial structures of Ramesses II and Seti I, at the Ramesseum and Qurna respectively (Stadelmann 1973, Figs. 3 & 5; Lacovara 1997, 33), existed as a '*non-residential, ceremonial palace*', where an absence of residential suites and storage areas is suggestive of a so-called '*dummy palace*'. This building would have been utilised by the living king during his participation in ritual activities connected with the temple and perhaps also during more public performances. However its true *raison d'être* was as a residence for the ka of the king after death, to allow the deceased ruler to symbolically participate posthumously in the rituals and festivals enacted by the temple associated with the funerary palace (O'Connor 1995, 280).

If such a structure existed, then one could reasonably argue that it was predominantly dedicated to the ceremonial and ritual activities of Amenhotep III during his lifetime, connected with his personal cult and those cults of other deities residing within the 'United with Ptah' temple. It would therefore have existed as a northern residence for the ka of the deceased king, in association with the southern palatial complex at Malkata and the Theban 'Mansion of Millions of Years' at Kom el-Heitan. The palace would also conceivably have been created as an additional '*architectural stage*' for the jubilee celebrations of this king in conjunction with the grand contemporary festivities at Malkata, when important rituals were enacted both within the Memphite temple and its palace for the symbolic renewal of the king (O'Connor 1995, 280). This idea of symbolic royal rejuvenation may have been physically reproduced in the palace with a raised floor level culminating in the throne-dais and a columnar hall exhibiting palm, papyri- and loti-form capitals, as a three-dimensional evocation of the primeval mound and the moment of creation comparable to the structure of the palace of Merenptah and the raised casemate palace of Apries to the north of the great Ptah temple (O'Connor 1991, 182; 1995, 290), both of which find resonance in Amenhotep III's jubilee palace at Malkata.

Concluding Remarks

The archaeological and textual evidence pertaining to the presence of Amenhotep III within the city of Memphis, most notably the 'autobiographical' inscription of Amenhotep-Huy, confirm the existence of at least two enigmatic cultic structures: the 'Mansion of Millions of Years' of Amenhotep III at Memphis named 'Nebma'atre United with Ptah', and an associated *sṯyt*-shrine designed to house the *ḥnw*-barque of Ptah-Sokar. However, the data does not allude to the presence of a temple-palace that may have been physically associated with the 'United with Ptah' structure, which, together with the absence of archaeological evidence, ensures that any conclusions concerning the Memphite palatial installation of Amenhotep III remain conjectural. One could logically argue that such a structure took the form of a cultic or ceremonial entity associated with the maintenance of the divine and royal cults within the temple, though this may well be disproved during future excavations.

It remains to be concluded whether the temple and the shrine were physically linked, and indeed what the precise nature of their relationship with the great Ptah temple was; however a tentative attempt at a physical reconstruction for both the temple and the shrine may be offered for the purposes of this study, based on the surviving documentary material.
The 'Nebma'atre United with Ptah' temple may have comprised:

- Entrance pylon
- One or more chapels to accommodate subsidiary cults
- Sanctuary at the rear of the temple
- Pillared hall(s) exhibiting papyriform and/or lotiform capitals
- Constructed from limestone and quartzite
- Enclosure wall
- Series of divine statues, and at least one royal statue
- Raised and sunk relief employed in the decoration.

And the barque-shrine for Ptah-Sokar may have contained:

- Small pylon-structure
- The *ḥnw*-barque of Ptah-Sokar, and the *mfḫ*-sledge associated with it
- One or more pillared halls
- Predominantly constructed from limestone
- Raised and sunk relief employed in the decoration
- Votive items deposited within the precinct of the shrine.

The significance of the Memphite building programme of Amenhotep III is best illustrated with material from later reigns. Haeny (2005, 106) suggests that Horemheb followed the precedent set by Amenhotep III in Memphis by establishing a temple near the great Temple of Ptah, in a comparable manner to the location of the 'Nebma'atre United with Ptah' structure. The fundamental outcome of this programme appears to have been the subsequent foundation of an enigmatic Aten temple under Akhenaten (Malek 1997, 95). During this time, surviving aspects of Amenhotep III's installation were subsequently defaced; a phenomenon best illustrated by the removal of the cartouche of the kneeling quartzite statue of the king discussed above.

However, following this turbulent period in Memphis, the cult of Amenhotep III appears to have been re-established and continued under Ramesses II. P. Sallier IV (Verso, 1, 8) affirms that the cult of '*Ptah who is under his moringa-tree of Nebma'atre United with Ptah*' existed together with the cults of 37 other contemporary deities, suggesting that the cult statue of Amenhotep III's temple, if not the temple proper, survived into the Ramesside Period (Gardiner 1937, 89; Aston & Jeffreys 2007, 75). During this time, Morkot (1990, 337) argues that the 'Chief Steward of Memphis' under Ramesses II, another Amenhotep-Huy, may have moved the scribal statue of Amenhotep III's steward to the area of the temenos of the great Ptah temple, in an '*act of piety by an official to a predecessor in office*'. Whether this theory can be established as historical fact remains to be seen; however one may also argue that through the reuse of relief blocks from Amenhotep III's Memphite structures, Ramesses II not only gained a useful source of building material, but also symbolically associated himself with the 18th Dynasty installation by incorporating the blocks into his own cultic structure as an act of piety by the king to a predecessor in office.

The building programme of Amenhotep III in Memphis succeeded in the production of great temples and colossal statues which, through the power of royal imagery, communicated what words could not successfully convey to the Egyptian population: the supreme power and universality of their pharaoh. The Memphite landscape was re-drawn to focus upon the position of the king as the centre of the cosmos, and was certainly '*no real estate development scheme*' (Kozloff & Bryan 1992, 5).

To quote Kozloff & Bryan (1992, 3): '*[Amenhotep III]'s wish, eventually written on a stele at Thebes in terms of an accomplishment, was to construct monuments "the like of which never existed before since the primeval time of the two lands"*'.

School of Archaeology, Classics and Egyptology
University of Liverpool

Acknowledgements

This paper is a result of an M.A. undertaken at the University of Liverpool. I am grateful to all the staff of SACE, and many thanks are also due to Prof. W. R. Johnson, Dr. D. Aston and Prof. K. Kitchen for kindly agreeing to review my M.A. dissertation in preparation for this article, H. Sourouzian and R. Stadelmann for their continued support, and to C. Price, G. R. Morgan and the anonymous peer reviewers whose comments on this paper were tremendously beneficial. However, the responsibility for the ideas expressed in this paper and any errors remain mine alone.

Bibliography

Aston, D. A., and Jeffreys, D. G. (2007) *The Survey of Memphis III: The Third Intermediate Levels,* London, Egypt Exploration Society.

Badawi, A. M. A. (1948) *Memphis als Zweite Landeshauptstadt im Neuen Reich*, Le Caire, Institut Français d'Archéologie Orientale.

Baines, J. and Malek, J. (2000) *Cultural Atlas of Ancient Egypt*, Oxford, Phaidon Press.

Bourriau, J. (1982) 'Three Monuments from Memphis in the Fitzwilliam Museum', *Journal of Egyptian Archaeology* 68, 51–59.

Bruyère, B. (1927) *Rapport sur les Fouilles de Deir el-Médineh*, Le Caire, Imprimerie de l'Institut Français d'Archéologie Orientale.

Dodson, A. (1990) 'Crown Prince Djehutymose and the Royal Sons of the 18th Dynasty', *Journal of Egyptian Archaeology* 76, 87–96.

Edwards, I. E. S. (1986) 'The Shetayet of Rosetau', in Lesko, L. H. (ed.), *Egyptological Studies in Honor of Richard A. Parker*, Hanover, University Press of New England for Brown University Press.

Eyre, C. J. (1994) 'The Water Regime for Orchards and Plantations', *Journal of Egyptian Archaeology* 80, 57–80.

Faulkner, R. O. (1964) *A Concise Dictionary of Middle Egyptian*, Oxford, Griffith Institute.

Gaballa, G. A., and Kitchen, K. A. (1969) 'The Festival of Sokar', *Orientalia* 69, 1–76.

Gardiner, A. H. (1937) *Late Egyptian Miscellanies*, Bruxelles, Fondation Egyptologique Reine Elisabeth.

Grandet, P. (1994) *Le Papyrus Harris I, BM 9999*, Le Caire, Institut Français d'Archéologie Orientale.

Haeny, G. (2005) 'New Kingdom 'Mortuary Temples' and 'Mansions of Millions of Years', Schafer, B. E., (ed.) *Temples of Ancient Egypt,* Third Edition, London, New York, I. B. Tauris.

Hayes, W. C. (1951) 'Inscriptions from the Palace of Amenhotep III', *Journal of Near Eastern Studies* 10, 1, 35–56.

Helck, W. (1958) *Zur Verwaltung des Mittleren und Neuen Reiches, Probleme der Ägyptologie 3,* Leiden, Koln.

Jeffreys, D. G., and Smith, H. S. (1988) 'Memphis and the Nile in the New Kingdom', in Zivie, A. P., (ed.), *Memphis et ses Nécropoles au Nouvel Empire: Nouvelles Données, Nouvelles Questions*, Paris, Éditions du Centre National de la Recherche Scientifique.

Jeffreys, D. G., and Tavares, A. (1994) 'The Historic Landscape of Early Dynastic Memphis', *Mitteilungen des Deutschen Archäologischen Instituts Abteilung Kairo* 50, 143–173.

Jefferys, D. G., and Bunbury, J. (2005) 'Fieldwork, 2004–5: Memphis', *Journal of Egyptian Archaeology* 91, 8–12.

Johnson, W. R. (1990) 'Images of Amenhotep III in Thebes: Styles and Intentions', in Berman, L. M., (ed.), *The Art of Amenhotep III: Art Historical Analysis*, Indiana, Indiana University Press.

Johnson, W. R. (1996a) 'Re-Used Amenhotep III Blocks at Memphis', *Egyptian Archaeology* 9, 3–5.

Johnson, W. R. (1996b) 'Amenhotep III and Amarna: Some New Considerations', *Journal of Egyptian Archaeology* 82, 65–82.

Johnson, W. R. (1996c) 'The Revolutionary Role of the Sun in the Reliefs and Statuary of Amenhotep III', *The Oriental Institute News and Notes* 151, 1–6.

Kees, H. A. J. (1977) *Ancient Egypt: A Cultural Topography*, Chicago, University of Chicago Press.

Kemp, B. J. (2006) *Ancient Egypt: Anatomy of a Civilization*, Second Edition, London, Routledge.

Kitchen, K. A. (1991) 'Towards a Reconstruction of Ramesside Memphis', Bleiburg, E., & Freed, F., (eds), *Fragments of a Shattered Visage: The Proceedings of the International Symposium of Ramesses the Great*, Memphis, Memphis State University.

Kitchen, K. A. (1996) *Ramesside Inscriptions: Translated and Annotated Vol. II Ramesses II*, Oxford, Blackwell Press.

Kitchen, K. A. (1999) *Ramesside Inscriptions: Translated and Annotated Vol. III Ramesses III and his Contemporaries*, Oxford, Blackwell Press.

Kozloff, A. P., and Bryan, B. M., (eds). (1992) *Egypt's Dazzling Sun: Amenhotep III and his World,* Bloomington, Cleveland Museum of Art.

Lacovara, P. (1997) *The New Kingdom Royal City*, London, New York, Kegan Paul International.

Mariette, A. (1882) *Le Sérapeum de Memphis*, Paris, Vieweg.

Malek, J., and Quirke, S. (1992) 'Memphis 1991: Epigraphy', *Journal of Egyptian Archaeology* 78, 13–18.

Malek, J. (1992) 'A Meeting of the Old and New Saqqara during the New Kingdom', in Lloyd, A. B., (ed.), *Studies in Pharaonic Religion and Society in Honour of J. Gwyn Griffiths*, London, Egypt Exploration Society.

Malek, J. (1997) 'The Temples at Memphis: Problems Highlighted by the EES Survey', Quirke, S., (ed.), *The Temple in Ancient Egypt: New Discoveries and Recent Research*, London, British Museum Press.

Morkot, R. G. (1990) 'Nb-Mt-R'-United-with-Ptah', *Journal of Near Eastern Studies* 49, 4, 323–337.

Nelson, H. H. (1942) 'The Identity of Amon-Re of United-with-Eternity', *Journal of Near Eastern Studies* 1, 2, 127–155.

O'Connor, D. B. (1991) 'Mirror of the Cosmos: The Palace of Merenptah', in Bleiburg, E., & Freed, F., (eds), *Fragments of a Shattered Visage: The Proceedings of the International Symposium of Ramesses the Great*, Memphis, Memphis State University.

O'Connor, D. B. (1995) 'Beloved of Ma'at, The Horizon of Re: The Palace in New Kingdom Egypt', in O'Connor, D. B., and Silverman, D. P., (eds), *Ancient Egyptian Kingship*, Leiden, Brill.

O'Connor, D. B. (1998) 'The City and the World: Worldview and Built Forms during the Reign of Amenhotep III', in O'Connor, D. B., & Cline, E. H., (eds), *Amenhotep III: Perspectives on his Reign,* Ann Arbor, University of Michigan Press.

Petrie, W. M. F., Wainwright, G. A., and Gardiner, A.H. (1913) *Tarkhan I and Memphis I*, London, School of Archaeology in Egypt.

Porter, B., and Moss, L. B. (1978) *Topographical Bibliography of Ancient Egyptian Hieroglyphic Texts, Reliefs and Paintings Vol. III: Saqqara to Dahshur*, Oxford, Clarendon Press.

Sandman Holmberg, M. (1946) *The God Ptah*, Lund, C. W. K. Gleerup.

Schafer, B. E. (2005) 'Temples, Priests and Rituals: An Overview', in Schafer, B. E., (ed.), *Temples of Ancient Egypt,* Third Edition, London: I. B. Tauris.

Schulman, A. R. (1965) 'The Berlin "Trauerrelief" (No. 12411) and Some Officials of Tut'ankhhamūn and Ay', *Journal of the American Research Center in Egypt* 4, 55–68.

Sethe, H. K. (1906) *Urkunden de 18 Dynastie IV*, Leipzig, Hinrichs.

Smith, H. S., and Jefferys, D.G. (1985) 'The Survey of Memphis, 1983', *Journal of Egyptian Archaeology* 71, 5–11.

Smith, H. S., and Jeffreys, D. G. (1986) 'A Survey of Memphis, Egypt', *Antiquity* 60, 88–95.

Sourouzian H., Stadelmann, R., Alvarez, M. S., Bavay, L., Becker, H., Bromblet, P., El-Amouri, M., Emara, S., Linke, J., Pernel, F., Schubert, F., Schubert, M., and Wenzel, F. (2004) 'The Temple of Amenhotep III at Thebes: Excavation and Conservation at Kom el-Hettân Third Report on the Fifth Season in 2002/2003, *Mitteilungen des Deutschen Archäologischen Instituts Abteilung Kairo* 60, 171–236.

Sourouzian, H. (2007) 'Three Seasons Work at the Temple of Amenhotep III at Kom el Hettan', *Annales du Services des Antiquités de l'Égypte* 80, 323–520.

Stadelmann, R. (1973) 'Tempelpalast und Erscheinungsfenster in den Thebanischen Totentempeln', *Mitteilungen des Deutschen Archäologischen Instituts Abteilung Kairo* 29, 221–242.

van Dijk, J. (1988) 'The Development of the Memphite Necropolis in the Post-Amarna Period', in Zivie, A. P., (ed.), *Memphis et ses Nécropoles au Nouvel Empire: Nouvelles Données, Nouvelles Questions*, Paris, Centre National de la Recherche Scientifique.

Varille, A. (1936) 'Colosse d'Amenophis III dans les Carrières d'Assouan', *Revue d'Égyptologie* 2, 173–176.

Wild, H. (1979) 'Une Stèle Memphite du Règne d'Aménophis III à Lausanne', in Vercoutter, J., (ed.), *Hommages à la Mémoire de Serge Sauneron*, Le Caire, Institut Français d'Archéologie Orientale du Caire.

Wilson, P., Jeffreys, D. G., Bourriau, J. D., Johnson, W. R., Martin, G. T., Nicholson, P. T., Kemp, B. J., Maxfield, V. A., Peacock, D., and Rose, P. (1998) 'Fieldwork 1997–8: Delta Survey, Memphis, Saqqara, Tell el-Amarna, Gebel Dokhan, Qasr Ibrim', *Journal of Egyptian Archaeology* 84, 1–22.

Wilson, P., Jeffreys, D. G., Bourriau, J., Johnson, W. R., Kemp, B. J., Nicholson, P. T., and Rose, P. (2000) 'Fieldwork 1999–2000: Sais, Memphis, Tell el-Amarna, Tel el-Amarna Glass Project, Qasr Ibrim', *Journal of Egyptian Archaeology* 86, 1–21.

Wilson, P., Spencer, J., Jeffreys, D. G., Nicholson, P. T., Johnson, W. R., Bourriau, J., Kemp, B. J., and Rose, P. (2001) 'Fieldwork 2000–1: Tell Mutubis, Delta Survey, Memphis, Tell el-Amarna, Qasr Ibrim', *Journal of Egyptian Archaeology* 87, 1–22.

New Technology or Regression? A Compositional Study of Faience Beads from Two Tombs in Abydos

Esme Hammerle

Introduction

This paper presents the results of a pilot study focusing on the dramatic technological changes undergone by faience during the Egyptian Middle and New Kingdom. The main question asks: did faience technology regress or progress during this period of some 970 years? This research will investigate the changes in faience technology (and chemical composition) as exhibited by beads from two tombs excavated at Abydos. Scanning electron microscopy coupled with an energy dispersive spectrometer (SEM-EDS) was used to analyse the samples in order to determine their chemical composition. The results from the analyses were then compared to determine whether Egyptian faience technology changed from one period to the next. One of the aims and objectives of this research is to apply analytical methods to Egyptology, and to create a working model which will enable archaeologists to identify variations in bead manufacture using SEM-EDS.

Background

Abydos

The site of Abydos was chosen because it is one of the largest and most continuously used cemeteries in Egypt and as such has produced a vast number of faience beads suitable for this research. This site was inhabited from the Predynastic Period into the Late Period and served not only as a settlement site, but also as a religious centre and as a cemetery for some of Egypt's royalty. The beads used for this project are part of the University of Liverpool's Garstang Museum collection. John Garstang excavated at Abydos from 1906 to 1909; the samples used in this research are from tombs excavated during the 1908 season. These tombs were selected for their dates, artefact assemblages, accessibility and relatively low level of disturbance. Unfortunately, the field notes from this season are currently unavailable and the tombs have, therefore, been dated based on their artefact assemblages.

Tomb 498 A'08 has been dated to the Middle Kingdom, though the precise location and method of construction remains unknown (Snape 1986, 261). The contents include a fragment of a blue faience hippopotamus decorated with purplish 'paint' (E128), beads of blue faience, green and yellow steatite, carnelian and lapis lazuli (E2383), ceramic, ivory, a few inscribed stone lintels and jambs (Snape 1986, 261). Tomb 498 can be dated to the Middle Kingdom by the faience hippopotamus fragment, which is very distinctive of this period. Hippopotamus figurines were common subjects for faience work at this time and symbolised the revitalising properties of the Nile (Nicholson 1993, 23).

Tomb 541 A'08 is dated to the New Kingdom and, similarly to Tomb 498, its location and method of construction are unknown. The contents include ceramics, ivory, bone, twelve links of copper, beads of steatite, light green faience, shell, light green stone, and lapis lazuli (Snape 1986, 274). Tomb 541 is dated to the New Kingdom by its contents: a Cypriot 'spindle-bottle' which is a foreign import dated to between the late Second Intermediate Period and the Eighteenth Dynasty (Fig. 1, Artefact 1). Artefact 2, a ceramic vessel with a heavy base, and artefacts 9 and 10, ivory clappers not seen before the New Kingdom, also aid in dating this tomb (see Fig. 1). There is, however, one anomaly, which has a different date to the rest of the contents in this tomb: artefact 7, an Anhydrite vessel dated to the Middle Kingdom. It is likely this vessel was either an heirloom or it may indicate that the tomb had been reused.

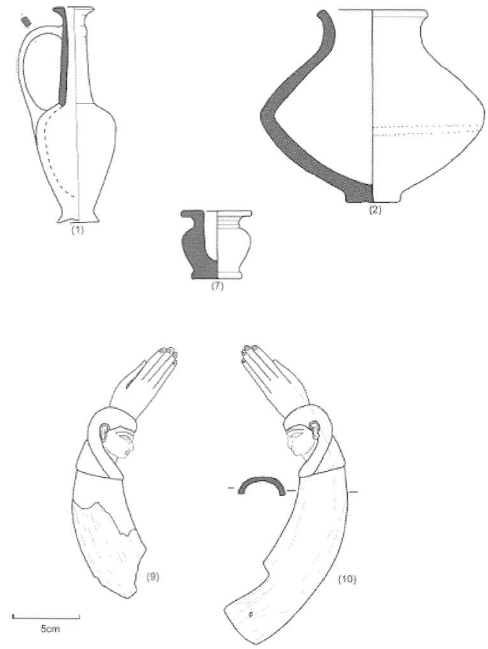

Figure 1. *Artefacts from Tomb 541 (adapted from Snape 1986).*

Faience

Faience was chosen as the topic of this research because of the many debates surrounding this material, such as its origin and its terminology. Since the composition of faience can only be determined by scientific analysis, there is a clear gap in information and much of the past work is speculative and based more on artistic qualities than on technology. What is known is that the production of faience dates back to 4000 BC in the Near East and Egypt and that faience has been used in Egypt continuously from the Predynastic Period to the fourteenth century AD.

Faience is considered the first high-tech non-clay ceramic, and is composed of crushed quartz or sand with small amounts of lime and either natron or plant ash added as an alkali (Noble 1969, 435; Renfrew and Bahn 2000, 338). The material consists of a layered structure, the thickness of which depends on the production method used. The layers are, i) a core of coarse quartz grain with little glass, ii) a quartz-free glaze, and iii) an interaction layer where the quartz grains are cemented together by glass (Shortland 2000, 3). The faience core material is produced by adding finely ground quartz to an oxide such as soda and lime, which is then glazed using one of three methods. The first two glazing techniques are considered to be self-glazing, for the glaze comes from within the faience material through either cementation or efflorescence. The third method is direct application glazing, which is applied to the core material with a brush or by dipping.

Faience was significant in Ancient Egypt and was used by all levels of society from the king to the poor being both part of daily life and used in the preparation for death. Many different objects were made from this material: it was used in architecture, for religious figurines, and adornment purposes (Aspinall *et al.* 1972, 27). Faience was produced in many different colours, including black, red, pink, yellow, green, and the most commonly found, blue. It has been suggested by many scholars that faience, due to its common blue colour, was created to imitate turquoise or lapis lazuli, which is very rare with only one single source known in antiquity: Badakshan in Afghanistan (Tite 1981, 209; Nicholson and Peltenburg 2000, 179). Textual evidence of the Egyptian name for faience is *thnt*, which means 'dazzling' or 'shining'. The same word is used for lapis lazuli, which possibly indicates that faience was intended as an artificial gemstone and prized in its own right for colour, and not necessarily as a lapis imitation (Nicholson and Peltenburg 2000, 179).

The materials used to produce faience were neither rare nor highly valued and the production methods were relatively simple; yet faience was important to the people of Egypt for its colour, and its magical, and religious significance. Faience may also have been regarded as culturally significant for its blue colour, which was a symbol of the Nile, life, and good health. Friedman (1998, 15) states that 'faience was not merely a cheap substitute for lapis, turquoise or any other material, its inherent associations with light, rebirth and fertility, through Hathor, gave it a meaning that far transcended its mundane composition'. The Egyptian goddess Hathor is the goddess of faience, turquoise, lapis, copper and associated mining activities. She would protect the Egyptians on their expeditions to procure the raw materials and minerals required in the production of these artefacts. These expeditions were probably organised by the Egyptian state to procure material for the king and the elite for the manufacture of luxury faience objects. The production of faience was an elite-dominated, institutionally affiliated craft due to its symbolic nature (Bianchi 1998, 23). Indeed, faience is commonly found in royal tombs in great quantity and even though the composition is basic and simple, the material far exceeds its actual production costs in significance because of ritual practices.

Middle vs. New Kingdom

Many general conclusions regarding the Middle Kingdom and the New Kingdom faience technology have been reached during previous research. These generalizations ranged from the most dominant colourant in Abydos beads (copper according to Tite *et al.* 2007) to the relative hardness of the faience. Such conclusions imply that there are differences in the chemical composition and the production methods between these two assemblages. The Middle Kingdom is considered the period of expansion and acceleration in the working and manufacture of Egyptian faience (Nicholson and Peltenburg 2000). The faience objects that were produced were the most diverse and experimental since the Predynastic Period. Cementation glazing was introduced as a common method for the first time, so that all three methods of production were utilized in this period. The glazes were bright and copper was the main colourant, with plant ash being the main alkali source (Nicholson and Peltenburg 2000).

The New Kingdom is considered the zenith of faience working and is characterized by the introduction of new colours and new types of larger objects being produced (Nicholson and Peltenburg 2000). These developments were built on the achievements of the previous periods and, with the aid of glass technology, led to the development of a stronger type of faience with greater hardness, more vitreous structures, and new colours. Production methods expanded to include drilling, piercing, incising, inlaying, and painting. During this period, faience objects were mass-produced in moulds. There was also a new alkali source being used – natron, and a different colourant – cobalt (Tite and Shortland 2003).

Samples
Eleven beads were selected from the Abydos tomb assemblages as samples for this study. Tomb 498 A'08 (E2383) was selected as representative of the Middle Kingdom beads and contained a total of fifty-nine beads, most of which were faience with a few natural stone beads. As there are fifty-nine beads within the collection, a sample size of six beads was chosen as representative of the total without significantly depleting the assemblage. Tomb 541 A'08 (E2377) was chosen as the New Kingdom representative and had a total of fourteen beads within its assemblage, a few of which were made of natural stone. A total of five beads were selected as the representative sample for this tomb and period. Beads were selected for their size, shape, and colour and these aspects were considered in order to properly represent the bulk of the assemblages.

All beads collected for this investigation underwent a complete recording. This included photographing of the samples using a digital camera equipped with super macro that has a focus range of 1 cm to 10 cm. The beads were then sketched in order to record the shape in more detail. A Munsell Colour Chart was used to record some of the bead colours in a standardised format. Unfortunately, the Munsell chart utilised in this research did not include the blue green spectra. Since the beads from the Middle Kingdom fall into this category, no Munsell coordination could be made. Measurements were taken using callipers and the weights were recorded in grams. Then, an inspection of the samples was conducted using a transmitted light microscope to distinguish any noteworthy features of the beads before they were prepared for the SEM-EDS analysis. Table 1 presents the initial observations of each bead by catalogue number and bead number. Snape (1986) ascribed numbers to a few of the beads; however, due to the difficulty in matching the beads used for this study with these numbers, the beads were given arbitrary numbers with a concordance to the original ones (Snape 1986).

Method

The main analytical method adopted for this study is the use of the scanning electron microscope coupled with an energy dispersive spectrometer (SEM-EDS) as this can provide excellent images of the microstructure and microtopography while also providing chemical analysis. The SEM is an imaging system that utilizes electrons, which are accelerated to an energy level of between 1 keV to 30 keV (Goodhew *et al.* 2001, 122). In this case, energy was at 25 keV, which is the maximum for the machine used. The beam passes through a series of magnetic lenses in order to de-magnify the beam and focus on the area of the sample to be analysed. The final lenses consist of two sets of magnetic coils, which cause the beam to scan over the surface of the samples (Tite 1981, 200). Due to complications over access to an SEM, two different machines were used for the SEM-EDS portion of this research, one of which was located in the University of Liverpool's Engineering Department. The Hitachi S-2460 N with Robinson backscatter detector was used to produce the images necessary for this research. Each bead sample was profiled from surface edge to surface edge and recorded in backscatter mode with the images taken with a field of view of 100 to 200 μm.

The second machine used was located in the University of Liverpool's Earth and Ocean Science Department. A Philips XL30 was utilised to produce the chemical analysis for this research because its Oxford Instruments Inca EDS system is capable of quantitative analysis. This machine was used at an accelerated voltage of 20 KeV with a working distance of 12.7 to 12.9 mm and using the mineral standards developed by the department. Corning Incorporated Glass Standards were analysed before the faience samples in order to establish the reproducibility and error of

Bag # Bead #	Shape	Colour	Weight	Snape 1986 #	Photographs
2383 - 1	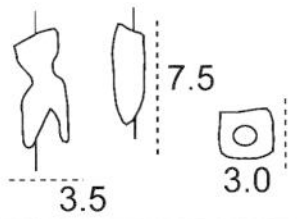	Blue/Green	0.092g	iii	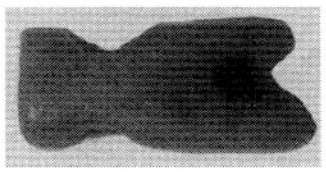
2383 - 2	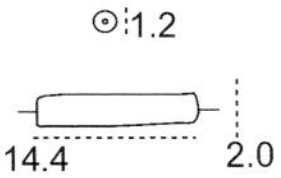	Blue/Green	0.088g	xv	
2383 - 3	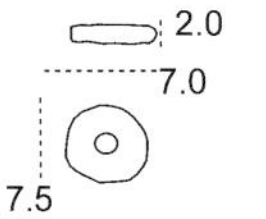	Blue/Green	0.121g	Unknown	
2383 - 4	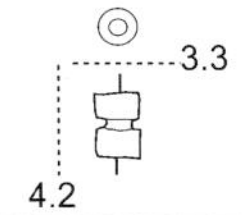	Blue/Green	0.042g	vi	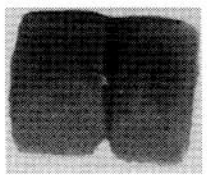
2383 - 5	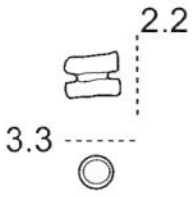	Blue/Green	0.022g	Unknown	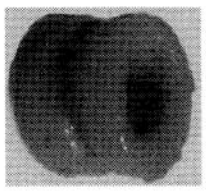
2383 - 6	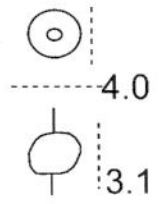	GLEY 1 7/1 Light greenish gray	0.054g	xi	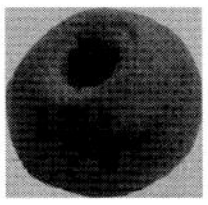

Bag # Bead #	Shape	Colour	Weight	Snape 1986 #	Photographs
2377 - 1	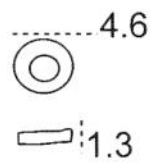	2.5 Y 8/2 Pale yellow	0.027g	iv	
2377 - 2	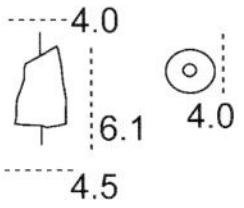	GLEY 1 7/1 Light greenish gray	0.109g	viii	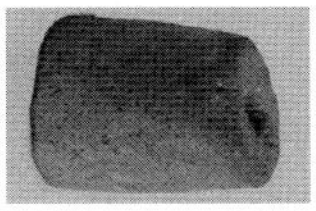
2377 - 3	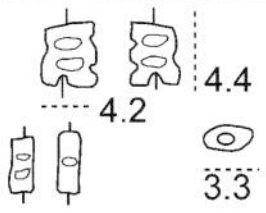	GLEY 1 5/1 Greenish gray	0.065g	i	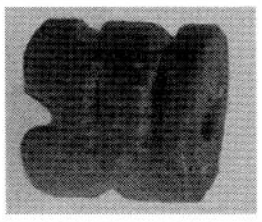
2377 - 4	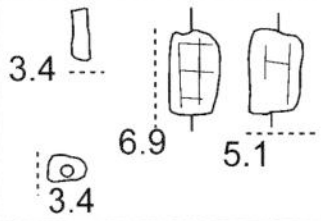	10YR 6/4 Light yellowish brown	0.129g	iii	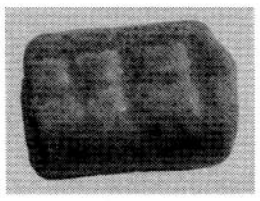
2377 - 5	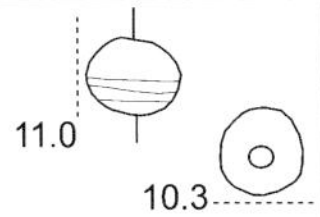	GLEY 1 8/1 Light greenish gray	1.081g	v	

Table 1. *Beads from Tomb 498 (2383) and 541 (2377).*

Oxides	% Error	Precision %
SiO_2	± 0.09	±6.41
Al_2O_3	± 8.91	±4.61
CaO	±13.49	±22.69
MgO	±7.47	±0.54
Na_2O	±8.05	±2.54
K_2O	±45.05	±37.93
Fe_2O_3	±29.36	±17.05
TiO_2	±38.75	±11.47
CuO	±25.00	±18.08
MnO_2	±16.95	±9.22

Figure 2. *Error and precision for the SEM as compiled from Corning Standard A.*

the EDS system based on internationally known and certified values. Corning Glass Standard A was used to calculate the precision and accuracy of the EDS system at the beginning of each session (Fig. 2). The results were then calculated with stoichiometry (oxygen) and normalised to be consistent with past research and to aid in calculating the degree of error. After the initial calculations of the Corning Standards and eventual normalizing of the results, spot analysis was done on each bead three times: one on the surface area, one within the interaction zone, and one within the core material. Spot analysis was chosen in order to penetrate between the silica particles to test the interstitial glass. The live time for each spot was 100 seconds with the dead time below twenty-five percent.

Results

SEM

SEM analysis helped to determine the glazing method and distinguish morphological features that aid in characterizing the faience beads from each period. The glazing method can be determined through backscatter images that enhance the different phases due to the differences in their atomic number, which is shown in various shades of grey (Fig. 3). The quartz appears dark compared with the higher atomic number of the glass phases, which appear as a lighter shade of grey, and the glaze being higher yet in atomic number can appear a very light grey (Tite *et al.* 1983, 26). The glazing methods can also be determined by the amount of interstitial glass present, for efflorescence has extensive interstitial glass whilst cementation has very little (Peltenburg 1987, 10; Tite *et al.* 1987, 128).

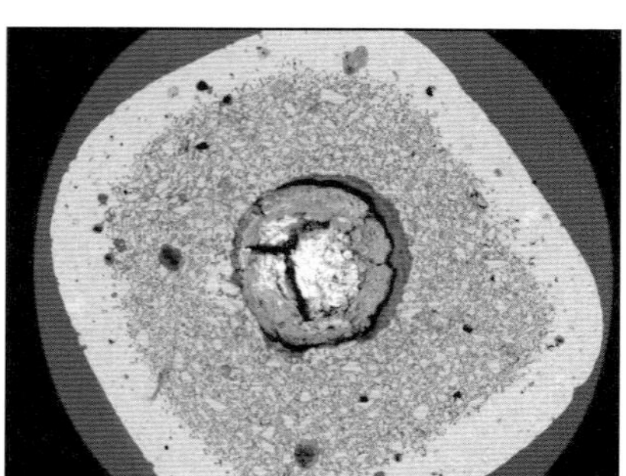

Figure 3. *Bead E2383–1 Middle Kingdom with distinctive layers.*

The SEM also brought to light an interesting phenomenon found only in the New Kingdom beads. Several beads have metallic iron prills that show up with the use of backscatter imaging (Fig. 4). The presence of this iron suggests that the beads were fired in a reducing atmosphere at very high temperatures.

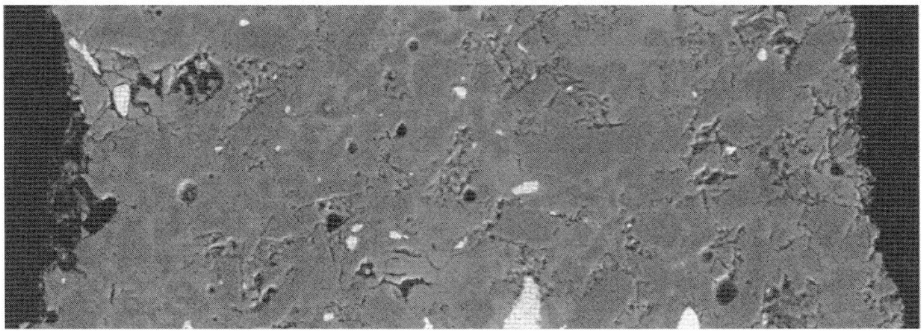

Figure 4. *Bead E2377–3 New Kingdom with Iron prills showing as white.*

EDS

The EDS system aided the identification of potential sources of silica, alkali, and colourant, through the analysis of the impurities and the minor elements that were present. Sand can be determined as the silica source due to impurities such as iron, aluminium and lime. Identification of the alkali source depends on the amount of magnesium and sodium present. The main colourant was also determined with the use of EDS and was found to be copper. Fig. 5 presents the results for the EDS analysis of the Middle and New Kingdom assemblages.

Based on the presence of common impurities, sand was considered to be the main silica source for the Middle and New Kingdom beads (Fig. 6). In typical Egyptian sand, the impurities are lime, alumina, manganese, titanium, and iron, all of which are present in these assemblages. However, the New Kingdom assemblage contains a very high iron content. Kaczmarczyk and Hedges (1983, 123) found that, in the majority, sand was used as a silica source for faience. The site of Abydos has a vast source of silica to the south east of the limestone plateau and consists of Pleistocene deposits of white and yellow quartz sand (Snape 1986, 2). The silica content for both periods ranged from 53% to 99%. The minimum is a little low (possibly due to spot analysis placement) but for the most part holding in line with what is considered to be typical faience.

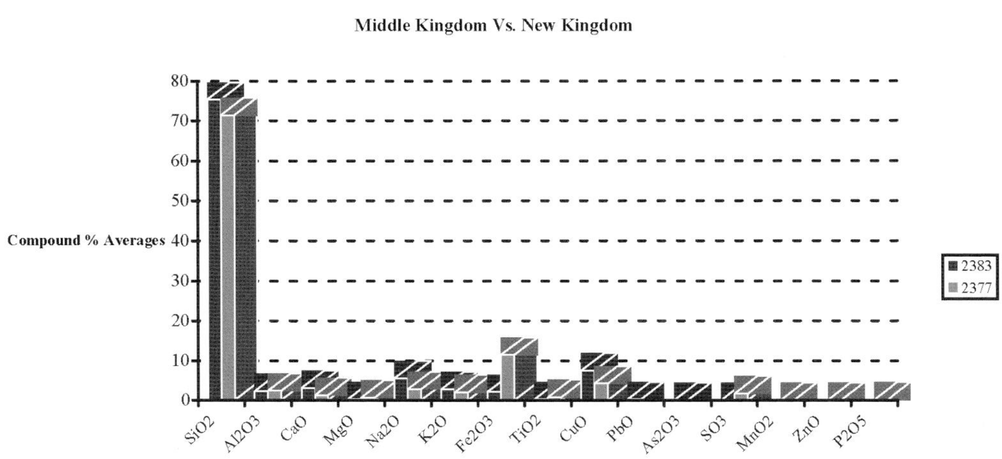

Figure 5. *Middle Kingdom (2383) bead compositions as compared to the New Kingdom (2377).*

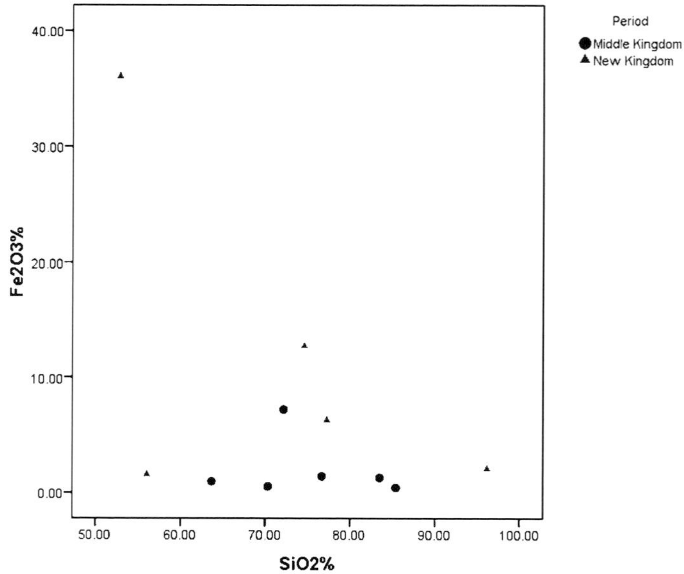

Figure 6. *Iron compound weight% against silica compound weight%.*

The samples in this research all have a mixed alkali composition due to the amount of sodium and magnesium present in the beads. The presence of the magnesium indicates that plant ash was used and the levels of sodium indicate that natron was also utilised. However, the results have shown that the sodium and potassium are correlated and therefore imply plant ash as the alkali source rather than Natron (Fig. 7, 8). Natron contributes only soda to the composition of faience whereas plant ash contributes significant amounts of magnesium, potassium, and calcium. The majority (probably all) of the beads in this assemblage utilised plant ash as their alkali based on the magnesium (0.23–4%) and potassium (0.19–9.25%) levels. Natron could have been added in order to supply a higher level of sodium (0.70–7.46%), but was not used independently of plant ash. There is a possibility that plant ash correlates with the use of copper for glazes as proposed by Shortland (2000, 46). Plant ash can be produced all over Egypt and was probably obtained locally in Abydos. Natron could have also been easily accessible due to the site's location at the mouth of a wadi and route leading to the Western Desert (Redford 1992, 14).

Copper was the colourant used in the production of the faience beads in this assemblage and is perfect for use with self-glazing methods because it can migrate through the silicate matrix of the faience. Tite *et al.* (2007, 1579) found that copper was a main colourant for Abydos beads and the results are consistent with these findings with a range of copper from 0.4%–33.2%. The sources were probably scraps from the metal industry, which obtained its copper supplies from the Eastern Desert and/or the Sinai Peninsula (Bard 1999; Shaw 2000). Some of the New Kingdom beads (2377–1 and 2377–2) have a pronounced presence of sulphur, which is correlated with copper. This could imply a potentially different source of copper for these two beads; however, sulphur could have also come from the plant ash alkali.

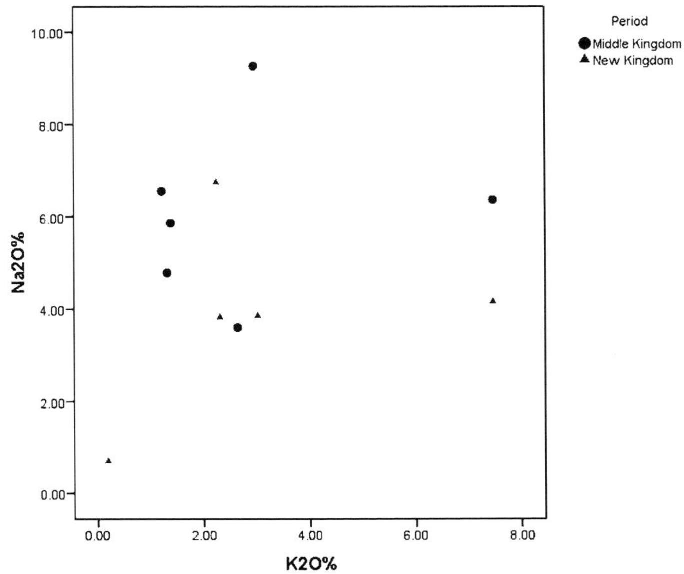

***Figure** 7. Sodium compound weight (%) against potassium compound weight%.*

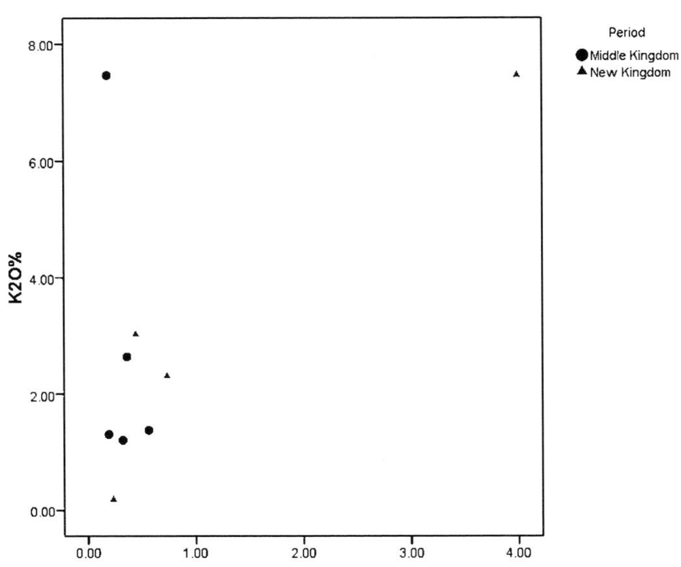

***Figure** 8. Potassium compound weight (%) against magnesium.*

Discussion

Middle Kingdom

The Middle Kingdom beads seem to be very similar to each other with just one oddity: bead E2383-5, which has a slightly different colour, higher glaze, and chemical composition from the rest of the beads (Fig. 9). Otherwise, the beads are consistently produced by the modelling method (determined by the simple designs and soft edges) and pierced, which concurs with the statements of previous researchers for this time period. Of the three glazing methods, only two were present in this assemblage: cementation and one case of efflorescence, which was determined by the presence of extensive interstitial glass. Dual characteristics of cementation and the presence of interstitial glass similar to the efflorescence glazing method have made it difficult to assign Bead E2383–5 to a specific glazing method.

Middle Kingdom beads were all produced using the same raw material sources; quartz sand for the silica as indicated by impurities such as iron, titanium, and aluminium. Plant ash was utilised as the alkali; albeit low, magnesia was present. Copper was used as the colourant, though at an exaggerated amount, far more than is necessary for the desired colour. The copper content is significantly higher in the surface layer, but is found throughout the body due to the self-glazing methods utilized in the production of these beads. Another anomaly with Bead E2383–5 is the chemical composition. This bead contains levels of lead and arsenic, which are only found in New Kingdom beads and not found in faience produced before the 18th Dynasty. This is either the earliest lead-containing bead ever found, or its presence indicates that the tomb has been disturbed. Since lead and arsenic is not found in the New Kingdom beads, it is possible that the origin of this bead differs from that of the rest of the entire assemblage.

Bead	Modelled	Pierced	C Glaze	E Glaze	Mohs Core	Mohs Glaze	Silica	Alkali	Colorant
E2383–1	√	√	√		7	8	Sand	Plant Ash	Copper
E2383–2	√	√		√	8	8	Sand	Plant Ash	Copper
E2383–3	√	√	√		7	7	Sand	Plant Ash	Copper
E2383–4	√	√	√		8	9	Sand	Plant Ash	Copper
E2383–5	√	√	?	?	8	8	Sand	Plant Ash	Copper
E2383–6	√	√	√		8	8	Sand	Plant Ash	Copper

Figure 9. *Middle Kingdom beads (C= cementation glaze, E= efflorescence glaze).*

New Kingdom

The New Kingdom beads appear to be very similar to each other and were all produced by the modelling method and pierced. This is the same method as that of the Middle Kingdom beads, and is very different from the expected moulding method suggested by past researchers. In the

New Kingdom bead assemblage, cementation and efflorescence were the only glazing methods represented. According to past researchers the glazing method of cementation was not utilised during this period. This is significant, considering that cementation is the method used for three of the five beads (Fig. 10).

The results of the analysis indicate that the raw material utilised for the production of these beads was sand for the silica source (due to the presence of impurities) and plant ash for the alkali source (due to the presence of magnesium). Copper was used at very high levels; again, more than was necessary, to obtain the desired colour. During the New Kingdom cobalt was suggested to have taken the place of copper, and natron was correlated with this change, although it does not appear to do so in this assemblage. The only anomaly in the New Kingdom bead composition, other than the high iron and copper content, is the presence of zinc. Zinc could have been added accidentally as either an impurity in the sand or from the copper source (Kaczmarczyk and Hedges 1983). Some copper ore from the Eastern Desert has a slight presence of zinc.

Bead	Modelled	Pierced	C Glaze	E Glaze	Mohs Core	Mohs Glaze	Silica	Alkali	Colorant
E2377–1	√	√	√		4	4	Sand	Plant Ash	Copper
E2377–2	√	√	√		7	7	Sand	Plant Ash	Copper
E2377–3	√	√		√	7	7	Sand	Plant Ash	Copper
E2377–4	√	√	√		7	7	Sand	Plant Ash	Copper
E2377–5	√	√		√	3	3	Sand	Plant Ash	Copper

Figure 10. *New Kingdom beads (C= cementation glaze, E= efflorescence glaze).*

Comparison

The Middle Kingdom and the New Kingdom faience beads were more similar in their production methods and chemical composition than originally thought. The primary production methods of both assemblages were modelling, piercing, and cementation with a few cases of efflorescence glazes. The EDS results have shown that the chemical variations are not as significantly different as at first suspected, and in fact, the two bead assemblages are very similar. The silica and alkali sources were similar in the sense that both sand and plant ash was utilised. Both periods utilised copper as the main colourant at a high percentage. The iron content fluctuated considerably from the Middle Kingdom to the New Kingdom, but this is relatively correlated with the presence of metallic iron prills in the New Kingdom beads.

The main difference between the two periods is that the Middle Kingdom beads seem to be much harder than those of the New Kingdom. This may have resulted from different firing methods or the slight differences in chemical composition, such as the higher copper content in the glazes, and possibly leads to the conclusion that technological change is not always for the better. New Kingdom faience beads are softer than Middle Kingdom beads and this is probably the result of changes in firing brought about by a greatly increased demand and diversification of colours suggested by the presence of reduced iron prills. The basic conclusion of the past research is that there was a marked continuity of technology throughout the 970 year period covered by the material analysed, at least based on this pilot project with a very small sample size.

Problems and Future Research

Several problems arose during the progress of this research, many of which were due to the small sample size and the actual dating of the tombs. The small sample size made it difficult to draw conclusions, especially when assessing generalizations made by past researchers. This small assemblage has thrown doubt on many of these generalisations, but no specific characterisation of the periods can take place without a larger sample. The problem of the dating of the tombs due to the lack of excavation records is an example of how the evidence from a single site and a single excavator's notes can limit analysis. In future research, these problems will be addressed utilising a much larger sample from better provenanced tombs. Other analytical methods will also be employed, such as isotopic studies and replication experiments.

These experiments will be related to the questions raised by the variations in hardness and the appearance of iron particles in the New Kingdom beads. Another aspect that has aroused great interest is the silica content and how to improve the scientific determination of its source. The current way of determining the silica source is by analysing the impurities or the angularity of the particles. Impurities, as discussed earlier in this paper, suggest that sand was used, as quartz pebbles are pure silica and would have none. The angularity of the particles indicates that they are from crushed quartz pebbles, as sand particles would be rounded from weathering. However, this research has shown that this is not always accurate and they are not mutually exclusive, since there was an over abundance of impurities and the particles were angular. An attempt will be made to use crystallography to source the quartz based on the homogeneity of the crystal. The more homogenous the quartz, the more likely it derives from a pebble; a less homogenous structure indicates the quartz is from sand. In addition, oxygen isotope analysis will aid in the determination of silica sources, though this method has so far only been applied to glass.

Conclusion

This research has shown how little faience technology changed from the Middle to the New Kingdom, as exhibited by beads from two tombs in Abydos. Throughout the existence of faience in Egypt, manufacturing techniques and composition were relatively constant. This could be due to the conservative nature of Egyptian society and the continued use of faience for over 5,000 years. Also many generalisations about faience have been questioned, with further research needed to create a new characterisation of each period.

In essence, did the production of faience progress or regress from the Middle to the New Kingdom? This question is much more difficult to answer than first believed. In quality and hardness, the Middle Kingdom faience was more durable and had a superior glaze than the New Kingdom items. Yet in the New Kingdom the use of faience expanded in colours and shapes and was mass-produced. Therefore, in the quality of finished objects the small sample size and the actual dating of the tombs, faience regressed. In terms of technology, with innovations from other sources such as glass, faience became a whole new technology.

School of Archaeology, Classics and Egyptology
University of Liverpool

Acknowledgments

I would like to thank my supervisor, Dr. Matthew Ponting of the University of Liverpool, School of Archaeology, Classics and Egyptology, for his guidance throughout the entire process of this research. I would also like to acknowledge Dr. Steven Snape and Miss Patricia Winker, for their guidance and help in providing adequate samples from the Garstang Museum at the University of Liverpool. Also, I am very grateful to Dan Boatright and Sara Smitherman for their help and advice. I would like to thank the University of Liverpool's Department of Engineering, and the Department of Earth and Ocean Sciences for providing access to their laboratory facilities. With a special thank you to Mr. David Atkinson, Dr. Peter Beahan, and Ms. Carmel Pinnington for their advice and time throughout this research.

Bibliography

Aspinall, A., Warren, S. E., Crummett, J. G., and Newton, R. G. 1972. 'Neutron activation analysis of faience beads', *Archaeometry* 14 (1), 27–40.

Bard, K. 1999. *The encyclopaedia of the Archaeology of Ancient Egypt*, London: Routledge.

Bianchi, R.S. 1998. 'Symbols and meanings', in Friedman, F. D. (ed.), *Gifts of the Nile: Ancient Egyptian Faience.* London, Thames and Hudson, 22–31.

Friedman, F. 1998. 'Faience: the brilliance of eternity', in Friedman, F. D. (ed.), *Gifts of the Nile: ancient Egyptian faience*. London, Thames and Hudson, 15–21.

Goodhew, P.I., Humphreys, J. and Beanland, R. 2001. *Electron microscopy and analysis*, London, Taylor and Francis.

Kaczmarczyk, A. and Hedges, R. E. M. 1983. *Ancient Egyptian faience: an analytical survey of Egyptian faience from Predynastic to Roman Times*. Warminster, Aris and Phillips Ltd.

Nicholson, P. T. 1993. *Egyptian faience and glass*. Buckingham, Shire Publications.

Nicholson, P. T. and Peltenburg, E. 2000. 'Egyptian faience', in Nicholson, P.T. and Shaw, I. (eds), *Ancient Egyptian materials and technology.* Cambridge, Cambridge University Press, 177–193.

Noble, J. V. 1969. 'The technique of Egyptian faience', *American Journal of Archaeology* 73 (4), 435–439.

Patch, D. C. 1998. 'By necessity or design faience use in ancient Egypt', in Friedman, F. D (ed), *Gifts of the Nile: Ancient Egyptian faience*. London, Thames and Hudson, 32–45.

Peltenburg, E. J. 1987. 'Early faience: recent studies, origins and relations with glass' in Bimson, M and Freestone, I. C. (ed.), *Early vitreous materials.* London, British Museum Research Laboratory, 5–29.

Redford, D. B. 1992. *Egypt, Canaan, and Israel in ancient times*. Princeton, Princeton University Press.

Renfrew, C. and Bahn, P. 2000. *Archaeology: theories, methods and practice*. London, Thames and Hudson.

Shaw, I. 2000. *The Oxford history of ancient Egypt*. Oxford, Oxford University Press.

Shortland, A. J. 2000. *Vitreous materials at Amarna: the production of glass and faience in the 18th Dynasty Egypt*. Oxford, British Archaeological Reports.

Snape, S. R. 1986. *Mortuary assemblages from Abydos*. Liverpool, University of Liverpool PhD thesis.

Tite, M. 1981. *Methods of physical examination in archaeology*. London, Seminar Press.

Tite, M. S., Freestone, I. C. and Bimson, M. 1983. 'Egyptian faience: an investigation of the methods of production', *Archaeometry* 25 (1), 17–27.

Tite, M. S., Freestone, I. C. and Bimson, M. 1987. 'The scientific examination of pre-Hellenistic faience from Rhodes', in Bimson, M. and Freestone, I. C. (eds), *Early vitreous materials*. London, British Museum Research Laboratory, 127–132.

Tite, M. S., Manti, P. and Shortland, A. J. 2007. 'A technological study of ancient faience from Egypt', *Journal of Archaeological Science* 34, 1568–1583.

Tite, M. S. and Shortland, A. J., 2003. 'Production technology for copper- and cobalt-blue vitreous materials from the New Kingdom site of Amarna – a reappraisal', *Archaeometry* 45 (2), 285–312.

Mass-Production in New Kingdom Egypt: The Industries of Amarna and Piramesse

Anna Kathrin Hodgkinson

Introduction

One of the main aims of this research is to establish the definition of the term 'capital city' for New Kingdom Egypt. In modern European terms it has been defined as '*The most important town or city of a country, usually where the central government operates from*' (Oxford English Dictionary of Current English 2005). In the Ancient Egyptian monarchical state, a city would have probably received temporary or nominal 'capital' status through the existence of a palatial building in occupation by the king (Franke 2003, 1). This could have been any settlement of considerable size, and these settlements have been classified as 'Royal Cities' by Lacovara (1997). This research is concerned with the nominal capital cities of New Kingdom Egypt: Memphis, Thebes, Amarna and Piramesse. Although the term 'capital city' has never been intensively discussed, these major settlements have traditionally been referred to as 'capital cities' in Egyptology. This problem was looked at during the initial stages of this research and it was decided that the question of capital cities in Ancient Egypt can only be answered by looking at the settlement as a whole, and by analysing the following aspects: the location of the settlement within the country and its natural surroundings, the time-span of occupation, the internal layout and the presence of a defining range of features within the city (see also Franke 2003).

This research concentrates on the economic and industrial landscape of each of these settlements, in order to allow an interpretation of the city's economic role within the state and give a deeper insight into its function as a capital. The aim is to create a structural network based on the existence of industries within the cities of New Kingdom Egypt and to produce a model of dependency between a New Kingdom capital city's status and its industrial activities.

Model

This model is based on the theory that certain features must be present within the city to give it 'capital' status: There must be evidence for one or more temples, at least one of large scale and dedicated to a state deity or a group of gods. Also, the main city requires a royal residence, domestic architecture, high and low status cemeteries, and, depending on the historical background, some military features (for the Ramesside Period, see Franke 2003, 10). In addition, a degree of infrastructure must be evident to satisfy the needs of the population, both in the shape of food production and, in many cases, industrial and commercial activities (Renfrew 1975, 27). Furthermore, the royal connection and presence will raise a city to the status of 'capital' (Hassan 1993, 555). All this evidence should be primarily based on archaeological, or, if this is not otherwise available, on textual or pictorial material. During the initial stages of this research, evidence for all these features within the key sites has been observed.

Working on the premise that a link exists between the need for mass-production and relative settlement size and importance, it must therefore be discussed whether any relationship existed between the individual production sites within the capital cities. A methodology for spatial analysis has been developed, which will provide some conclusions concerning the physical relationships between, and distributions of, the industries within the cities on the one hand, and the inter-relationship of the cities, if contemporary, on the other hand, and allow analysis of their economic landscapes.

It is important to consider the length of time for which these industries continued to be used. Dating is sometimes problematic, as it is not always definite and in some cases in need of review. For example, Pusch discusses the possibilities for dating the installations for metal-working at Thebes. Although he does not absolutely contradict Scheel's Ptolemaic date, he points out that if the stratigraphy had been interpreted and described more accurately, the dating of the installations might have been different (Scheel 1988a, 1988b; Pusch 1994, 147). In other cases, the production sites were abandoned and built over just after their period of usage had been terminated, and thus their context and continuity becomes less clear (Pusch 2008, 25).

Terminology

The term 'mass-production' has been defined for this research, this term being valid if either one of the following characteristics applies: Firstly, objects should be very similar or equal in size, constitution and weight, whilst not necessarily existing in large archaeological quantities, as states of conservation may vary. Secondly, the evidence for the accessibility of objects throughout all social strata, or a large amount of finds in one stratum, can form an indicator for mass-production. Thirdly, it can be indicated by the existence of large scale workshops that are capable of quickly producing a large quantity of goods, either through technological standards proven to have been used at this site, or the distribution of elements of production on the site, such as kilns, which were easily accessible throughout the production area. This corresponds to the modern understanding of mass-production, according to which craftspeople undertake a small, simple task in the production process, rather than producing the finished product itself, which saves time and labour costs (Hounshell 1985, 306–7) or '*the production of large quantities of (a standardized article) by an automated mechanical process*' (Oxford English Dictionary of Current English 2005). In this study, workshops are defined by both structural remains and archaeological finds assigned to a specific type of industry. These can be either multifunctional or fulfil one single function. The absence of a workshop does not, in this context, indicate the absence of a certain type or form of industry.

Methodology

These issues are being monitored by means of a database into which all available evidence for industrial activity within New Kingdom capital cities is being entered, known either through archaeology or literature. The primary data resource is published material, with new data being entered as soon as available. In addition, a spatial analysis will aid the understanding of distributions of industrial sites and other features across the individual cities.

Problems

The main problem encountered during the initial stages of this research is that the archaeological material for large-scale industrial sites is not abundant, as is the case at Memphis and Thebes. Ideally, many more urban sites should be excavated with a focus on industrial areas within the boundaries of the settlement. In terms of excavated material Amarna and Piramesse are rather different from one another in nature, and it is yet to be established whether a direct comparison as attempted below is at all justifiable. Other material is derived from textual or pictorial sources and is not as reliable as first-hand archaeological material. In addition, the variety of techniques and standards applied in excavation and publication in the past and in recent years makes the comparison more difficult, as the reliability of the evidence varies. Despite these problems, I am confident that the amount of material (recently) excavated or located in museums, is sufficient for the current level of approach. Future fieldwork with an intense focus on industrial activities is, however, needed.

Case Studies: Amarna and Piramesse

This research commenced with a brief analysis of the industrial and economic character and landscape of Amarna and Piramesse. Both cities functioned during the New Kingdom and considerable amounts of archaeological data have been made available for both in recent years, revealing a large amount of material related to large scale, mass-producing workshops and industrial activities in smaller workshop areas attached to domestic buildings. The following is a brief overview of the material considered as useful for this research to date, focusing on the production of vitreous materials, such as glass and faience, metal-working, and the production of textile goods.

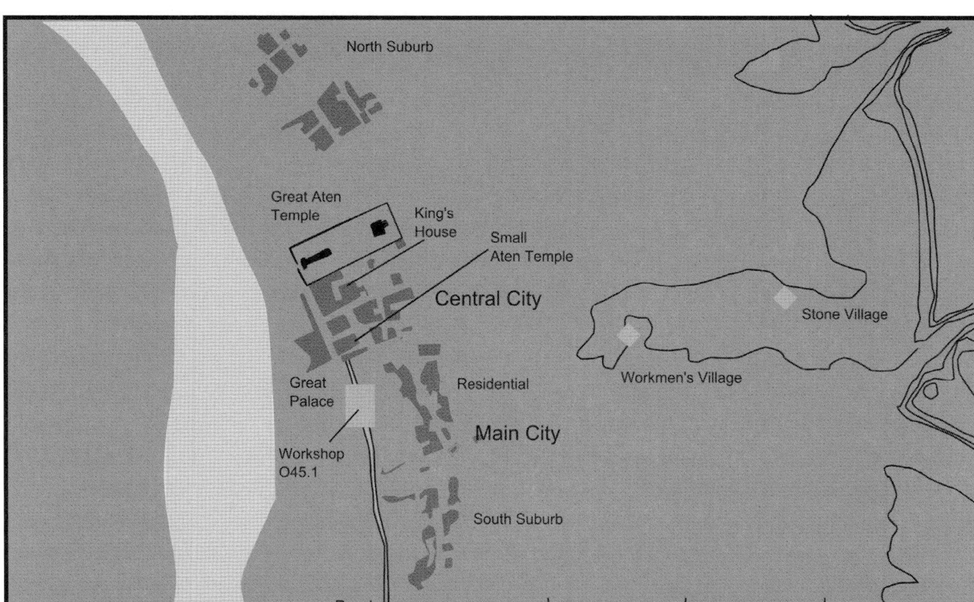

Figure 1. *Map of Amarna with the sites relevant to this study. The scale bar measures 2km. (After Nicholson 2007, Courtesy of the Egypt Exploration Society).*

Amarna

Glass and Faience

The production of vitreous materials at Amarna is not the earliest in Egypt, as there is evidence from Lisht, Malkata and Gurob amongst other places (Fig. 2). Furthermore, glass vessels have been found in burials before production commenced at Amarna, as in the case of the tombs of Thuthmosis III and Amenhotep II, which contained around 11 and 76 glass vessels respectively (Nolte 1968, 46–62; Shortland 2000, 4). These vessels were core-formed and most probably produced from raw materials imported into Egypt (Nicholson 2007, 6). This sudden development has been termed an innovation specific to New Kingdom Egypt, as the production of glass is

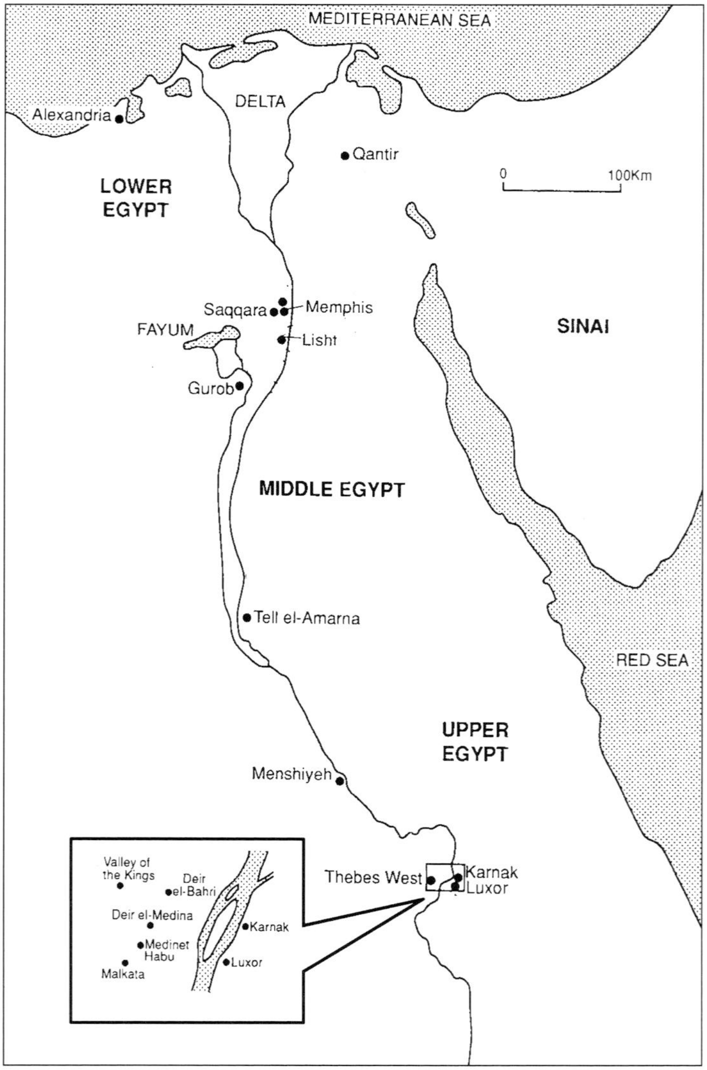

Figure 2. *Glass producing sites in New Kingdom Egypt (Courtesy of the Egypt Exploration Society).*

previously unknown (Shortland 2000, 5; 2001, 220) and lighter shades of blue dominated the general colour scheme, although many other colours were produced (Nicholson 2007, 5).

A portion of the evidence at Amarna, namely the site of building O45.1 excavated by Nicholson in the 1990s (Nicholson 2007), incorporates a workshop which is located south of the Small Aten Temple. It is surrounded by a series of mudbrick walls forming an open courtyard, which is a common phenomenon in New Kingdom Egypt (Shaw 2004, 16). This workshop is located in the general area examined by Petrie in the 1890s and described by him as an 'area of moulds' (Petrie 1894, pl. xxxv). Petrie believed furthermore that he had located "... the sites of three or four glass factories, and two large glazing works..." although he is not clear about their locations and whether the two lie together (Petrie 1894, 25; Shortland 2000, 66). Many of these finds from Petrie's excavation related to the glass industry came from the Palace dumps, and only very few from the Palace itself, although the larger portion of the evidence was not contexted, as it had been found and brought to him by local children from sites around Amarna. Thus, the site O45.1 cannot be the only possible location for Petrie's workshops. During Petrie's excavations some heating trays were found which he does not mention due to lack of recognition (Nicholson 2007, 140). Furthermore, monochrome glass rods and pieces of crucibles have been found in this and other areas of the city containing evidence for glass and faience working.

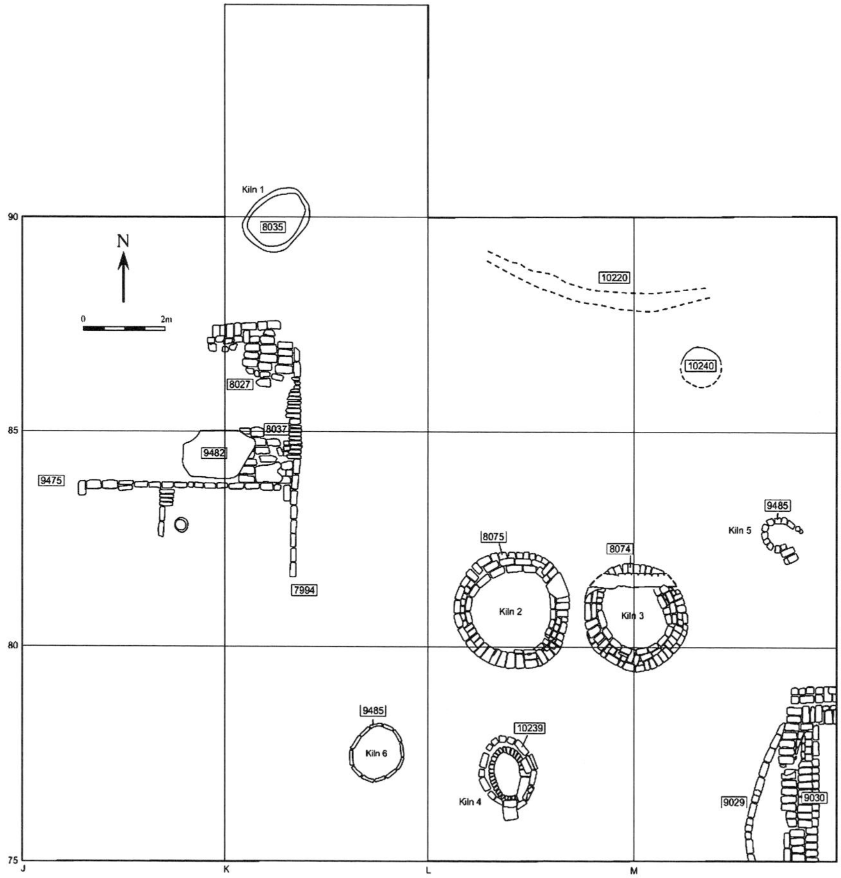

Figure 3. The main industrial phase at site O45.1 (Courtesy of the Egypt Exploration Society).

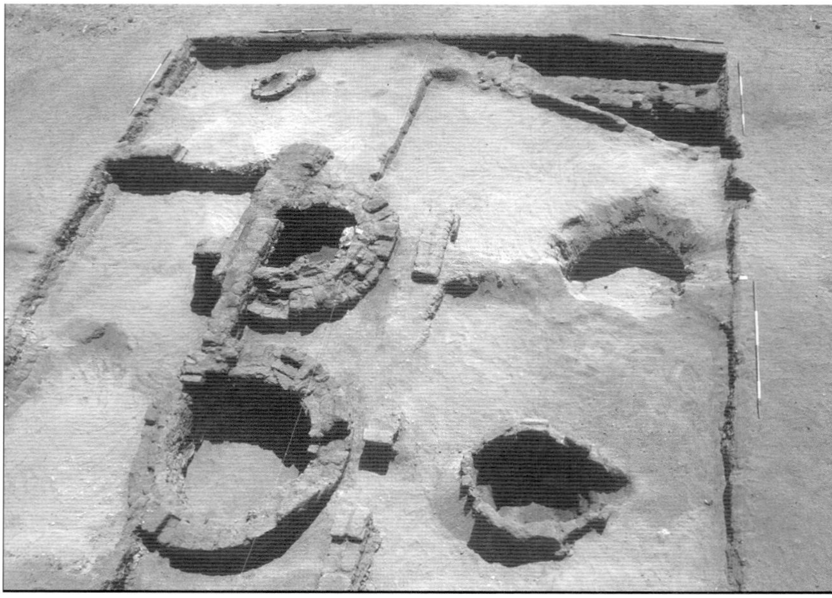

Figure 4. *General view over O45.1, looking east (Courtesy of the Egypt Exploration Society).*

The production site excavated by Nicholson lies over an earlier cemetery, the exact dating of which is yet to be determined, although it appears to have been disturbed by the main industrial phase of the workshop (Nicholson 2007, 31) (Figs. 3, 4). The tombs from this cemetery are very similar in size and shape to those currently under examination by Kemp's team at the Stone Village at Amarna and can therefore be dated to the Amarna Period (Stevens and Dolling 2007).

The main industrial phase consists of four kilns, which were cut into sterile sand (Nicholson 2007, 72). According to the excavator, this workshop was initially used for the production of faience and glass, with a later phase, for which its layout was changed. The function of the second phase is not certain, although it is likely that the workshop was used for the production of pottery (Nicholson 2007, 33). Two of these kilns (kiln 2 [8075] and 3 [8074]) measure approximately 2m in diameter, compared to the other two smaller ones (<2m in diameter). The large kilns incorporated vitrified mudbricks with slags attached, and Nicholson has proved through experiments that they were potentially able to produce temperatures high enough for the manufacture of raw glass (Nicholson 2007, 83; Shortland 2000, 7). The kiln he built during the course of these experiments was directly based on one of the large kilns at O45.1. Simultaneously, Nicholson states that this experiment does not validly prove that raw glass was produced at Amarna – but only that the potential existed. Pusch (2008, 142) agrees with this being potentially possible, but does not draw the conclusion that kilns 2 and 3 were glass-production kilns, as there is insufficient evidence for this. He also argues that the workshops at Amarna produced mainly finished glass products from raw glass in white (colourless) and cobalt blue (Fig. 5), and that only small amounts of raw material were produced at Amarna itself. Despite this interpretation, most ingots from the Ulu Burun Shipwreck (Nicholson *et al.* 1997, Rehren and Pusch 2007, 231) fit the crucibles from Amarna perfectly, which increases the likelihood of raw glass manufacture at Amarna. Shortland (2000, 55) states that only one 'true' colourless piece of glass has been attested at Amarna, which leads to the conclusion that the production of blue glass must prevail.

The manufacture of faience is closely related to the glass industry at Amarna. Shortland's study shows that some of the glass objects were found in the same context as faience moulds from baked clay in workshops throughout the city (Fig. 6). Glass rods derived from courtyards of houses, especially in the Main City, but evidence also exists from the North Suburb (Fig. 7). The areas analysed by Shortland revealed clusters of houses with particularly high quantities of faience moulds in the Main City (mainly in its northern part) and North Suburb, although most houses seem to have had at least one or two moulds. Faience works have also been found to function in connection with other industries, such as jewellers or sculptors, and some workshops have been associated with the house of the sculptor Thutmose (P47.1–3) (Shortland 2000, 69). The moulds appear more frequently in the outer courtyards of these houses, which were usually located to the south of these buildings, where kilns have been found in the Main City, but not in the North Suburb (Shortland 2000, 67). It can therefore be concluded that house-based workshops, in some cases family-run, would have undertaken their own manufacture of faience products, mainly beads and amulets, in the courtyards of their houses (Shortland 2000, 66).

Figure 5. *Piece of (blue) glass. Amarna: Site O45.1 (Courtesy of the Egypt Exploration Society).*

Figure 6. *Faience mould: Possibly a design of a bunch of grapes. Amarna: Site O45.1 (Courtesy of the Egypt Exploration Society).*

Figure 7. *Cylindrical vessel with blue glass attached. Amarna: Surface find from the Palace Dumps (Courtesy of the Egypt Exploration Society).*

Textiles

Another branch of industry at Amarna to be considered in this context is the manufacture of textile goods, published by Kemp and Vogelsang-Eastwood (2001). The evidence for this, as in the case of the larger portion of the faience production, is based on finds from individual houses, occurring mainly in the Workmen's Village, but also in the North Suburb. This form of production has been classified a '*cottage industry*' (Kemp and Vogelsang-Eastwood 2001, 449). Spinning bowls and socket blocks for the upright New Kingdom looms, alongside a variety of smaller finds related to the industry, have been found, providing evidence for all stages of textile production. Furthermore, linen cloth of variable quality, and often in an extremely good state of preservation, has been found in both the Workmen's Village and the North Suburb. The finds of finished goods suggest that the '*untailored cloth*' was produced in a range of qualities and degrees of thickness in the houses in order to be worn as a '*voluminous garment*' by the recipients (Kemp and Vogelsang-Eastwood 2001, 450). Furthermore, a high number of functional goods were found, such as ropes and lamp wicks (Kemp and Vogelsang-Eastwood 2001, 226). A high number of linen garments were found in the tomb of Tutankhamen, and these include loin cloths, tunics, kilts, belts, jackets, socks and gloves of various degrees of thickness. Most of these are undecorated, but some garments, in particular some of the (at least) twelve bag tunics, revealed intricate weaving patterns and embroidery. One tunic (Carter 261a) is said to have previously belonged to Akhenaten (Vogelsang-Eastwood 1999, 54). It was discovered around the neck of the Anubis statue and the titles of Akhenaten can be found embroidered into the cloth. Its sides are decorated with bands which form part of the weaving pattern. There is a high likelihood that this tunic, and possibly some of the others found in the tomb, were produced at Amarna.

Piramesse

Glass and Faience

Work undertaken by the team from the Roemer und Pelizaeus Museum, Hildesheim under Eggebrecht and Pusch in the 1980s revealed a series of large workshops, all of which are located in a large area to the south of the New Kingdom city centre (Fig. 8). The site QIV revealed most evidence for the production of glass, mainly in its raw form, whilst large scale, multifunctional workshops were found at QI (Pusch 1990a; Pusch and Rehren 2008; Figs. 9, 10), containing metal, and leather workshops amongst other specialities, but also some evidence for glass production. The site QV contained some glass related waste (see below). Due to its location in the Delta on the Pelusiac Nile Branch, the city was built up on a series of turtlebacks (Bietak 1975; Hodgkinson 2007) and this limits space and enhances the need for clustering these workshops. No structural evidence for the glass workshops has been located, as any evidence of kilns or other walls potentially belonging to a workshop, is missing. However, an abundance of vitrified ceramic vessel fragments, slags, tripods and glass objects have been recovered from the area. A total of 851 fragments of glass crucibles (including 300 base fragments), and beer jars with glass attached were found during the excavations at QI, QIV and QV (Rehren and Pusch 1997, 127; Pusch and Rehren 2008, 136; Fig. 11). The reason for the absence of any structural remains connected to the glass workshops is that these were levelled, and the area QIV redeveloped for the royal horse stud (Pusch 1999, 117). As a result, a thick series of layers of 'glass debris' remained which can be split into two areas on sites QIV & QI. The glass layer dates to the late 18th Dynasty until at least the early part of the reign of Ramesses II, whilst the horse stud came into being during the reign of Seti II at the latest, but may have already developed

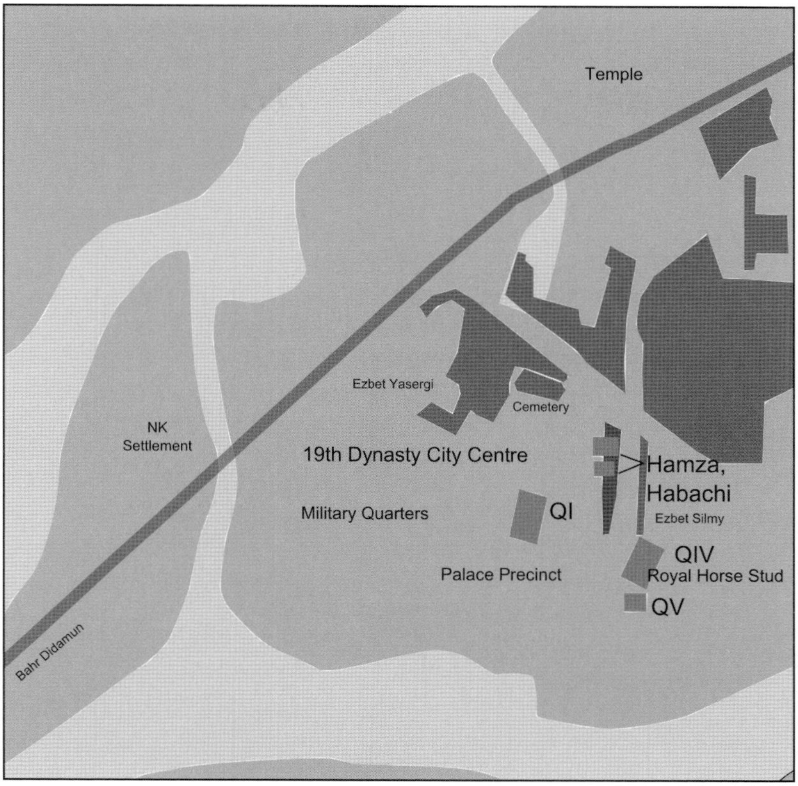

Figure 8. *Map of Piramesse with sites relevant to this study (after Pusch and Rehren 2008).*

Figure 9. *Structural remains at site QIV (Pusch and Rehren 2008).*

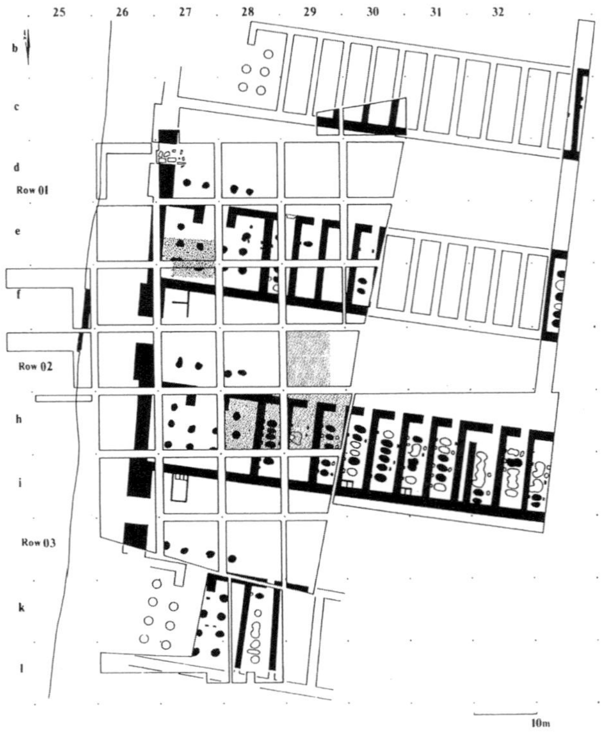

Figure 10. *Structural remains at site QI (Pusch and Rehren 2008).*

Figure 11. *Beer jar from the excavations at Qantir: QV (Pusch and Rehren 2008).*

during the later part of the reign of Ramesses II (Pusch 1999, 119; Pusch and Rehren 2008, 32). Huge lumps of slag which were found out of context, have been interpreted as having formed the lining of melting pits for raw glass. Rehren, who conducted a very detailed study of the objects related to the glass industry at Qantir, argues that structures capable of reaching temperatures high enough for production of glass from raw materials would have been in place (Pusch and Rehren 2008, 147). Red ('Ruby') glass predominates here, in comparison to Amarna where mainly blue glass was produced (see above), whilst there is a striking absence of finished products, and an abundance of objects related to the production of raw glass (Rehren and Pusch 2007, 232). This particular colouring of the glass has been said to be connected with the adjacent metal workshops at QI, with the copper being used as a colourant (Rehren *et al.* 2001, 227).

In addition to the above, large faience workshops, were uncovered by Hamza in 1928 to the West of modern 'Ezbet Silmy, in the direct vicinity of the sites QI, QIV and QV, and he also found the first indicators of the glass workshops, including an ingot of red glass, now in the Cairo Museum (JE64296) (Hamza 1930; Fig. 11). These workshops were capable of mass-producing faience products, and it is certain that they were integrated into the other industrial establishments in the area (Rehren and Pusch 1997, 140). The production of Egyptian Blue has also been associated with the site due to the fact that some fragments of this substance were found here (Pusch 1999, 111; Pusch *et a*l., forthcoming).

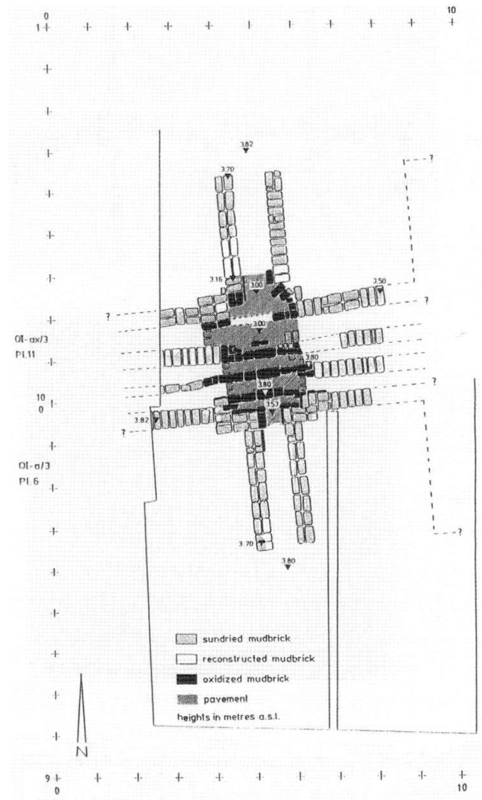

Figure 12. *Plan of one of the cross-furnaces excavated at QI (Pusch 1993).*

Metal-working and multifunctional workshops

The site QI at Qantir – Piramesse revealed the multifunctional and metal workshops that were established between the reigns of Horemheb and Seti I (Pusch 1990b, 78). After the reign of Ramesses II, the metal workshops were integrated into the military quarters which covered the area and encompassed a chariotry and other buildings of military function. The Piramesse workshops revealed evidence for mass-production, as Herold

Figure 13. *Metal-working scene from the tomb of Rekhmire (TT100) (Author's own).*

(1998, 16) analyses the bits belonging to horse bridles and other metal objects used within the context of metal-working, such as shield moulds believed to be of possible Hittite origin and an abundance of tools for the shaping of metals and other purposes (Pusch 1990b, 104).

The four 'cross-furnaces', excavated by Pusch in 1982–87 (Pusch 1990b, 1994; Fig. 12), were dug into sterile sand as can be observed at other sites of similar character (see above, Amarna). These furnaces can be very closely compared to those depicted in the tomb of Rekhmire (TT100; Davies 1935, Fig. 13). The paintings show the workmen operating a series of linear furnaces, which bear a striking resemblance to those excavated by Scheel (1988a and b) in two of the north-eastern courtyards in the mortuary temple of Seti I at Qurna on the Theban West Bank. The furnaces from Thebes have been dated to the Ptolemaic Period, but the evidence is problematic. In my opinion these furnaces are very well integrated into their settings. Therefore it seems likely that the structures could very well have been contemporary with the primary phase of the temple.

Discussion

Need and purpose for production

It can be established that the industrial sites of the New Kingdom capital cities existed due to a need for the finished products, which must have existed to some extent in the city. A workshop would have been built in order to produce enough glass to decorate the palace and temple in the main city, as can be seen in the case studies of Amarna and Piramesse. The location of the glass and faience workshops at Amarna, especially, within the Main City, and the fact that large quantities of waste came from the Palace dumps, leads to the conclusion that most produce would have been controlled, and administered, by palace and temple staff who would consequently distribute the finished products further. The inclusion of faience and glass workshops into sculptors' workshops meant that composite statues could be produced more easily, with the finished products easily accessible (Shortland 2000, 69).

The same can be concluded with the glass workshops at Piramesse. In addition, they lay in the vicinity of a large palatial complex which is known to have been decorated with faience tiles (Hayes 1937), which allows one to conclude that, at least in the case of Piramesse and its geography, distance would have been a factor for the glass workshops' location. It is uncertain why most workshops were abandoned during, or just after, the reign of Ramesses II, leaving only the multifunctional ones operating. It is possible that the need for such goods was no longer present, but it is much more likely that the workshops were relocated (this has also been suggested by Pusch and Rehren 2008, 159). Simultaneously, metal workshops, and the other industries related to the military quarters, would have been necessary to equip the local military bases, a factor not necessarily applicable to Amarna. It is probable that high status goods, such as glass and faience, were produced mainly for a royal and elite context.

Infrastructure and organisation of production

At this stage it is worth asking whether it is at all possible to reconstruct the infrastructure of the production facilities. The location of the workshops at Amarna is relatively central within the Main City and North Suburb, both central areas, accessible and visible to much of the population. Kemp (2006) observed that large, high status residences can be found amongst lower status houses, which were organised in groups of industrial units. This corroborates Petrie's description of the area around site O45.1 as 'low status dwellings' (Petrie 1894, 15–16). In addition, the low status cemetery in O45.1 could indicate the same, especially if it dates to the Amarna Period as suggested above.

It has been suggested that the faience and glass workshops at Amarna were organised into groups which were differentiated by ranking. Shortland (2000, 70–72) has divided these workshops into possible high status workshops that may have been more specialised in their production, and others organised in family groups, producing goods which required less technical specialisation. Workshops would have specialised in modes of production, such as that located in house Q46.1, which would have produced glass for inlaying into jewellery. It can be assumed that the faience manufacture which took place in larger workshops, such as that excavated by Hamza (1930) in Piramesse, produced more specialised goods and would have been responsible for mass-producing large quantities of faience, such as the palace decoration described by Hayes (1937). No records concerning the internal organisation of manufacture are known from Amarna or Piramesse, and at this stage it can only be assumed that the structure of royal and elite control over high status goods and their manufacture resembles that of other New Kingdom economies (Shortland 2000, 72).

In all cases of urban industry described above, a certain degree of centralisation, either in factory location or organisation, can be established. Most of Petrie's finds of finished glass and faience products came from the Palace area, which meant that the main branch of this industry would have been under royal and elite control. The central location of the workshops at Piramesse supports this, and furthermore the organisation of the process of manufacture is facilitated due to the fact that the workshops were grouped in one area.

The resources needed for production would have been easily accessible through good routes of transportation, which would have consequently facilitated the transportation of the finished products, either as intended or unintended surplus, off the site. Raw materials for the production of glass would have been available within or just outside the boundaries of Amarna. Other goods, such as copper, lead, and cobalt colourants and natron would have been imported (Shortland 2000, 52). Both Amarna and Piramesse are, like most cities in Egypt, conveniently located on the Nile or one of its branches, with harbours and good trade connections. None of the raw materials were perishable, and thus could withstand a multitude of conditions for prolonged periods. The import of specialised goods used for the sole purpose of the production of glass would have been subject to the king issuing expeditions or awaiting foreign trade partners and glass production would thereby be subject to royal control. The Amarna Letters give evidence of glass being used as a high status trade article during the Amarna Period (Moran 1992, 72–84, 235; Oppenheim 1973; Shortland 2000, 6).

In the case of the Amarna and Piramesse glass workshops, a network of production has already been suggested. Rehren and Pusch (2007, 232) propose that during the Late Bronze Age glass workshops throughout the Mediterranean area specialised in the production of different colours of glass depending on their natural resources and the need for a certain type of product (Rehren *et al.* 2001, 229). In addition, the workshops would have specialised in either the production of raw glass or the post-processing of the same for the finished products. This theory is strengthened by the fact that the workshop at Piramesse revealed only a small quantity of finished products, although this could be due to a lack of archaeological evidence. Furthermore, the discrepancy in date of both industries makes this model difficult to prove. Whilst there is evidence for the Amarna glass industry working until after the Amarna Period, there is none for it functioning as late as the Ramesside Period. At the same time, the earliest date that can be assigned to the

Piramesse glass industry, at least at QI, is late Dynasty 18 (Pusch and Rehren 2008, 25). This being the case, the production techniques at both sites are very similar, and there is no reason why the industry at Amarna should not have relocated after the end of the Amarna Period (see also Nolte 1968). When regarded in the light of other Late Bronze Age glass production sites, and in comparison with the evidence of the Ulu Burun Shipwreck (Nicholson *et al.* 1997; Rehren and Pusch 2007, 231), this theory can be tentatively accepted. At least at this level it can be believed that industries and settlements co-existed and were related to one-another on both national and international levels.

Comparison

The evidence for production as compiled for Amarna and Piramesse has been presented in Tables 1 and 2 below. The production of pottery has been intentionally omitted as it will be discussed separately on another occasion.

Amarna

Material	*Location within settlement*	*Organisation of production*	*Usage of final products*	*Control of production*
Glass	Concentrated in Main City Visible to some degree in North Suburb	Production in specialised workshops, possibly part of a national or international network Workshops could be integrated into living areas	Used in settlement as high-status goods: archaeological material from Palace, sculptors' workshops exported	Traded at high political level – production, therefore probably controlled by elite / king
Faience	Throughout settlement but concentrated in Main City, North Suburb	Production in (specialised) workshops Workshops could be integrated into living areas	Used on site as high-status goods Possibility for objects being available throughout all social strata	Produced for local population of all social strata Control depended on production site
Textiles	Throughout city but concentrated in North Suburb, Workmen's Village	Production mostly in domestic dwellings	Used on site as high-status goods, but finished textile items available throughout all social strata	Produced for local population of all social strata, partly controlled by elite

Table 1. *Evidence for the production of materials at Amarna.*

Piramesse

Material	*Location within settlement*	*Organisation of production*	*Usage of final products*	*Control of production*
Glass	South of Qantir, outside New Kingdom centre	Production in specialised workshops, in connection with multifunctional workshop, possibly part of a national or international network	Used in settlement as high-status goods: archaeological material from Palace exported	Traded at high political level – production therefore probably controlled by elite / king
Faience	South of Qantir, outside New Kingdom centre	Production in (specialised) workshop within multifunctional workshop	Used on site as high-status goods, but objects probably available throughout all social strata	Control depended on production site
Metal	South of Qantir, outside New Kingdom centre	Production in specialised workshop within multifunctional workshop	Objects probably available throughout all social strata	Necessary for military establishments, therefore probably controlled by elite but accessible to lower social strata

Table 2. *Evidence for the production of materials at Piramesse.*

Conclusion

It can be observed that at both Amarna and Piramesse mass-production took place in accordance with the definition of the term provided above in the introduction. The archaeological evidence at Piramesse revealed glass, metal, and multifunctional workshops which appear clustered in one area south of the New Kingdom city centre and were later partly built over when they were abandoned and/or replaced. At Amarna such a large cluster of workshops has not been revealed, either due to lack of archaeological investigation or actual absence of material, although there is evidence for the multi-functionality of the house level workshops excavated throughout the city, as they were used for the production of faience goods and would have been able to produce glass. This would be time and space economical.

Glass can be classified as a high status product, which, produced at both Amarna and Piramesse, was primarily used in the decoration of major buildings, such as palaces and temples, but can also be found in the context of – mainly royal – burials. There is evidence for the finished products being exported to and from Amarna, which exists on a textual basis in the Amarna letters and probably, on an archaeological basis, in the Ulu Burun context. At Amarna the industrial sites are far more integrated into the city's main urban built-up areas. The proximity of the glass workshop uncovered by Nicholson suggests that the need for the final products to reach their destinations, i.e. the main palace and temples, was urgent and short routes of transportation were necessary.

The variation in quality of the linen products found at Amarna suggests that textiles were produced for a number of purposes and were distributed accordingly. The production of textiles which is both clustered within the Main City area and the Workmen's Village, also reveals a reasonable spread throughout the city as a whole, and indicates the possibility of a local use of the end products, with only the surplus and garments of high status, such as those found in the tomb of Tutankhamen, being used for trade purposes. Finished goods may have been collected in an unknown location and transported elsewhere from Amarna.

At Piramesse the industrial areas are concentrated in one area to the south of the central city. The fact that this industrial area coincides with the location of military establishments indicates the intentional placement of these features around an area of potentially lower social stratification. It furthermore improves the accessibility of the products, due to shorter routes of transportation and immediate control. In fact, the multifunctional workshops facilitate the production of high-temperature goods and their post-processing with the creation of finished products. Another reason for the location of these multifunctional workshops within Piramesse is the geographical situation of the city, as the settlement was built up on a series of turtlebacks, protecting it from the Nile floods and external threat (Hodgkinson 2007).

It is too early at this stage to classify the definite use of the finished products and to reconstruct an entire infrastructure on the basis of the material presented above. The material is still too unclear and requires a great deal more attention. Nevertheless, it can be concluded that a dependency existed between the city as a whole and the city's industries. In both cases production takes place in an easily accessible location within the city, and plays an important role in its infrastructure. High status goods were produced mainly for royal and elite use in a local context. This fact establishes a connection between the industrial evidence within a settlement and its status as a capital city. The evidence for the export of goods from these cities further enhances their status within the country's economical network and their international role.

School of Archaeology, Classics and Egyptology
University of Liverpool

Acknowledgements

I would like to express my gratitude to Barry Kemp, Paul Nicholson and Edgar Pusch for invaluable help and inspiration with the Amarna and Piramesse materials and for permitting me to use their images for this publication. I would furthermore like to thank my PhD supervisors, Ian Shaw and Steven Snape for their support.

Bibliography

Bietak, M. (1975), *Tell el-Dab'a II, Der Fundort im Rahmen einer archäologisch-geographischen Untersuchung über das ägyptische Ostdelta*, Untersuchungen der Zweigstelle Kairo des Österreichischen Archäologischen Institutes; Band 1, Denkschriften der Gesamtakademie; Band 4, Vienna, Verlag der Österreichischen Akademie der Wissenschaften.

Davies, N. de Garis (1943) *The Tomb of Rekh-mi-Re at Thebes*. Metropolitan Museum of Art Egyptian Expedition 11, New York, Publications of the Metropolitan Museum of Art Egyptian Expedition.

Franke, D. (2003) *Theben und Memphis – Metropolen in Ägypten.*

Hamza, M. (1930) 'Excavations of the Department of Antiquities at Qantir (Faqus District)', *Annales Du Service Des Antiquités De L'Égypte*, 30, 31–68.

Hassan, F. (1993) 'Town and Village in Ancient Egypt: Ecology, Society and Urbanization', in Shaw, T., Sinclair, P., Andah, B. and Okpoko, A. (eds), *The Archaeology of Africa: Food, Metals and Towns.* London, Routledge, 551–586.

Hayes, W. (1937) *Glazed Tiles from a Palace of Ramesses II at Kantir*, Metropolitan Museum of Art Papers; No. 3, New York, Ayer Company Publishers.

Herold, A. (1998) 'Gegossen-Geschmiedet-Tordiert', *Metalla*, 05.1, 1998, 3–21.

Hodgkinson, A. (2007) 'The Final Phase of Per-Ramesses: The History of the City in the Light of its Natural Environment', in Cannata, M. (ed.), *Current Research in Egyptology VII: Proceedings of the Seventh Annual Symposium.* Oxford, Oxbow Books, 99–115.

Hounshell, D. A. (c.1985) *From the American system to mass production, 1800–1932: The development of manufacturing technology in the United States,* Baltimore, Johns Hopkins University Press.

Kemp, B. and Vogelsang-Eastwood, G. (2001) *The Ancient Textile Industry at Amarna*, London, Egypt Exploration Society.

Kemp, B. (2006) *Ancient Egypt: Anatomy of a Civilization*, London, Routledge.

Kemp, B. (2008) 'Tell el-Amarna, 2007–8', *Journal of Egyptian Archaeology*, 94, 1–68.

Lacovara, P. (1997) *The New Kingdom Royal City,* Studies in Egyptology, London, Kegan Paul International.

Moran, W. L. (1992) *The Amarna Letters*, Baltimore and London, Johns Hopkins University Press.

Nicholson, P., Jackson, C. and Trott, K. (1997) 'The Ulu Burun glass ingots, cylindrical vessels and Egyptian glass', *Journal of Egyptian Archaeology*, 83, 143–153.

Nicholson, P. (2007) *Brilliant Things for Akhenaten: The Production of Glass, Vitreous Materials and Pottery at Amarna, Site O45.1*, London, Egypt Exploration Society.

Nolte, B. (1968) *Die Glasgefässe im alten Ägypten*, Münchner Ägyptologische Studien 14, Berlin, Verlag Bruno Hessling.

Oppenheim, A. L. (1973) 'Towards a history of glass in the ancient Near East', *Journal of the American Oriental Society,* 93, 259–66.

Petrie, W. M. F. (1894) *Tell el–Amarna*, Methuen, London.

Pusch, E. B. (1990b) 'Metallverarbeitende Werkstätten der frühen Ramessidenzeit in Qantir Piramesse/ Nord', *Ägypten und Levante, I*, 75–113.

Pusch, E. B. (1993) 'Recent work at Northern Piramesse: Results of the Excavations by the Pelizaeus–Museum, Hildesheim', in Bleiberg, E. and Freed, R. (eds), *Fragments of a shattered Visage: The Proceedings of the International Symposium on Ramesses the Great.* Monographs of the Institute of Egyptian Art and Archaeology 1, Memphis State University, Institute of Egyptian Art and Archaeology, 199–220.

Pusch, E. B. (1994) 'Divergierende Verfahren der Metallverarbeitung in Theben und Qantir? Bemerkungen zur Konstruktion und Technik', *Ägypten und Levante,* IV, 145–170.

Pusch, E. B. (1999) 'Glasproduktion in Qantir', *Ägypten und Levante,* IX, 111–120.

Pusch, E. B. and Rehren, T. (2008) *Hochtemperaturechnologie in der Ramses-Stadt. Rubinglas für den Pharao.* Forschungen in der Ramses-Stadt 6, Hildesheim, Gerstenberg Verlag.

Pusch, E. B., Rehren, T. and Schmidy, H. (forthcoming), *Hochtemperatur in der Ramses-Stadt – Ägyptisch Blau und Fayence (Forschungen in der Ramses-Stadt).*

Rehren, T. and Pusch, E. B. (1997) 'New Kingdom Glass-Melting Crucibles from Qantir-Piramesses', *Journal of Egyptian Archaeology*, 83, 127–142.

Rehren, T. and Pusch, E. B. (2007) 'Glas für den Pharao – Glasherstellung in der Spätbronzezeit des Nahen Ostens'. in Wagner, G. (ed.), Fortschritte der Archäometrie, Heidelberg, Springer Verlag, 215–235.

Rehren, T., Pusch, E. B. and Herold, A. (2001) 'Problems and possibilities in workshop reconstruction: Qantir and the organisation of LBA glass working sites', in *The Social Context of Technological Change* 1, 223–239.

Renfrew, C. (1975) Trade as Action at a Distance: Questions of Integration and communication. In Sabloff, J. and Lamberg-Karlovsky, C. (eds), *Ancient Civilization and Trade*, Albuquerque, University of New Mexico Press, 3–59.

Scheel, B. (1988a) 'Metallverarbeitung in Theben', *Archaeologie in Deutschland,* Heft 2/1988, 18ff.

Scheel, B. (1988b) 'Fundobjekte eines Ptolemäerzeitlichen Metallverarbeitungsstätte in Theben und Vergleichsfunde anderer Vorderorientalischer Ausgrabungsplätze', *Studien zur Altägyptischen Kultur*, 15, 243–254.

Shaw, I. (2004) 'Identity and occupation: how did individuals define themselves and their work in the Egyptian New Kingdom?', in Bourriau, J. D. and Phillips, J. (eds), *Invention and Innovation: The Social Context of Technological Change 2*. Oxford, Oxbow, 12–24.

Shortland, A. (2000) *Vitreous Materials at Amarna*, British Archaeological Reports International Series, Oxford, Archaeopress.

Shortland, A. (2001) 'Social influences on the development and spread of glass technology', in Shortland, A. J. (ed.), The Social Context of Technological Change: Egypt and the Near East, 1650–1550 BC. Oxford, Oxbow, 211–22.

Soanes, C. and Stevenson, A. (eds) (2005) *The Oxford Dictionary of English* (revised edition). Oxford, Oxford University Press.

Stevens, A. and Dolling, W. (2007) 'The Stone Village', in Kemp, B. J., 'Tell el-Amarna', *Journal of Egyptian Archaeology* 93, 1–11.

Vogelsang-Eastwood, G. M. (1995) Die Kleider des Pharaos, *Die Verwendung von Stoffen im Alten Ägypten*, Hannover / Amsterdam, Kestner-Museum / Batavian Lion.

Vogelsang-Eastwood, G. M. (1999) Tutankhamun's Wardrobe, *Garments from the tomb of Tutankhamun*, Rotterdam, Van Doorn & Co.

The Veterinary Papyrus of Kahun

Conni Lord

Introduction

The field of veterinary medicine is a little researched area of ancient Egyptian medical knowledge and the reason for this is that the evidence has simply not survived. A Middle Kingdom text, the Veterinary Papyrus of Kahun UC32036 (Quirke & Collier 2004, 54–57), is the only solid proof for animal healing in ancient Egypt and this has largely been ignored by Egyptologists, probably due to the severe fragmentation of the original document. The ancient Egyptians possessed all the necessary components for veterinary care of a scientific nature to flourish; they had relatively sophisticated proficiency in medical procedures and knowledge of herbal remedies from early pharaonic history. The wall paintings from tombs throughout the Dynastic Era show that animal husbandry procedures were established and portray a culture that enjoyed a rich interdependent relationship with their animal counterparts, but only the Veterinary Papyrus allows us any substantiation of animal healing. An analysis of the Papyrus reveals that the ancient Egyptians did recognize animal disease as well as a need for human intervention for certain animal ailments. The surviving case studies in the Papyrus describe a logical approach to animal healing, with some of the treatments still having validity in modern veterinary practice. Despite its damage and the problems with translation, the Veterinary Papyrus of Kahun gives a tantalizing idea of the application of animal healing in ancient Egypt and, considering the importance of animals throughout Egyptian history, it is an area that certainly deserves attention.

In the late 1880s, Flinders Petrie was excavating a site at the eastern edge of the Fayum which was at the pinnacle of its importance during the Middle Kingdom (2055–1650 BC) (Chronology used is Shaw & Nicholson 1995, 310–312), housing the pyramid workers, and later the priests and officials, of the royal funerary monuments of Sewosret II. In one of the Kahun houses, Petrie discovered a cache of papyri, their contents ranging from religious and medical texts to personal communications and administrative documents (David 1986, 115–120). One of these documents was the unique Veterinary Papyrus of Kahun, the only text that can be used as evidence for the proposal that the ancient Egyptians recognised animal disease and saw the necessity of human intervention when an animal was ailing.

The Papyrus is severely fragmented and all that remains coherent is a main section that appears to be outlining three treatments for ailing bulls. There are also a few small fragments that seem to relate to dogs and fish; however, their overall positioning in the Papyrus is unknown. The main fragment measures 25 inches in length and 5½ inches in width, with 48 columns and 3 horizontal headings. The script is written in cursive hieroglyphs, which is a method usually reserved for religious documents. From the content of the Papyrus, there is nothing to suggest it had religious significance so the use of such a script remains a mystery. The text reads in columns from right to left.

Veterinary knowledge in the ancient world

The first evidence for animal healing through human intervention comes from Mesopotamia, around 2200 BC, in the form of a clay seal (Fig. 1) found in the tomb of a Sumerian king (Dunlop & Williams 1996, 55). The seal names Urlugaledenna and describes him as a doctor and one who assists mother animals when they are giving birth. Dating to around 1930 BC, another Mesopotamian text, the Laws of Eshnunna, appears to contain the first evidence of an animal disease, in this case Rabies, with a statement regarding the harsh fine someone will be liable to if their rabid dog bites another person, resulting in that person's death. During the reign of the Babylonian King, Hammurabi (1730 BC) a new set of laws was introduced – The Code of Hammurabi. This code is preserved on a diorite stela, housed in the Louvre. Within this Code comes a statement regarding payment incurred for veterinary services, suggesting that this was a well-established service. The Code states in Articles 224 and 225:

> If the veterinary surgeon performs a serious operation on an ass or an ox and cure it, the owner shall pay the surgeon one sixth of a shekel as a fee. If he performs a serious operation on an ass or an ox and kill it, he shall pay the owner one fourth of its value (Dunlop and Williams 1996, 55).

Produced at around the same time as this Codex, comes the first evidence for animal healing of an entirely more sophisticated nature. The Veterinary Papyrus of Kahun is completely original in that it shows what appears to be a logical and scientific approach to animal illness.

That the ancient Egyptians had knowledge of human illness and healing can be seen in the surviving medical papyri. Of the twelve most important medical papyri, most are written in a mix of scientific and, what we would call magical, treatments. To the ancient Egyptians, however, this separation of magic and science would not have existed, both being seen as integral parts of the complete cure. That said, some of the papyri lean more heavily one way or the other. This can be seen in the section 3 of the Chester Beatty III papyrus, which concerns itself with prescriptions that are largely magical in nature. The Chester Beatty VII papyrus is focused on how to combat the bite of scorpions, with the cures being incantations and 'magical' intervention rather than 'scientific' and the London Medical papyrus contains 61 paragraphs, 36 of which are magical (Nunn 1996, 24–41).

The Edwin Smith Surgical Papyrus, however, differs from most of the other medical papyri with its logical approach to healing, mainly victims of trauma. It reads like an instruction book for doctors and other healers. According to Nunn (1996, 29) the Edwin Smith Papyrus has 'instant appeal to the doctor of today'. It is this papyrus that is the most comparable to the

Figure 1. *Clay seal describing Urlugaledenna as 'one who assists mother animals giving birth' (Dunlop & Williams 1996, 54).*

Veterinary Papyrus of Kahun, in which the three surviving paragraphs read like a set of case studies rather than simply a collection of remedies. The approach and content of the Veterinary Papyrus, like that of the Edwin Smith, testifies to the likelihood of its practical use rather than simply an object of historical curiosity.

Other evidence for veterinary practice in ancient Egypt

The Veterinary Papyrus of Kahun remains the only tangible substantiation for the idea of ancient Egyptian recognition of animal disease and the need for human intervention, in an attempt to save such valued commodities from death and dysfunction. However, there is some tantalising circumstantial information given in other literary forms that can be used, alongside the Papyrus, as support for the hypothesis that animal healing was practiced in ancient Egypt in a sophisticated manner. The first of this circumstantial evidence can be seen in a piece of graffito found at the alabaster quarries at Hatnub dated to the 12th Dynasty (Nunn 1996, 129). Pictured in this graffito (Fig. 2) are two men, who describe themselves as *wab*-priests of Sekhmet. The priests of Sekhmet have long been thought to be associated with human healing, acting as intermediaries for the people punished by their goddess of death and destruction, Sekhmet. The larger of the two graffito figures, Hery-Shef-Nakht, states that he is chief of the king's physicians and records his expertise in diagnosing the sick, all fairly standard achievements for a *wab* priest of Sekhmet with his titles. It is his colleague, Aha-Nakht (drawn smaller and therefore probably Hery-Shef-Nakht's subordinate) who is of interest in regards to the argument for veterinary practice. He does not bear the title '*swn.w*' (doctor), however he describes his work in a similar way to Hery-Shef-Nakht, with one important addition – he is '*rekh kau*' or 'one who knows bulls'. It is possible that this means Aha-Nakht used his diagnostic and healing skills to ensure the health of ancient Egyptian cattle.

Aha-Nakht is not the only *wab*-priest of Sekhmet to be suggested as a possible ancient Egyptian veterinary surgeon. From the Old Kingdom three Sekhmet priests are pictured in tomb scenes presiding over sacrificial butchery of offering cattle. The priest's role here is to pronounce

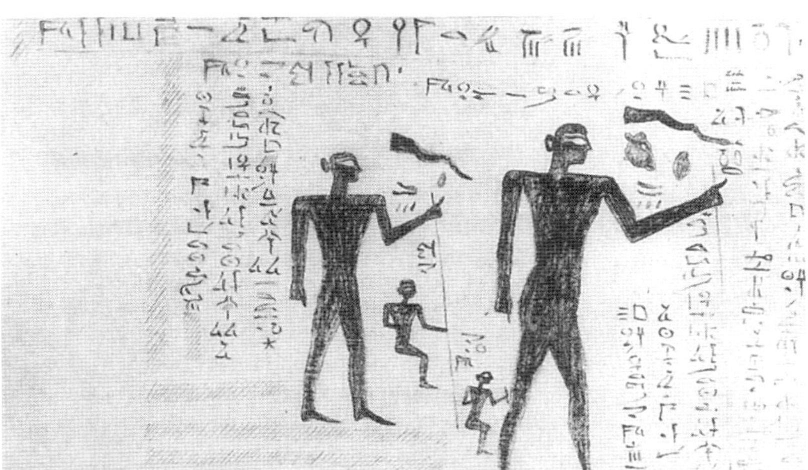

Figure 2. *Aha-Nakht (smaller of the two main figures) is the 'one who knows bulls' (Nunn 1996, 129).*

the sacrificed animal as clean and the blood as pure. Scholars such as Ghalioungui (1983, 13) believe that this is the proof for the priests of Sekhmet being the most likely candidates for the role of veterinary surgeon. An inscription from the much later Ptolemaic Period is, in this author's opinion, a much stronger indication of the involvement of the priests of Sekhmet in animal matters. It is found in the tomb of Petosiris at Tuna el-Gebel, the necropolis for the ancient city of Thoth (Hermopolis). In this text, Petosiris's daughter says to him:

> 'Your herds are numerous in the stable, thanks to the science of the priest of Sekhmet' (Ghalioungui 1983, 12)

Tomb scenes throughout dynastic history portray animals in their natural and domesticated state. These scenes reveal a wonderful understanding on the part of the artists of not only many different species but also the particulars of animal behaviour. The rich relationship between man and beast can be evidenced in many kinds of tomb scene but probably never more so than in the agricultural scenes depicting field animals and their carers.

Today, the care of animals, especially cattle and other herd animals, is divided into two areas of responsibility. Firstly, for everyday treatment and care of field animals, experienced herdsmen have responsibility. Only if an animal is very ill, is a veterinary surgeon called in. With the evidence available, this concept can be transferred to ancient Egypt. In agriculturally based societies, a close association between people and animals can develop; ancient Egyptian herdsmen would have known their animals extremely well and, through experience, would be able to deal with many animal husbandry issues. Tomb reliefs give evidence of this with many images depicting herdsmen assisting with cows giving birth, branding of cattle and the force-feeding of animals. There is no evidence of veterinary surgeons caring for these herds. It is obvious from archaeological remains and tomb reliefs that animals were indispensable for the function of ancient Egyptian agriculture, and it is likely that experienced herdsmen carried out most animal needs. As these herdsmen would have mostly been illiterate, any skills and knowledge would not have been written down in a form such as the Veterinary Papyrus but was passed down orally or learnt by trial and error.

In many scenes involving herdsmen and their charges, the men can be seen making magical gestures of protection toward the animals. Dialogue attached to these scenes includes simple charms aimed at protecting both the animals and their carers. There have been suggestions that these herdsmen may have been part-time priests who obtained their knowledge of protection charms from the temple books (Ghalioungui 1983, 13; Schwabe 1978, 160). However, the herdsmen are depicted in such a way that indicates that these men were not of a high enough status to belong to any sector of the priesthood. Like the practical knowledge of animal husbandry, the basic magic involved in the protection spells would have been passed down orally from generation to generation (Pinch 1994, 59).

Content of the Veterinary Papyrus of Kahun

The Veterinary Papyrus of Kahun remains the only solid evidence for a scientific approach to animal disease and healing by human intervention, and it is the very 'scientific' nature that makes the papyrus problematic. The specialist vocabulary, like that of much of the medical papyri, is extremely difficult to translate and so the exact nature of the illnesses described, and the following treatments, remain uncertain. It is not easy to use the medical papyri as a basis for interpretation of the Veterinary Papyrus as the treatments offered for such general symptoms,

Figure 3. *The second case study of the Veterinary papyrus begins with the title using the determinative of the wind-filled sail on the right hand side (Quirke and Collier 2004).*

such as fever, differ from any contained in the medical papyri. It is possible to make a hypothesis from this: that healing/medicine for people and that for animals were different areas of ancient Egyptian understanding.

By concentrating on the second of the three remaining case studies (Fig. 3), it is possible to see how diagnosis and treatment progressed (based on the translation by Quirke and Collier 2004, 55–56).

Title – Eye examination of a bull with an airborne disease

There is no doubt about the patient in this case study as 'ka' or bull is named in the title. The word to describe the disease '*nft*' uses the determinative of the wind-filled sail, usually connected to words concerning sailing, storm, wind or breath. Although rare, the word, in this form, is seen in some of the medical papyri (Von Deines and Grapow 1962, 459).

Symptoms

The symptoms named in the second case study are easily recognisable to the modern reader;

- 'its eyes are running, its tears heavy' – the bull is suffering from eyes running probably with thick mucal discharge
- 'the roots of its teeth reddened' – swollen red gums
- 'it's neck taut' – swollen lymph nodes.

From the general symptoms given, it seems clear that the bull has some sort of fever and ocular distress and this is confirmed by the recommended treatment. Most scholars who have analysed the Veterinary Papyrus are in agreement regarding a possible diagnosis for case study two (Dunlop & Williams 1996, 55; Lord 2005, 69; Walker 1964, 198–200). Even with the limited and non-specific symptoms named, the virus Bovine Malignant Catarrh (BMC) is a strong possibility. BMC is still present throughout the world today and is spread by a number of reservoir hosts, such as wildebeest, wild and domestic sheep and goats as well as oryx. Sheep are the most common cause of the spread of the disease to domestic cattle (New South Wales Department of Primary Industries, 2009). In ancient Egypt, domestic cattle would come into contact with contaminated grass, water and/or faeces left behind by wild or other species of domestic animals. Even today, there is no effective vaccine for BMC and what is recorded in the Veterinary Papyrus is exactly what veterinary surgeons of today would do – treat the individual symptoms.

Treatment

The bull is put on its side and sprinkled with cool (fresh) water. Its eyes and body are then rubbed with one or other of two plants (*khenesh* or *shu* plants). These two plants are not seen in any of the surviving medical papyri although from the context, it would seem clear that they are being utilised because of cooling properties, just as cucumber and aloe vera are used today. The bull is kept out of the damp and again rubbed with a type of plant (the *khenesh* part of the *qadet* plant). Nunn (1996, 154) suggests that '*qadet*' may be the word for the Hederacea plant, the essential oil of one form of which, *Glechoma hederacea*, has many potent medicinal properties. It is used as a general tonic for coughs and colds, relieves congestion of the mucous membranes and has anti-inflammatory properties, all of which fit the context of symptoms in case study two.

The bull is then bled. Bloodletting, or phlebotomy, was, in the past, a common treatment for fever, as it was believed to aid in the expulsion of toxins. It was practiced among diverse ancient peoples including the Mesopotamians, Greeks, Mayans and Aztecs. Interestingly though, there is no evidence in the medical papyri of it being practised by the ancient Egyptians.

Prognosis

After recommending a course of treatment, a prognosis is stated; 'The bull will live from it or he will die from it', meaning that he, the veterinary surgeon, is hardly likely to be proved wrong. However, this bet each way idea is in keeping with the modern day prognosis of BMC where 50% of animals live and 50% die (although if the symptoms go untreated, this mortality rate can rise to 100%).

Re-inspection and further symptoms

The bull obviously starts to suffer from additional symptoms, such as further ocular distress and lethargy or depression. Both of these auxiliary symptoms agree with the above-suggested diagnosis of Bovine Malignant Catarrh.

Further treatment

According to the Papyrus, in order to alleviate the bull's ocular distress, the eyes must be bandaged in fine, warm linen. Today, for the same condition, the veterinary surgeon would use eye patches or sew up the third eyelid to protect the eyes from the light. While the heating of the linen is not necessary, it may have increased blood flow to the eye area. The second case study ends at this point.

The Veterinary Papyrus of Kahun is a unique document. It gives us a tantalising hint of how the ancient Egyptians identified and treated disease in their animals and it remains the only solid evidence for this. However, it is also a frustrating text in that it is impossible to gain the exact meaning of the content, with so many words unused anywhere else and therefore unable to be effectively translated. It is fragmented and fragile but there is enough remaining to suggest that at least some ailing animals were subjected to human intervention of a logical or 'scientific' nature. In the remaining treatments, it is remarkable to find that 3700 years later, veterinary surgeons are still treating some symptoms in the same way. Considering the importance of animals in ancient Egypt, the advanced medical knowledge possessed for an ancient people of that time and the evidence (mainly from tomb scenes and models) of admirable skills in animal husbandry, it is hard to imagine the ancient Egyptians not establishing some form of veterinary care. Added to this, the presence of the sacred bull cults throughout dynastic history, including the famous Apis bull, that were so strongly linked to the pharaoh, it is almost impossible to think that if one of these animal gods fell ill, it would not be cared for by one of its priestly carers using any healing knowledge they had at hand. However, evidence for all this remains elusive.

While many of the twelve best-known medical papyri are a blend of science and 'magic', the Veterinary Papyrus is more comparable to the medical papyri that are concerned with what we would deem today as practical, such as the Edwin Smith Surgical Papyrus and the Ramesseum V. The remaining case studies of the Veterinary papyrus follow the logical progression of title, symptoms, treatment, prognosis, re-inspection and new symptoms and finally further treatment. Unfortunately, the identity and/or title of the person conducting the treatment is not recorded so we have no way of knowing if there was ever a word for veterinary surgeon as there was 'swn.w' for 'doctor'.

As with many agrarian cultures, animals and humans enjoyed a close relationship in ancient Egypt. It is evidenced in tomb scenes and models, jewellery, furniture and literature. It is impossible to have a complete understanding of the life, diet, disease and death of the ancient Egyptian people without the corresponding information regarding their animal counterparts. However, until further archaeological evidence is uncovered, the questions surrounding the concepts of animal disease and/or veterinary care must remain unanswered. That the ancient Egyptians had an understanding of such things, there can be no doubt, thanks to the surviving content of the Veterinary Papyrus of Kahun; however, how widespread this was or what form it took, can only be assumed. We can but hope that one day this will not be the case and more information regarding this intriguing facet of ancient Egyptian society will come to light.

KNH Centre for Biomedical Egyptology
University of Manchester

Bibliography

David, A. R. (1986) *The Pyramid Builders of Egypt.* London, Routledge.

Donovan, L. and McCorquodale, K. (2004) *Egyptian Art – Principles and Themes in Wall Scenes,* Sydney, MU Press.

Dunlop, R. and Williams, D. (1996) *Veterinary Medicine.* St. Louis, Mosby.

Lord, C. (2005) *How Now Sick Cow.* Unpublished Master's Dissertation, University of Manchester.

Ghalioungui, P. (1983) *The Physicians of Pharaonic Egypt.* Cairo, Al-Ahram Center for Scientific Translations.

New South Wales Department of Primary Industries. (2009). *www.agric.nsw.gov.au* sited May 2009

Nunn, J. (1996) *Ancient Egyptian Medicine.* London, British Museum Press.

Pinch, G. (1994) *Magic in ancient Egypt.* London, British Museum Press.

Quirke, S. and Collier, M. (2004) *The UCL Lahum Papyri: Religious, Literary, Legal, Mathematical and Medical.* London, Archaeopress.

Schwabe, C. A. (1978) *Cattle, Priests and Progress in Medicine.* Minneapolis, University of Minnesota Press.

Shaw, I. and Nicholson, P. T. (1995) *British Museum Dictionary of Ancient Egypt*, London, British Museum Press.

Von Deines, H. and Grapow, H. (1959) *Wörterbuch der Ägyptischen Drogennamen.* Berlin, Akademie Verlag.

Walker, R. (1964) 'The Veterinary Papyrus of Kahun' in *The Veterinary Record*, 76, 198–200.

A Brief Presentation of the Egyptian Collection at the 'Accademia dei Concordi', Rovigo, Italy. A look at published and unpublished objects

Simone Musso and Simone Petacchi

The Accademia dei Concordi, Rovigo, was founded in 1580 by Count Gaspare Campo, a local patron of the arts and was established as a permanent art collection by the Doges at the end of seventeenth century. The collection was further enhanced during the eighteenth and nineteenth centuries by donations from other art and antiquities collectors, one of whom was Giuseppe Valsé Pantellini (1826–1890), (Fig. 1) born in Rovigo, who emigrated to Egypt, where he acquired a number of prestigious hotels, and was appointed by the Khedive to organize the grand ceremonial banquet for the opening of the Suez Canal (Dolzani 1969, 5).

Because of his influential position in Egypt he was approached by the Director of the Accademia with a view to acquiring Ancient Egyptian artefacts and, in 1878–79 he despatched to Rovigo five wooden boxes containing antiquities (Turri 2005, 103–109). The collection was subsequently expanded by the addition of pieces donated by other collectors such as G. Miani and E. Piva. However, it is unfortunately not possible to link specific artifacts with specific donors because of insufficient data in the academy's archives.

There are approximately five hundred pieces in the Egyptian collection, the majority of which are thought to have formed part of the contents of the original wooden boxes despatched from Egypt. The new catalogue now under preparation will comprise both those on display and those held in storage, in contrast to the thirty five percent of the collection published in the first edition edited by Claudia Dolzani in 1969. Also, the two mummies in the collection (a female adult and a baby) will be scientifically analysed by CAT scans, DNA testing and radiocarbon dating.

The Egyptian collection of Rovigo spans the periods from the Old Kingdom to the Graeco-Roman occupation of Egypt. The Accademia dei Concordi holds five epigraphic stelae: four funerary and one votive. Three of the funerary type are family stelae. The first (Dolzani 1969, 25, pl. 12) (Fig. 2) (24 cm × 10.8cm), of limestone, is

Figure 1. *Portrait of G. Valsé Pantellini by G. Cessi (courtesy of the academy's archives).*

Figure 2. *Family stela, Middle Kingdom, ACCE 00120.*

Figure 3. *Stele of Tyty, Middle Kingdom, Hermitage Museum, St. Petesburg, accession n°8729. After www.globalegyptianmuseum.org*

roughly rectangular in shape, with inscribed recessed border. It is ascribed to Ameny and dates to the Middle Kingdom (12th–13th Dynasty). It is roughly inscribed, as evidenced by the cursive form of writing, in sunk relief filled by a greenish powder, possibly malachite. The inscription contains the standard offering formula to Osiris and the standard list of names to whom it is addressed. The majority of personal names confirm the date of the stela, but neither the title of the tomb owner nor his family members are given. This stela, however, is of exceptional rarity for the reversed falcon markings under the *wadjet* eyes in the lunette.

Similar in shape, inscription and decoration is the stela of Tyty from Abydos, in the Hermitage Museum, St. Petersburg (Fig. 3). The method of engraving and cursive style of the hieroglyphs would date both stelae to the same period. The same provenance, however, cannot be assumed, as confirmed by the recent study of Rosati (2003, 91).

Also in the Rovigo collection is a fragment of a funerary stela of Ramesside date (Dolzani 1969, 14–18, pl. 8) (Fig. 4). The right-hand side of the lunette is inscribed with six standing and barefoot figures (two male and two female), facing inwards. The elongated figures, their long figure-hugging garments, pointed sleeves, and tripartite wigs date the object to the 19th–20th Dynasty.

Figure 4 (above). *Virtual reconstruction of the Ramesside family stela, ACCE 00117.*

Figure 5 (right). *The Ibis-Thoth stele, New Kingdom, ACCE 00133.*

A further fragment (Dolzani 1969, 24) (Fig. 5) would originally have formed the centre of a stela with similar lunette. Its purpose was votive and it is dedicated to Thoth, who is shown here in the centre of the stela as the sacred Ibis on its standard before an offering table. Despite the surface damage, the refinement of line and superbly drawn naturalism of the bird can clearly be observed. To the left of the offering table is a podium with cavetto cornice, from which emerges a portion of tail, perhaps belonging to the figure of another god associated with Thoth, but this is difficult to confirm with certainty.

The lower register portrays two erect male figures with bare torsos and shaven heads, possibly priests, facing towards the right. The right hand figure, with raised hands and hunched shoulders appears to be in the act of adoration. The second, whose pleated kilt has also been preserved, bears a bouquet of papyrus and lotus flowers which touch the shoulders of the figure in front. Stylistically and iconographically – for example in the elongated shape of the skull and attitude of adoration – this stela reflects the art of the Amarna Period. The date, therefore, is likely to be the beginning of the 19th Dynasty.

Fig. 6 shows the painted wooden funerary stela of Pa-Wer (Dolzani 1969, 20–22, pl. 11) which belongs to a group of commemorative or decree-type stelae of the Ptolemaic Period, and which would originally have rested on a pair of stepped plinths which have not been preserved. The decoration is divided into three registers framed by a coloured border. The lunette depicts a *djed* pillar with scarab beetle supporting a winged sundisk with four pendant uraei. This is flanked by two couchant and confronted jackal figures representing Wepwawet or Anubis as guardians of the deceased. In the pictorial register, Pa-Wer is presented by Anubis to Osiris attended by Isis and Nephthys, who hold up their right hands in a gesture of protection. Anubis leads the deceased by his right hand and, in his left, holds the papyrus containing the above-mentioned decree.

Also dating to the Ptolemaic Period is the large central portion of a wooden stela executed in a cursory style (Dolzani 1969, 23–24) (Fig. 7). The panel has been plastered and decorated with three painted scenes and is pierced with five holes into which pins, some of which are still extant, were inserted to affix it to a further board, thus forming the entire stela. The lunette is decorated with a winged sundisk, Horus the Behedite, and two mirror-image uraei, of which only that on the right is preserved, facing an offering table. The lunette is separated from the register below by a frieze of alternately coloured rectangles and darts. The pictorial register holds a scene of five mummiform figures, of which only the first is crowned with a sundisk, and facing towards the right. Each bears a *w3s*-sceptre and elongated red band. The first figure, on the right, is falcon-headed, the second, ape-headed, the third and fourth, human-headed and the fifth has not been preserved. The lower register of the stela is badly preserved but the extant part of the hieroglyphic text can be identified as the funerary *ḥtp di nsw* formula, together with the names of the gods Osiris, Anubis, Isis and Nepthys. The offering itself can be read as *Kbḥ mw* – 'cool water'.

Figure 6. *Stele of Pa-Wer, Graeco-Roman Period, ACCE 00118.*

Figure 7. *Mummified figurines on the Graeco-Roman stela (a detail), ACCE 00136.*

The Rovigo collection also holds several important items of funerary equipment: a series of amulets, including scarabs inscribed with various motifs and royal names (Thutmosis III, Amenhotep I, Amenhotep III, Seti I, Ramesses II), seventy examples of ushabtis (although some are fragmentary), made of moulded terracotta or faience, an ushabti case inscribed with the name of its royal owner (Dolzani 1969, 11–14, pl. 7–8; Vandersleyen 2005, 43, 83) (Fig. 9), three lids of canopic jars and one complete jar inscribed with the name of Psametjekseneb (Dolzani 1969, 18, pl. 9) two fragments of coffin cartonnage with rishi band decoration dated probably to the 25th Dynasty (Dolzani 1969, 25–28, pl. 13–14) (Fig. 8), and a wooden mask of similar or later date. (Fig. 10).

The well-preserved ushabti coffin (Fig. 9) may justifiably be deemed the masterpiece of the Rovigo collection. It is carved from a single block of Lebanese cedar wood

Figure 8. *The two cartonnage fragments with rishi friezes, 25th Dynasty, ACCE 00436a on the left and ACCE 00436b on the right.*

which attests to its use as a luxury item and exclusive privilege of the royal family in a period of constraints. The lid is decorated lengthwise with sections of greenish-blue alternating with unpainted sections. The longer sides are decorated with three panels separated by inscribed columns, emulating the 'palace-façade' type of decoration. The uninscribed central sections of the panels were originally covered with gold leaf.

The only title extant on this piece is *s3 nswt smsw* – 'the elder son of the king,' ie, the heir to the throne, who unfortunately died at about six years old. If, therefore, the owner of this case was Iahmes-Sapair (the second part of the name being acquired later), the son of Seqenenre-Djehuty-Aa, the last king of the 17th Dynasty, as Vandersleyen (2005, 9–34) indeed thought this to be, then this piece is one of only two objects bearing his name – the other being a statue

Figure 9. *Iahmes Sapair's ushabtis case, 17th Dynasty, ACCE 00463.*

Figure 10. *Coffin mask, Late Period, ACCE 00464.*

on display in the Musée du Louvre, E15682 (Vandersleyen, 2005, 14).

Fig. 10 shows the wooden funerary mask (Dolzani 1969, 28) (32.5 cm × 28 cm) of an unknown person probably dating to the Late Period. Here, the eye and brow sockets would originally have been inlayed with semi-precious stones such as obsidian and limestone, but these have been removed in antiquity and the cavities subsequently painted in white with black pupils. The chin is indented, probably for the insertion of a false beard. The earlobes are pierced, probably for the insertion of earrings, which may suggest that the deceased was female. The wig is composed of alternate yellow and green horizontal lines. At neck level, a light blue line, which is still visible, may be what remains of a *wesekh*-collar. The tenon on the crown would have attached the mask to the sculpted wig, which has not been preserved.

A series of three cult objects on display in Rovigo, namely three obelisk-shaped shrines dating to the Ptolemaic Period (Dolzani 1969, 31, pl. 14, 16) (Fig. 11) merit particular attention, not only for their rarity, but also for their function, which remains unclear. Made of limestone, they are decorated in bas-relief and portray an image of a standing Osiris figure wearing an *atef* crown, either alone or accompanied, in the lower right-hand corner, by a female figure – perhaps Isis. Some remaining traces of colour indicate that these figures were originally painted in red and yellow. The interiors of two of the shrines (Fig. 11, ACCE 0098, centre, and ACCE 0099, right) have been hollowed out at the back, and the third (Fig. 11, ACCE 0097, on the left) has a roughly circular hole in the base. These cavities may have held some relevant object, such as a relic, associated with the Osiris figure sculpted on the front. The absence of any trace of holes

Figure 11. *Osiris' shrines. Left: ACCE 0097, Centre: ACCE 0098. Right: ACCE 0099.*

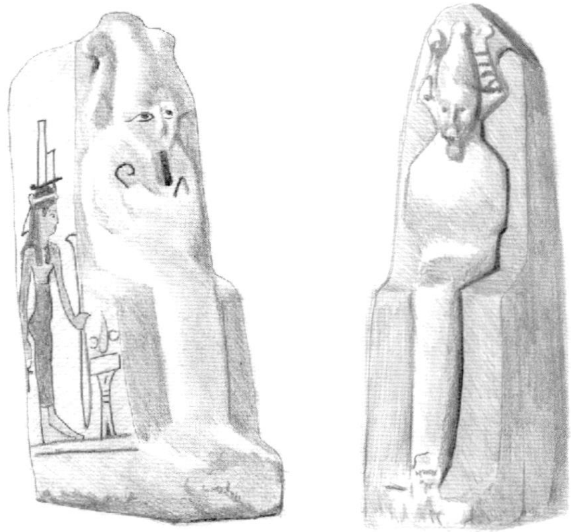

Figure 12. *Left: ÄOS 951. Right: ÄOS 955, Kunsthistoriches Museum, Vienna (drawing by S. Musso).*

along the edge, or of any resin or damage on the surface, would seem to indicate that the cavity remained uncovered, and leads to speculation that this type of object was intended to be propped up on a domestic altar or inserted into a niche within a temple. Some parallels can be drawn with examples in other Egyptian collections – for example, six pieces in the Kunsthistorisches Museum, Vienna (Satzinger 1998, 419) (Fig. 12) and two in the Museum of Fine Arts, Budapest (Nagy 1999, 84–85) (Fig. 13 and Fig. 14). The Vienna examples represent a variant of this type of shrine, showing an enthroned Osiris carved from a block of wood instead of limestone and, in some cases, decorated with gilded plaster.

These shrines can be classified into two types:

Type 1 is represented by the lone standing figure of Osiris on the façade as per ACCE 0099 (Fig. 13, Upper), which is similar to its wooden counterpart in Vienna (Fig. 13, Lower) containing unidentified organic material, oblong in shape.

Type 2 is represented by a standing Osiris on the façade accompanied by a smaller proportioned female figure on his left (Fig. 14.). In both examples presented here, the figures are painted in red, and perhaps ochre, for the shrine in Budapest (Fig. 14, right), and in yellow-brown for the Rovigo example (Fig. 14, left).

A further variant of Type 2 comprises an Osiris figure carved inside a niche with, on his left, a presumed Isis figure (Fig. 15.), again in smaller proportions but now carved within a second, smaller, niche. A third figure, kneeling, is sculpted on the back of the shrine, perhaps representing another goddess.

An inevitable question is where were these objects deposited? Unfortunately we do not have any information about their provenance, neither in the academy archives nor in the catalogue entries of the museums of Vienna and Budapest. Moreover, in only three of the examples were

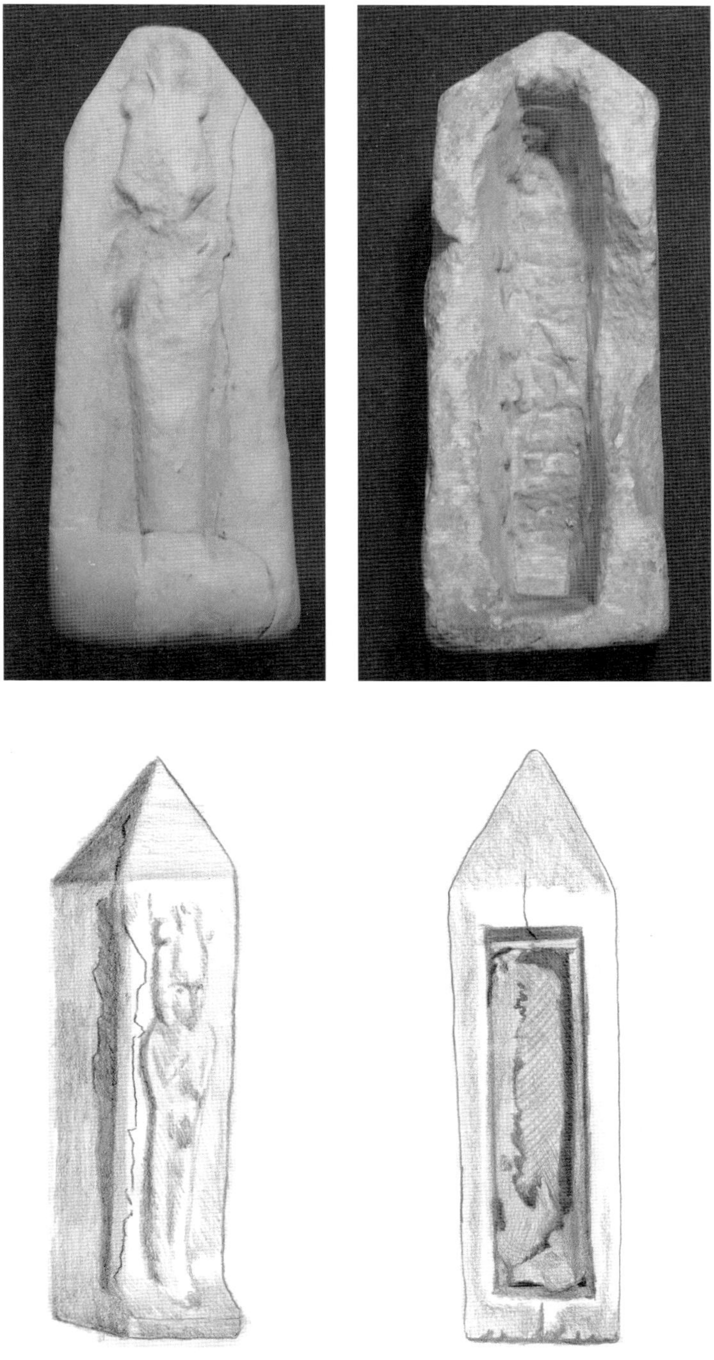

Figure 13. *Type 1. Upper: ACCE 0099. Lower: ÄOS 956, Kunsthistoriches Museum, Vienna (drawing by S. Musso).*

Figure 14. *Type 2, Left: ACCE 0098. Right: 2003. 19E, Museum of Fine Arts, Budapest, (courtesy of Dr. I. Nagy). Lower: detail of mummified figurines on both shrines.*

their contents preserved, and these are not identical. The gilded plastered example in Vienna (ÄOS 951) held a papyrus roll, whilst the undecorated example (ÄOS 956) contained an unspecified organic material.

It seems likely that this last example could be related to the Hungarian example, which contained a mummified foetus. Foetus mummies are very rare in Egypt and this series of containers does not reflect a specific custom. Why was an obelisk, a solar emblem, used perhaps in a funerary rite? To which votive tradition could it be associated? Further investigation is required and it is hoped that future fieldwork will contextualize these objects and provide some answers.

Figure 15. *A variant of type 2, ACCE 0097.*

Acknowledgements

We would like to express our gratitude to Ms. Bocchia for proofreading the English manuscript of the first draft and Mrs. Corbelli for the language re-drafting in the final version.

Bibliography

Dolzani, C. (1969) *La collezione egiziana del Museo dell'Accademia dei Concordi in Rovigo*, Rome.

Nagy, I. (1999) *Guide to the Egyptian Collection, Museum of Fine Arts*, Budapest.

Rosati, G. (2003) 'La stele Rovigo n°12' in *Comunicazioni dell'Istituto Papirologico 'G. Vitelli'*, n°5, Florence.

Satzinger, H. (1998) 'Osirianische Obelisken in der Wiener Sammlung' in Clarysse *et al.* (eds) *Egyptian religion. The last thousand years. Studies dedicated to the memory of Jan Quaegebeur*, Leiden.

Turri, A. (2005) 'Giuseppe Valsé Pantellini' in Romanato G. *et al.* (eds) *Giovanni Miani e il contributo veneto alla conoscenza dell'Africa... Atti del 27° convegno di studi storici, Rovigo, 14-15-16 novembre 2003*, Rovigo.

Vandersleyen C. (2005) *Iahmès Sapaïr fils de Séqénenré Djéhouty-Aa et la statue du Musée du Louvre E 15682*, Bruxelles.

Embodiment Theory and the Body in Ancient Egypt

Emily Iona Stewart

Introduction

The Ancient Egyptians were enamoured with the idea of the conservation of the personal image often in an idealised form, through the preservation of the corporeal self. Their unique views on the afterlife and the construction of the self, have in part, led to the rich material record that characterises the study of Egyptology, wherein the body formed a central aspect of both daily life and funerary beliefs (Brecklinghaus 2002, 121). The Ancient Egyptian theology concerning matters of the body ran contra to traditional Western views, which were characterised by a bifurcation of body and mind, often called 'Cartesian' (Turner 1990, 9), This concept of a distinction between body and mind which typified much of 17th and 18th century thinking in the West, has been largely disregarded by modern scholars of the social sciences, who now prefer to work with models such as the 'corporeal phenomenology' of Merleau-Ponty (2000). Whilst the social sciences, and more recently archaeology, have embraced this move away from 'Cartesian' duality, into more in depth studies of embodiment, Egyptology has been accused of seeming resistant to many strands of 'methodological progress', in particular that of archaeological theory (Jeffreys 2003, 5).

A consideration of current work in Egyptology, however, indicates that the body has been considered in Egyptological discussions in a number of ways. It is surprising that the wealth of evidence provided by the Egyptological record may be among the last to be utilised as an analogous framework in the wider arena of theoretical discussion. Therefore, it is the hope within this work to look at the theoretical framework surrounding the study of the body in social sciences rather than the artefactual (osteoarchaeological, etc), and to indicate the extent of knowledge already available about the ancient Egyptian body. By doing so, some ways will be suggested by which the schism between theorists and the Egyptological record might be amended by examining the ways other disciplines have approached the question of the body, and how, in turn, our rich understanding of this topic in Egyptology can benefit this debate.

The body in social sciences and archaeology

Within the realms of the social sciences (especially those of anthropology and sociology) the use of the body as a frame of discourse has become increasingly important. The discussions of individuals such as Bourdieu (1991), Merleau-Ponty (1962) and Foucault (1972; 1974) have served to re-position dialogue about the body away from the dichotomies of mind and body, in favour of a view of an integrated, symbiotic relationship between body and mind. Instead, the two are supposed to be 'inextricably linked' (Shilling 1993, 12); with conscious or unconscious thought processes' influencing the body, while the actions of the body may contribute to the socialisation of the mind. This acceptance of the body as a conduit for socialisation ran in opposition to the views of mainstream sociological thought for some time, which, until recently, held the mind as that which 'defines humans as social beings' (Shilling 1993, 8).

Similarly in anthropology, whilst the body has been of importance to studies since the 19th century (Turner 1991, 1), an element of this kind of thinking was also prominent. Concerns about language, culture and interpersonal relations were thought to exist in the realm of behaviour, and therefore governed by the 'mind' (Blacking 1977, 2). These views have been reconciled in sociology, anthropology and even psychology, by admitting that all the keystones of these studies are essentially *embodied*. That is to say, that the mind cannot be separated from the body, the biological features in 'the invention of culture' while the body is shaped and influenced by the culture it inhabits (Blacking 1977, 2).

Within archaeological investigations, bodies have been largely, though not exclusively, regarded as another form of material record. As Hoffman & Whittle put it: 'typically, archaeology is catching up with debates carried out in other subjects' (2008, 287). Having said this, there has been a recent percolation of the theoretical approaches conceptualised within other social studies, demonstrated by such works as Sofaer (2006), Whittle (2003; 2008), Meskell (1998a; 1999), Hamilakis *et al.* (2002) and more recently Borić & Robb (2008). Studies of bodies within archaeology have been largely characterised in two different formats; the first is a scientific viewpoint, by which the body is studied osteologically within the set parameters of scientific methods. These are typically fixed in order that 'analysis and comparisons between bodies' can be achieved leading to 'conceptualisations [being] necessarily fixed, universal and transhistorical' (Sofaer 2006, xiii). Remains are often looked at in order to obtain age and sex, upon which assumptions and translations are made. Material interpretations often look to grave goods and/or burial style, or, on a more theoretical level, 'reconstructions of social formations and… gender relations' (Whittle 2003, 26) The second of these methods (and the focus of this study) is the discourse that has recently surrounded body studies in the realms of the social sciences which 'increasingly view the body as a social construction that is contextually and historically produced' (Sofaer 2006, xiii). With this constructionist view, scholars of the social sciences and archaeology have begun to look at the outward bodily manifestations of the self.

Biological phenomena have been found wanting as the only explanation for the appearance of bodies, which can now be viewed as 'somehow shaped, constructed and even invented by society' (Shilling 1993, 62). Self decoration, gender, dress and embellishments, movement and performance, shape, content and even the boundaries of the body (Douglas 1970, 69), are all now at issue as aspects of the self that cannot be explained away by biology. Meskell puts forward the proposition that whilst this holds true, embodiment and being embodied should be viewed as a number of 'related experiences' (Meskell 1999, 37), from one's own unique experience of living in their own body, the shared experiences of being human, to the 'identity markers' that embellish our own and others perceptions of ourselves (See Table 1).

These summary points present interesting possibilities for the archaeological investigation of individuals and their societies. Borić and Robb propose that the body may be seen as a 'museum of long term historical processes that…structure the conditions of social existence' (2008, 2) With this in mind we may be able to begin to twine together existing empirical knowledge, with theoretical investigations of embodiment. The manifestations of the body as given by Meskell (1999, 37) assume a certain degree of commonality for the experience of embodiment throughout time-scales and geography. However, as Joyce (2005, 147) points out, 'constructing credible models of past experiences of embodiment becomes more difficult once universality [of human

Type of Embodiment	Manifestations
Materiality of the body	The way people eat, sleep, bleed, menstruate, feel pain, *etc*
Elements of Construction	Social setting, constitution of the body, cultural context, *Corporeal Style* e.g. for some the body is not skin bound but may connect to other bodies, ancestors, spirits *etc*
Identity Markers	Sex, Gender, sexuality, age, race, ethnicity, disability *etcetera*
Individual Dimension	Unique individual experience of living in and through our own bodies. Concepts of identity, singularity and uniqueness.

***Table 1**. The dimensions of embodiment after Meskell, 1999 & Brecklinghaus, 2002 (Author's own).*

experience] is questioned, because the archaeologist cannot begin by assuming the position of a typical person'. And this remains a troubling aspect of body theory.

To speculate on the 'construction of the body' we may employ a number of archaeological tools; from the observation of texts and imagery, to the observance of trends and anomalies in individual interments. Similarly the investigation of identity markers may be aided by textual and artefactual evidence, but may also be postulated on through analogous investigations and individual cases. The individual dimension provides the most valuable methods of acknowledging the agency of individuals. Evidence may be drawn from empirical investigations of the body, as well as artefactual and written indications. It is this individual element which brings both a unique dimension to bodies displayed in collections, and helps us discover more about the 'lived' experience of society at large.

As in any archaeological investigation, we should acknowledge that certain constraints exist when applying the concepts of Table 1. Unlike the other social disciplines like anthropology and sociology, archaeology's subjects are not living, moving, producing bodies. We must also acknowledge that a disparity may be present, between the treatment of the body in death, and the reality of the lived body for that individual. This does not however mean that archaeology and Egyptology do not have a great deal to contribute to embodiment discussions taking place within the other social sciences. Rather than view ancient individual experience as inaccessible we should, instead, through the present material residues of those lives, suppose archaeology to be 'well placed to make similar (to the social sciences) cultural comparisons with the added interpolation of long term depth to add another dimension of complexity in terms of social difference and possibility' (Meskell & Joyce 2003, 1). To this end, adroit ways have had to be found for investigating the body in antiquity by archaeologists, who employ a number of methods and interpretations.

One such way that scholars of archaeology have approached the body, is as a theoretical framework on which to base phenomenological discussions. Once again these discussions frequently focus on the universality of the human body as a standpoint from which to create inferences about the embodied and sensory experience of environment. Using this discourse, it has been proposed by archaeologists that a certain amount of insight may be gained as to how their subjects 'encounter[ed] and underst[ood] the world' (Sofaer 2006, 21), and in particular how individuals 'experience monuments and landscapes as they move through them and carry out practices in them' (Hodder 2000, 24). These phenomenological discussions of embodiment serve to underpin discussions of nature and culture, mind and body, and structure and agency as collaborative forces at work in shaping experience in both individual and societal settings.

Treherne, in his 1995 study on the European Bronze age, discusses the changing concepts and constructions of the self through the medium of adornment, or more specifically, the appearance of grooming articles such as razors or tweezers at specific times in history. Treherne argues that the presence of such articles, as well as further bodily adornment, horses, hunting and the imbibing of alcohol all indicate a growing sense of individualism and the rise of the 'beautiful warrior' and growing status attributed to the new social group (Treherne 1995, 106). A particularly interesting aspect of this study is Treherne's postulation on this 'embodied' practice becoming a distinct identity over time, giving rise in part to aspects of the feudal order in Europe, thus giving a sense of wider social practice over time.

As body theory has principally been used by Prehistorians as a framework, Robb's 2008 discussion of the differences between the Native North American Huron and the Jesuit colonists, as recorded textually by the latter, provides an interesting case study of the scope of body theory when applied with textual historical sources. Within his article Robb looks at the body as a stage for world order, and its place within so called 'meaningless violence' (Robb 2008, 87). Comparisons are drawn between the French Jesuit's perceptions of the body, and the Huron's perceptions. Boundaries are analysed; with the Huron's limits between human and non-human bodies illustrated with the Jesuit's surprise at the human treatment by which some dogs became inclusive of the village, to the extent that 'Huron women [fed] favourite dogs with food from their mouths as they did with children' (Robb 2008, 92). Further to these observations about the dogs, the author points out that, just as some dogs were 'favourites', there were also dogs 'destined for the cooking pot'. In the same way human war captives were often destined for consumption, from which Robb postulates that the Huron did not distinguish rigid categorisations between human and non-human bodies; 'nor edible and non-edible ones' (Robb 2008, 92).

Further interesting comparisons are drawn between the Huron beliefs about the spiritual, corporeal and the boundaries in-between (See Robb 2008, 93). As readers of this piece and of 'body theory' in general, work like this does beg the question; would such an in-depth analysis and comparison be attainable if not for the textual evidence to back up the archaeology of these peoples?

Body Studies in Egyptology

It would be easy to dismiss Egyptology as being 'hostile [to] archaeological theory taking place in most of the rest of the world' (Jeffreys 2003, 5), but whilst Egyptologists have only just begun to take tentative steps towards this sort of methodological analysis, they have been, consciously or unconsciously, writing theory implicitly into their work for many decades now. In the many text books that broadly deal with 'daily life' of ancient Egypt, the body is approached as a form of material culture (Sofaer 2006, 88), and largely dealt with in two different ways. In the first instance, the embalmed remains are studied after the osteological fashion, being seen to provide access to information about embalming, health (or paleopathology, as discussed in Brier 1996, 174–193), nutrition *etc.* (see Fleming *et al.* 1980). Secondly, corporeal remains are studied in conjunction with visual data. Wall paintings, iconography, motifs, jewellery and ornamentation, as well as posture, gesture, costume, sexuality and representation are utilised in order to build up a picture of the average Egyptian person.

An excerpt from a children's book, entitled 'Egyptian Mummies: People from the Past' (Pemberton 2000) achieves just this. It takes the information supplied by the remains of Katebet, now in the British museum and presents them in a way we would typically expect of social constructavists, looking at adornment in the form of wigs, and the sort of emotions she might have experienced as a consequence of loosing her teeth (Pemberton 2000, 17).

The most explicit author combining body studies and Egyptology at this time, is Lynn Meskell who has sought to actively incorporate archaeological theory into her studies of the New Kingdom settlement site of Deir el-Medina. This has been achieved with various levels of success, with works such as those that feature in the Montserrat (1998) Wyke (1998) edited books, falling a little short of a standard later set by her own 1999 *Archaeologies of Social Life*. It is clear from these aforementioned works that Meskell is most at home discussing issues of sex and gender, rather than the body. Her 1999 book may be, to date, the most comprehensive assimilation of information that pulls together both knowledge of ancient Egyptian ideas about the body, and contemporary social studies in this field, but it is marked in its deficit of actual application of these ideas.

Finally, aside from a lack of authors explicitly dealing with body studies within their discussion of Egyptian *bodies,* and the tendency to engender and embody women above men, one major problem must be addressed. When writing the aforementioned 'daily life' variety of book, authors often draw from a vast range of sources. As Jeffreys puts to us; 'One must be cautious about assuming too great a uniformity in the ethnicity and shared cultural experience of Egyptian society now, or for that matter, at any time in the past' (Jeffreys 2003, 15). It is for this deficit of caution, that we often find pictures of the 'average' Egyptian emerging, which are drawn from sources with very little discrepancy. In turn, this is why a study of this sort remains so valid, as it enables us to 'bring flesh to the bones' of the ancient Egyptians, one citizen at a time.

Embodiment in ancient Egypt: Why Egypt is a suitable sphere for this kind of study

The presence of the well-preserved corporeal remains of the human beings that inhabited Ancient Egypt imbue this sort of study with a good level of validity. Unlike many other disciplines within archaeology, the beliefs and climate of Ancient Egypt have led to its human remains retaining many of the elements that would have made up the physical appearance of the person in life. Many of the bodies retain their physical shape, and reflect choices in bodily adornment, from hairstyle and cosmetics, to body modification in the form of tattoos and piercings (see Gilbert 2001, 11). In addition to the availability of the mortal remains of some of Ancient Egypt's inhabitants, their civilisation has left behind a wealth of pictorial (reliefs, sculptures, illustrations *etc*) and textual evidence, all of which can help 'embody Egyptian individuals in the manner specific to their own culture, [giving] our interpretations…some measure of legitimacy' (Meskell 1999, 113).

It is from this sort of evidence that we are able to establish just how different the beliefs of the ancient Egyptians were from our own, particularly with regard to the body. The evidence suggests that dualistic views of the body and the 'soul' are not valid in this sphere of study. It is noted by Assman, that the 'essential distinction within the totality of the person [was] not that between the body and the soul, but...between the individual self and the social self' with the bodily and soulful element of the self including the *Ba* and the shadow, while the social self comprised of the *Ka* and the name (2005, 14).

The ancient Egyptian beliefs on the components of the self transcended life and death, and could hold different characteristics in these states. Throughout this state of flux however, the body was held as 'the essential link between the deceased and his former earthly existence' (David 1999, 187), and, as such, complex rituals such as mummification evolved in order for the deceased spirit to recognise and remain linked to the corporeal form.

During life, the self was thought to be made up of up of five active components; the *Ba,* the *Ka,* the *Name*, the *Shadow* and the physical body (Shaw & Nicholson 2008, 51), while other components were thought to be present but dormant until the individual's entry to the afterlife. These elements were all thought to be necessary to the existence of a person both in life and death. The *Ba*, during the individual's lifetime, was similar to our concept of personality; it was thought to be non-corporeal and could also be used to describe a concept of power. There are suggestions that although the *Ba* is acknowledged as part of the person during one's lifetime and could even be viewed as a 'separate physical mode of existence' (Allen 2001, 161), the rarity of reference to it in the context of one's lifetime indicates that its independence seems only to be asserted upon death (Brier & Hobbs 1999, 45). Despite the apparent parting of body and *Ba* in death, the *Ba* nevertheless, was not divorced from the body in the way the spirit might be in Cartesian thought, but was essential to the physical body's continued survival with physical needs like food and drink, while the *Ba* and the body had to be reunited each night. The concept of the *Ba* appears to act as a reassurance both for those who would die, and the relatives of the deceased. Pyramid texts of the Old Kingdom inform the Gods that the deceased is 'a *Ba* among you' while the deceased is informed that 'your *Ba* is within you' (Allen 2001, 161), demonstrating the dual ability of the *Ba* to be both within and without upon death.

In death, the *Ba* took on the responsibility of travelling to meet the *Ka* in the place of the physical body which could no longer do this. The *Ka* had an almost unparalleled meaning, roughly translating as 'sustenance' or 'vital force' (Meskell 1999, 112). It was bound up with the physical self, and was thought of as a sort of double created at the same time as the individual, which preserved the person's physical image, 'memories of experiences, perceptions, thoughts and mental images' (Brecklinghaus 2002, 177). Its conception was tied up with the unique nature of the person, seen to embody their qualities and characteristics (David 1999, 187), and thus has been described somewhat like our definition of personality. Unlike this ideal, however, its continued existence was tied up with the bodily needs of sustenance, while simultaneously being thought of as separable from the owner's physical person (Gardiner 1950, 7, in te Velde 1990, 95). In contrast to the *Ba*, the *Ka* was not linked to the deceased corpse but was rather a vessel for restoring the individual's 'status, honour and dignity'. As such, the *Ka* dealt with the 'self' of the person, and was akin to a 'soul, protective spirit and doppelgänger' simultaneously (Assman 2005, 97). It was not supposed that upon death the *Ka* underwent any conceptual change, as its existence was independent to that of the body and *Ba.* Instead, to ensure a link between the *Ka* of the deceased and his other elements, figures and statues of the deceased would be erected in the tomb, with the aim of encouraging the *Ka* to recognise the person and take up residence in these statues, becoming, through them, the deceased's eyes and ears when visits were paid to the tomb (Budge 1973, 118). The *Ka* was sustained by the tomb offerings of food and liquid, and was thought to imbibe their spirit doubles. As such it was thought vital to continue provisions for the *Ka* in either physical or magical ways, in order to ensure the continued existence of the overall self (David 1999, 140).

The shadow was also an important part of the living person's 'self', and, in both life and death, represented an abstraction of shade and protection (Shaw & Nicholson 2008, 300). Budge through analysis of texts and ethnographic data (1973, 127) has shown that a number of beliefs about the shadow may be discerned; principally that:

1. 'there were believed to exist certain evil shadows that would do harm to their fellow shadows if they could'.
2. 'the shadow was associated with the soul.'
3. 'the shadow had the power to move about and go where it liked. The difference between the spirit body and the shadow is...slight'.

and finally, that the shadow could be stolen or lost, or cease to be cast should the owner take sick or be dying. In death, it was made clear that without one's shadow, resurrection of the spiritual body would be impossible. Like the *Ba* the shadow was thought free to wander, but returned to the person at night. It appears that upon death, the shadow became more independent of the composite whole of the person than in life and took on a more 'separate mode of existence' (Allen 2001, 277). As in life, it seems that it was feared that the shadow could become entrapped or harmed by malignant forces.

The name was also viewed as a vital element of individual being, viewed as just as integral to the being as the body. One's name acted as a means to convey identity, and occupied spiritual, corporeal and social spheres, whilst also having ritual connotations. Writing or reading one's name was thought to grant access to continued existence in the hereafter, but may also have given the knower of the name insight into his being and power over the named being (te Velde 1990, 87). Similarly, it was thought tantamount to the continuation of the person in the afterlife for the name to come to no harm. Such was the importance of the name in one's afterlife that in a passage relating to a man's lament that his soul cannot enter the West (the afterlife), he has cause to say:

> 'Look my name reeks.
> Look, more than the smell of bird droppings
> On summer days when the sky is hot...' (Parkinson 1997, 160).

In this case, the name is associated with rotting smells and the corruption of the self and can be read as a commentary on the man's inability for continued existence. Names given in life (at birth) were sometimes ritually significant to the continuance of the individual upon their death, such as; 'Wehemkai' or 'my *Ka* repeats itself' (te Velde 1999, 95). Thus we may deduce that, like the shadow, the name could have protective properties activated upon death, as well as encapsulating important elements of the self.

The Egyptian view of the body during life was no less different to western ideals as those of the other components of the body, nor was the body thought to be any less a vital part in the construction of the self. The ancient Egyptians believed that, prior to their conception, their bodies were shaped, along with their double (their *Ka*), on the God Khnum's potters wheel who subsequently breathed life into his creations (Pinch 2002, 154). Although the body was viewed as coming into existence as a cohesive whole, it is argued by Assman (2005, 26) that the ancient Egyptian view of the body was not of unified entity, but rather as 'an aggregated multiplicity of individual limbs'. Following the line of argument given by German historian Brunner-Traut (1996), Assman postulates that to the ancient Egyptians the body was seen as a collection of parts not unlike a 'marionette', mirroring an overall disjointed way of viewing the world.

Unifying this apparently disjointed view of the body were a number of beliefs pertaining to the physical and the spiritual, which were not necessarily divorced. The ancient Egyptians seemingly had the ability to 'let stand side by side contradictory creation myths and [lump] together seemingly incompatible theological concepts' (Najovits 2004, 121), including those pertaining to the physical and spiritual constitution of mankind and the fate of these components upon death. For example, the heart was thought of as a separate entity, primarily functioning as the source of human wisdom, a contributing factor to the personality and the centre of emotions and memory. It was also the centre of 'free will' and evidently could display a personality and agency of its own. Despite appearing to be described as, not only a separate part of the body, but, in some cases, a controlling force, it has also been identified by the French physician and Egyptologist Thierry Bardinet as a crucial factor to the unification of the disarticulated body. He postulated that physical cohesion was ontologically envisaged to have been facilitated by the blood and its circulation (Assman 2005, 28). While the body is seen to be made up of disconnected parts, the blood and blood vessels act as an integrating element, binding the limbs and *jb* (the collective term for 'insides') into a composed, living entity (Bardinet 1995, 70 trans Hawass & Pinch Brock 2003, 193)

Yet, despite its independent manifestation, it was frequently the only internal organ left inside the body in death, since it was felt that the heart could reveal a person's true character. This practice may also allude to a feeling of wishing to keep the cohesive element to the body, despite the disintegrating process of mummification. Enabling the heart and the blood to achieve this act of bonding the separate parts together, the ancient Egyptians believed the body to hold a substance called *Mwt.* The Papyrus Ebers tells us that the *Mwt* was thought to be a number of physical elements that include blood vessels, ducts, tendons and muscles, and was thought to transport blood, urine, air and semen (Nunn 1996, 44). It was believed that through the *Mwt* the heart was able to communicate with the limbs (Meskell, 2002, 61), and as the blood vessels were so closely associated with this perception, it is reasonable to think that these concepts were closely interlinked with ideas of cohesion. The evidence also indicates that the *Mwt* was believed to act as a conduit to both benevolent and malevolent spirits, demonstrating the dual physical and spiritual nature that ancient Egyptians contributed to their body and bodily functions.

As mentioned, one of the major problems we may identify with body theories aims is that they start out from the interpretive point of view of the modern archaeologist, and tend to assume a degree of homogeneity in aspects such as how the human body experiences pain/discomfort etc. The ancient Egyptians furnished their texts with a few accounts of corporeal experience, and even phenomenological perceptions. For instance; a poignant description of old age from the instructions of Ptahhotep, 8–21 describes the embodied experience of ageing:

> Frailty has come, old age has arrived,
> Weakness has come, childish helplessness returns,
> Strength diminishes, for my heart is weary.
> The mouth is silenced and speaks no more,
> The eyes are dim, the ears are deaf,
> sleep comes with difficulty, day after day;

the heart is forgetful, it no longer remembers yesterday,
the bone aches due to the length (of years)... (Assman 2005, 28)

While bearing in mind that textual evidence may often possess hidden agendas, and represent only the thoughts and experiences of the literate few, these accounts of phenomenological experiences lend some insight into both the similarities and differences of embodied experience, between our own and those of other cultures. Textual, pictorial and physical evidence may also contribute to our knowledge of those 'identity markers' (see Table 1) embodied in one's corporeal existence, and give us insight into the ways in which these affected lived experience.

It would be fair to observe that these identity markers may be split into two categories, the first of which is biologically or environmentally determined, and therefore out of the sphere of control of the individual. The second consists of those elements which are chosen by the individual, or are a result of societal norms or trends. These have been ordered into the table below (Table 2), with the elements shown in the middle as those which may be influenced by both. Included are those elements which, as we have shown, the ancient Egyptians would have felt to be identity markers.

Biologically or environmentally determined factors		**Identity markers added to the self through personal or societal choice.**
Sex	Gender	Mode of dress
Biological age	Social age	Hair style
Height/Weight	Race	Body decoration (semi permanent e.g. makeup/body paint)
Ba	Name	Body modifications (tattoos, piercings, etc)
Shadow		*Ka*
		Name

Table 2. *The three spheres of identity markers (Author's own).*

One of the most prominent, and well-explored aspects of these 'identity markers', is that of gender. Rightly or wrongly, the study of ancient bodies has become synonymous with that of gender studies (see Gilchrist 1999, 54–78 & Joyce 2008), and, although these types of studies often have very different agendas to those of body theory, some works on this topic in Egyptology may cast an interesting take on the lived body in Ancient Egypt. Studies pertaining to gender in Ancient Egypt have shown that masculinity and femininity, and the outward manifestations of sex, would have had an impact on the lives of the ancient Egyptians. It dictated what roles were expected, such as the wife and mother 'within the family unit, producing children and ensuring the continuality of the family' (Robins 1993, 178), or the preferred masculine trait of the 'silent man who shows moderation'. Furthermore, works such as Janssen & Janssen's Growing up in Ancient Egypt (1990) and Getting Old in Ancient Egypt (1996), address the issues surrounding both social aging processes, such as the transition from childhood to adulthood, to biological ageing, its symptomatic elements and its social ramifications.

On top of these abstract views of what made up the self in death, the ancient Egyptians perceived the living and the dead body in different, but not necessarily divorced, ways. Words to express these concepts such as *ẖt* for the living body and *ẖꜣt* for the deceased body, portray abstract concepts of the flesh, self and person, and the 'theological concept of the body, the eternal form which transcends the living body' (Meskell 1999, 111) respectively. The *Akh* might also fall under this category. The result of a successful reunion of the *Ba* with the *Ka*, once created, the *Akh* was considered enduring and unchanging for eternity. Its basic meaning seems to have been 'effectiveness' which may have referred to the ability of an individual to function effectively in both life and after death (Shaw & Nicholson 2008, 21). In life, it appears that the *Akh* functioned only as an implication of this effectiveness that it was seen to take on in the afterlife; e.g. an act which was seen to be well performed or pleased the Gods could be referred to as *Akh* effective (Friedman 2001, 47). Thus it could be said that this was largely a dormant characteristic that asserted its full potential upon the individual's death, virtually becoming an altogether new component of the person.

Conclusion

What it is hoped has been achieved in this brief overview of a potentially vast topic, is to show the scope of potential for the marriage of body studies and Egyptology. Key to this is the richness of Egyptian data with regard to bodies. With only a few exceptions, other disciplines within archaeology and history lack the opportunities to look into the faces, and indeed bodies, of their chosen subjects. While Egyptology is a fantastic platform in itself for this kind of study, its contribution to other fields of theoretical archaeology has much potential. An investigation into the ancient Egyptian views of the body is not only interesting in itself, but also serves to highlight how ideas about the body may differ in different societies and different time periods.

The purpose of this study has been to briefly demonstrate that by applying these sorts of ideas to the study of Ancient Egypt, we may be able to begin to conjecture about embodiment in other cultures, and perhaps present a sensible exemplar, on which to base analogous studies. Similarly, studying people and bodies in this way, presents us with a context easily accessible through its commonality. Embodiment is familiar to us, was familiar to past cultures and is indeed common to all people: the experience of living inside a body, of being *embodied*. It is the author's belief that this sort of study has significantly more to contribute to both the study of Ancient Egypt, and the sphere of theoretical thought in other areas of archaeology. It is regretted that case studies could not be provided in this brief overview of the topic, from a wealth of information as complex and intriguing as the data provided by the bodies of the ancient Egyptians.

School of History and Archaeology
Cardiff University

Bibliography

Allen, J. P. (2001) 'Ba' in Redford, D. B. (ed.) *The Oxford Encyclopaedia of Ancient Egypt*, A-F. Oxford, Oxford University Press, 161–162.

Assman, J. (2005) *Death and Salvation in Ancient Egypt,* translated by David Lorton, New York, Cornell University Press.

Blacking, J. (1977) 'Towards an Anthropology of the Body' in J. Blacking (ed.), *The Anthropology of the Body,* London, Academic Press, 1–28.

Boric, D. and Robb, J. (eds.) (2008) *Past Bodies: Body Centred Research in Archaeology.* Oxford, Oxbow Books.

Bourdieu, P. (John B. Thompson translation) (1991) *Language and Symbolic Power*. Harvard, Harvard University Press.

Brecklinghaus, H. G. (2002) *The Human Beings Are Awoken, You Have Set Them Upright. Body Structure and Conception of Man in Ancient Egyptian Art and the Present Day,* Germany, Lebenshaus Verlag.

Brier, B. (1996) *Egyptian Mummies: Unravelling the Secrets of an Ancient Art*, London, Michael O'Mara Books.

Brier, B. and Hobbs, A. H. (1999) *Daily Life of the Ancient Egyptians*. California, Greenwood Publishing Group.

Brunner-Traut, E. (1996) *Frühformen des Erkennens: Aspektive im alten Ägypten*. Darmstadt, Wissenschlaftliche Buchgesellschaf Auflage.

Budge, E. A. W. (1973) *Osiris and the Egyptian Resurrection,* New York, Courier Dover Publications.

David, A. R. (1999) *Handbook to Life in Ancient Egypt*, Oxford, Oxford University Press.

Douglas, M. (1970) *Natural Symbols: Explorations in Cosmology*, London, The Crescent Press.

Fleming, S., O'Connor, D., Silverman, D. & Fishman, B. (1980) *The Egyptian Mummy: Secrets and Science,* Philadelphia, University Museum, University of Pennsylvania.

Foucault, M. (1972) *The Archaeology of Knowledge*. Translated by A. M. Sheridan. London, Tavistock.

Foucault, M. (1974) (4th edn) *The Order of Things: an Archaeology of the Human Sciences*. London, Routledge.

Friedman, F. M. D. (2001) "Akh" in D. B. Redford (ed.), *The Oxford Encyclopedia of Ancient Egypt*, Vol. 1, Oxford, Oxford University Press, 47–48.

Gilbert, S., Gilbert, C. & Oguri, K. (2001) *Tattoo History: A Source Book: an Anthology of Historical Records of Tattooing Throughout the World*, California, Juno Books.

Gilchrist, R. (1999) *Gender and Archaeology: Contesting the Past.* London, Routledge.

Hamilakis, Y., Pluciennik, M. & Tarlow, S. (eds) (2002) *Thinking through the Body: Archaeologies of Corporeality*, New York, Kluwer Academic.

Hawass, Z. & Pinch Brock, L. (2003) *Egyptology at the Dawn of the Twenty-first Century: Language, Conservation, Museology* (2nd edition), Cairo, American University in Cairo Press.

Hodder, I. (2000) 'Agency and Individuals in Long-Term Processes' in Dobres, M. A. and Robb, J. E. (eds), *Agency in Archaeology,* London, Routledge, 21–33.

Hoffmann, D. and Whittle, A. (2008) 'Neolithic Bodies' in A. Jones (ed.) *Prehistoric Europe: Theory and Practice*. Edinburgh, Wiley Blackwell, 287–311.

Janssen, R. and Janssen, J. J. (1990) *Growing up in Ancient Egypt,* London, Rubicon Press.

Janssen, R. and Janssen, J. J. (1996) *Getting Old in Ancient Egypt,* London, Rubicon Press.

Jeffreys, D. (2003) 'Two Hundred Years of Ancient Egypt: Modern History and Ancient Archaeology' in D. Jeffreys (ed.), *Views of Ancient Egypt Since Napoleon Bonaparte*, London, UCL, 1–18.

Joyce, R. (2005) 'Archaeology of the Body', *Annual Review of Anthropology 34*, 139–58.

Joyce, R. (2008) *Ancient Bodies, Ancient Lives: Sex, Gender and Archaeology*. New York, Thames & Hudson.

Merleau-Ponty, M. (2002) *Phenomenology of Perception: An Introduction*, translated by Smith, C., London, Routledge.

Meskell, L. (1998a) 'The Irresistible Body and the Seduction of Archaeology' in D. Montserrat (ed.) *Changing Bodies, Changing Meanings: Studies if the Body in Antiquity,* London, Routledge, 139–161.

Meskell, L (1998b) 'Intimate Archaeologies: The case of Kha and Merit', *World Archaeology* 29, 363–379.

Meskell, L. (1998c) 'Engendering Egypt' in Wyke, M. (ed.), *Gender and the Body in the Ancient Mediterranean*, Oxford: Blackwell Publishing 173–178.

Meskell, L. (1999) *Archaeologies of Social Life: Age, Sex, Class etcetera In Ancient Egypt*, London, Blackwell Publishing.

Meskell, L. (2002) *Private Life in New Kingdom Egypt,* New Jersey, Princeton University Press.

Meskell, L. and Joyce, R. (2003) *Embodied Lives: Figuring Ancient Maya and Egyptian Experience*, London, Routledge.

Montserrat, D. (ed.) (1998) *Changing Bodies, Changing Meanings: Studies on the Human Body in Antiquity.* London, Routledge.

Najovits, S. R. (2004) *Egypt, Trunk of the Tree: A Modern Survey of an Ancient Land.* New York, Algora Publishing.

Nunn, J. F. (1996) *Ancient Egyptian Medicine,* London, British Museum Press.

Parkinson, R. B. (1997) *The Tale of Sinuhe and Other Egyptian Poems,* Oxford, Clarendon Press.

Partridge, R. B. (1994) *Faces of the Pharaohs*, Guildford, Biddles Ltd.

Pemberton, D. (2000) *Egyptian mummies: people from the past*. London, British Museum.

Pinch, G. (2002) *Handbook of Egyptian Mythology*. Oxford, ABC-CLIO.

Robb, J. (2008) 'Meaningless Violence and the Lived Body: The Huron – Jesuit Collision of World Orders' in D. Borić and J. Robb (eds) *Past Bodies,* Oxford, Oxbow Books, 89–100.

Robins, G. (1993) *Women in Ancient Egypt,* London, British Museum Press.

Shaw, I. and Nicholson, P. (2008) *The British Museum Dictionary of Ancient Egypt* (2nd edition) London, The British Museum Press.

Shilling, C. 1993, *The Body and Social Theory,* London, Sage.

Sofaer, J. R. (2006) *The Body as Material Culture,* Cambridge, Cambridge University Press.

te Velde, H. (1990) 'Some Remarks on the Concept 'Person' in Ancient Egyptian Culture' in Kippenburg, H. G., Kuiper, Y. B. and Sanders, A. F. (eds), *Concepts of Person in Religion and Thought,* Berlin, Mouton de Gruyter, 83–102.

Treherne, P. (1995) 'The Warrior's Beauty: The Masculine Body and Self-Identity in Bronze Age Europe', *Journal of European Archaeology* 3(1), 105–144.

Turner, B. S. (1991) 'Recent Developments in the Theory of the Body' in Featherstone, M., Hepworth, M. and Turner, B. S. (eds), *The Body: Social Process and Cultural Theory,* London, Sage, 1–35.

Whittle, A. (2003) *The Archaeology of People; Dimensions of Neolithic Life,* London, Routledge.

Wyke, M. (1998) *Gender and the Body in the Ancient Mediterranean,* Oxford, Blackwell Publishing.

House to House. A Comparative Study of Ancient Egyptian Houses from the New Kingdom to the Ptolemaic Period (1539–32 BC)

Ben van den Bercken

Introduction

This article forms a short discussion of the results of analyses carried out on ancient Egyptian Architecture, using a new computer application, and aims to shed more light on the ancient Egyptian domestic architecture of the New Kingdom down to the Ptolemaic Period for the whole of Egypt and the northern part of the Sudan. These structures have only become a topic of interest in the last few decades due to the work of Kemp at Amarna (1977, 1986), Bietak at Tell ed-Dab'a (1991; 1996), Arnold and O'Connor at Kahun and Elephantine (Arnold 1989, 2003; O'Connor 1998), Soukiassian at Ayn-Asil (2002), Welsby at Kawa (2001; 2002) and a still growing number of other projects throughout Egypt and the Sudan. All of these are contributing to a better understanding of how the ancient Egyptians lived, how they built their houses, how they behaved and possibly offer a look into how they thought.

It was decided that this paper should take an archaeological point of view. The choice was made to exclude an analysis and discussion of the textual and pictorial evidence. The reason for this is that 1) there was not enough space available to properly discuss all the known material; and 2) a comprehensive investigation of the archaeological dataset is, at the moment, particularly interesting as it has received relatively little attention until recently, while the other two datasets have already been investigated by others (e.g. Roik 1988, pictorial; Lesko 1994, textual; Menu 1998, for the sale of houses, textual; Toivari-Viitala 2003, textual; Černý 2001, textual and Demarée 2006, textual).

The aim of this article will be twofold. First, to show some of the results of this analysis. Second, to introduce a new tool which has proved to be useful in the analysis of ancient Egyptian (domestic) architecture namely 'Space Syntax Analysis' (SSA).

Goals and methods

The main aim of this analysis was to investigate the extent to which a continuous line of development is visible in the structures in all the above mentioned regions and periods. In addition to this, a set of smaller questions was aimed at investigating the relationships between public and private space. The relationship between the semi-permanent installations (Kent 1990, 13) and the house itself (how was the house equipped with furniture or features like hearths) was examined, in addition to looking at the use of space in general.

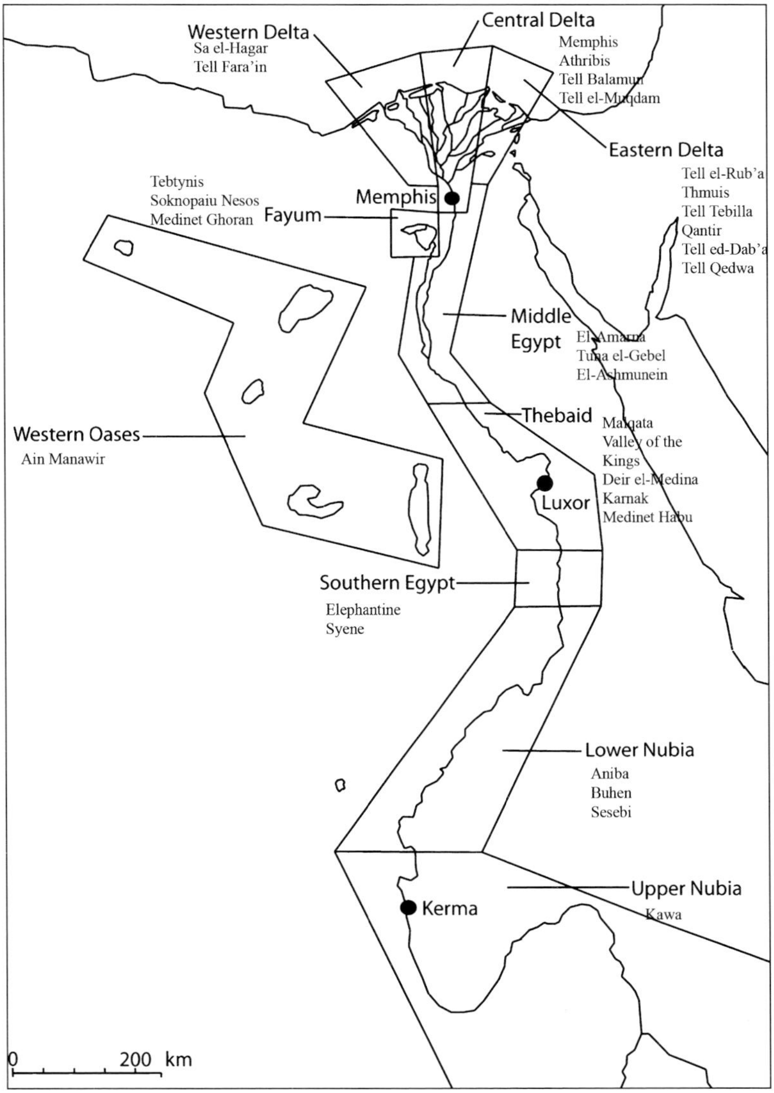

Figure 1. *Schematic map of Egypt including the regional divisions and overview of all the sites used for this paper.*

The most appropriate way of handling the above questions seems to be to put together a comprehensive dataset of structures. All the data available on these specific structures was investigated and a critical examination produced an objective corpus of sites ordered by topographical region (Fig. 1) and a comprehensive overview of all the literature involved. This corpus should still, of course, be seen as (at best) a selection of the material that should ideally be available. Three main problems occur; firstly, most of the publications are from the 19th century and are almost never re-examined or re-published. Our goals at present are of course different from those of scholars like Lepsius, Mariette and Petrie who initially excavated these sites. Secondly, many of those publications did not discuss the architecture at all. Their emphasis was often on the more spectacular finds rather than the structures interpreted to be houses which were only discussed in a few lines of text with limited illustrations (e.g. Petrie 1909). Finally, a problem that sadly occurs much too often is the total absence of publication, a problem that affects many issues in Egyptian Archaeology. On completion of this corpus of sites, the results were correlated in order to enable comparisons to be made, firstly by region, to ascertain whether regional trends were visible, and secondly by period, to discern possible continuity and developments. This comparison was done mainly on the basis of several factors. Firstly the architectural layout; wall thickness, geography of the structure, development of the structure and above all, the articulation of the different parts of the structure (how did they interact/function together). Secondly, archaeological features; hearths, ovens, silos, bins, sanitary installations, etc. were examined, as was artefactual evidence; investigating which objects were associated with which rooms (very thoroughly assessed by Koltsida (2007) for Amarna and Deir el-Medina).

Space Syntax Analysis

Introduction

In order to better visualize trends and phenomena, as well as add an extra dimension to the analysis, it was decided to use the concept of 'Space Syntax Analysis' to support the comparative approach. The Space Syntax Analysis was first advocated by Hillier and Hanson (Hillier 1984) and has continuously been improved, allowing for complicated analyses. In short, the method involves mathematical analysis of the spatial properties of a structure (or town), on the basis of lines or polygons. By using logarithms it provides a possible reconstruction of human motional behaviour in these structures. This can be done in a variety of ways (as discussed by Turner 2001).

The history of Space Syntax Analysis

Space Syntax Analysis is a concept that started to develop after the 'invention' of the 'isovist'. An isovist is the two-dimensional area that is visible to a person from a certain point (or node) (Benedikt 1979). Depending on the number of degrees of sight one takes into account, this will often be a polygon (Fig. 2). This is the most important parameter in this discussion. After an initial silence, the publication by Hillier and Hanson (Hillier 1984) had great impact and since then Space Syntax Analysis has gained ground as an analysis that focuses on the spatial properties and relationships of bordered spaces. The analysis was subsequently refined and the concept augmented

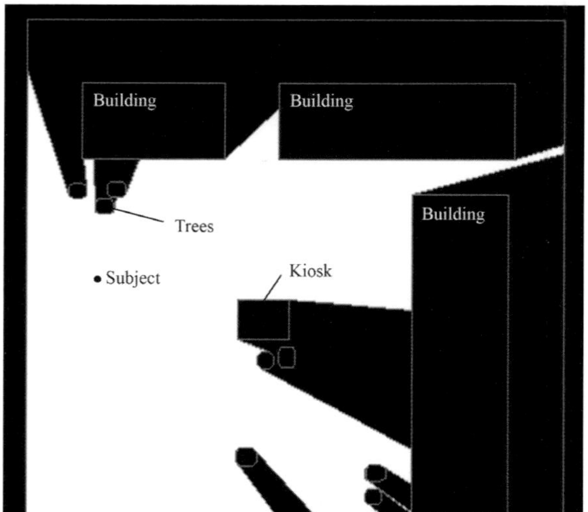

Figure 2. *The subject has an overview of the square with his 360-degrees isovist, limited only by the buildings and the trees.*

(articles by Van Nes 2004; 2009). Most of these analyses were integrated in the 'Depthmap' software (developed at the University College London), which enabled an automated approach of the Space Syntax Analysis. Turner (2004) describes a number of different analyses among which 1) 'axial analysis' (analysing lines of sight) 2) 'visibility analysis' (analysing isovists) 3) 'segment analysis' (analysing a set of lines of sight (i.e. a segment)) and 4) 'agent analysis' (visualization of possible walking patterns through a structure or street system). Because of this set of analyses it became easier to analyse the structures and settlements that were of interest. Some key articles concerning this program are by Turner (Turner 2001; 2004).

Visibility Graph Analysis (VGA), the use of the 'isovist' and the 'isovist area analysis'
The type of analysis that we will be dealing with here is that which is best for the analysis of individual structures or large open spaces in general, 'Visibility Graph Analysis' or 'VGA'. The basis of this analysis does not rely on lines of sight or segments but on individual points that can be made visible by laying out a raster over the plan of the structure (Fig. 3). A point is located in the centre of each square in the raster. The scale of the raster is determined by the accuracy or detail required, not by the scale of the original plan. These points will then be the basis for the Depthmap VGA to calculate the isovist(s) of one's choice (Fig. 4).

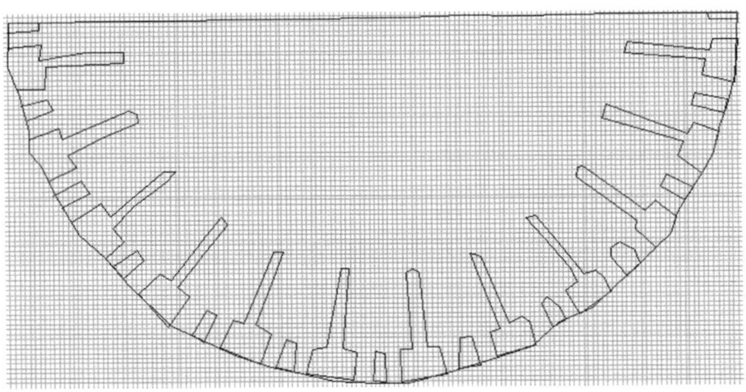

Figure 3. *Plan of the 'Panopticon'-building (modified after Hillier 1984:188). In this plan one can see the raster-overlay over the original vector drawing-plan.*

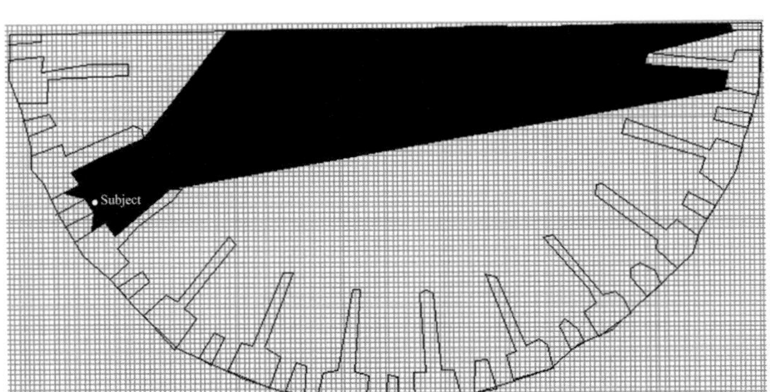

Figure 4. *Plan of the Panopticon with a raster overlay showing an isovist for a person (a node) from one of the rooms to the left toward the centre of the structure. We see that from this position only a small part of the structure can be overseen.*

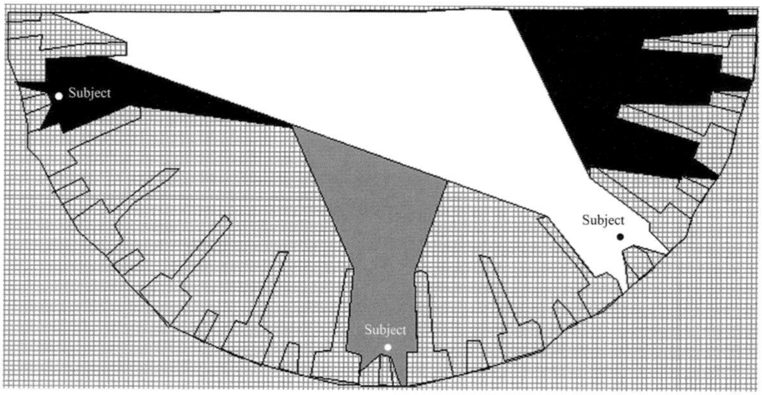

Figure 5. *The Panopticon with the raster overlay showing isovists from some of the smaller rooms giving an indication of where the maximum overlap will be.*

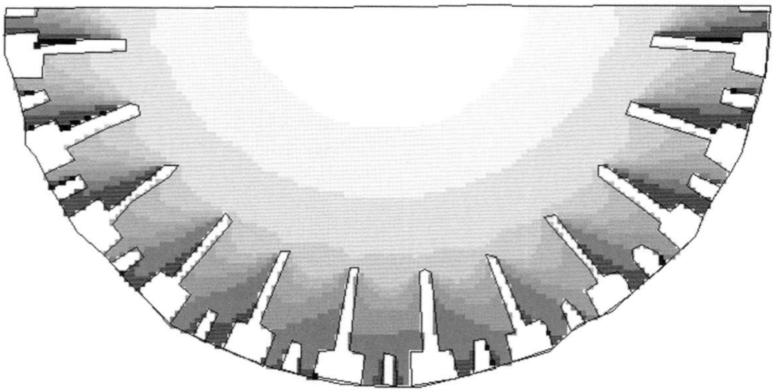

Figure 6. *The Panopticon (without raster overlay) showing the 'isovist area analysis' results (black is a low value, white is a high value). One sees that the highest values are in the centre of the building. The Panopticon was a prison which explains its peculiar design (see also Hillier 1984:188): from the centre one could oversee all the different cells in the semi-spherical building.*

Visibility Graph Analysis itself is subdivided into a number of tools available in Depthmap (Turner 2004) of which 'Isovist Area Analysis' was used. This tool will indicate in a colour-scale (or black and white) where the overlap between the isovists from all other nodes is the highest (in which each node functions as a point of view, (Fig. 5), meaning the area that can be seen from most other nodes (red or white = high; blue or black = low) (Fig. 6). These areas are generally interpreted as areas where interaction between people is most likely to take place (Van Nes 2009, 120:3), locations to which a person is urged to move in order to get the best overview of the structure.

Case studies

In order to better visualize the above process and connect it to the archaeological record, some examples need examining before looking at the overview of results that the comparative approach, combined with the SSA, accomplished. The Amarna houses will not be used as examples here since their archaeological context and analysis are already extensively described elsewhere (Peet 1923; Frankfort 1933; Pendlebury 1951; Ricke 1967; Borchardt 1980; Kemp 1986; Hamza 2000; Koltsida 2007), and receive attention in the paragraph about general results (see below). The aim of this case-studies-section is to provide a varied picture.

Deir el-Medina, house NE XIII (18th–19th Dynasty, Fig. 7)

The entrance of this house, with wooden doorjambs and a limestone threshold, led to a room (1) which once had a column in the middle to support the roof. The floor consisted of compacted mud and was plastered, while the lower part of the walls had a white-plastered band. In the northeast corner was a *lit clos* (possibly a house-shrine, Bruyère 1939, 50 and 55 ff.) with remains of Bes-figure paintings (Bruyère 1939, 260). Via a door with limestone jambs, which were painted red and still had some inscriptions on them, one could enter the next room (2). In this space the lower parts of the walls were also plastered white (Bruyère 1939, 259) and the floor was again of compacted mud and plastered. In the north-wall there was a small niche of which the function is not clear. Against the east-wall there was a 'divan' or bench which was still well preserved showing the elaborate, colourful, modelled decoration of its sides. In front of this divan was an oven set into the floor with a re-inforced wall of bricks (this contained much ash, charcoal and pottery).

On both sides of the divan there were doors leading to other parts of the house; on the north there was a passage into a small room (3) which did not give any clear indication of its function. According to Bruyère it might have been some sort of storage space. The other passage led into a small L-shaped room (4). The small side chamber contained pieces of amphora and mortar.

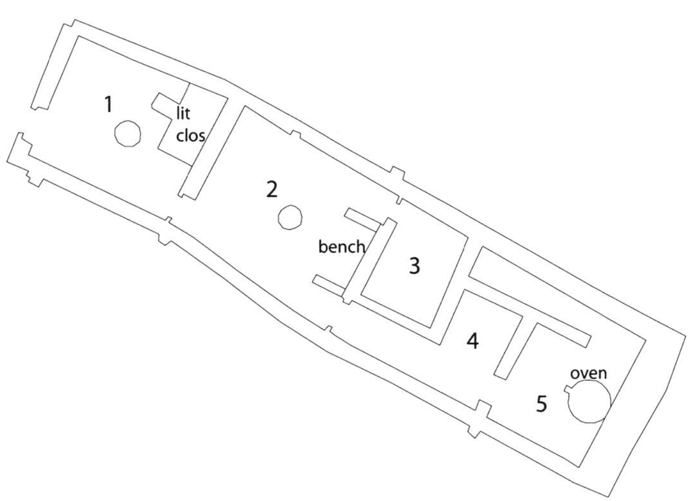

Figure 7. Schematic representation of house NE XIII at Deir el-Medina showing the most important features and the room numbering (after the original by Bruyère 1939).

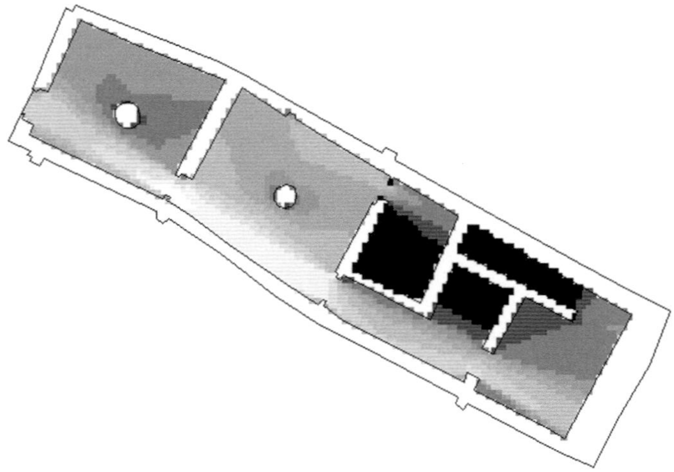

Figure 8. *Graph showing the results for the isovist area analysis at the Deir el-Medina house NE XIII.*

Perhaps this area was related to the area at the back where the food preparation took place. The final space was designated as the "kitchen" by Bruyère (5). There were traces of a large oven of 90 cm in diameter located against the centre back wall. The room was also roughly L-shaped since the small recess in the northeast contained a passage leading to the stairs that ran up to the west. This room seems to have had a food preparation function.

Looking at the isovist area analysis (Fig. 8) for this structure, a pattern that seems representative for the Deir el-Medina houses becomes apparent. The first two rooms have relatively high values as does the corridor running all the way to the back. The door from the first room to the second room seems to be a point where interaction must have taken place. This fits with the general assumption that the first room was more open to the public. Generally, the positions of the *lits clos* in the different Deir el-Medina houses are away from the main isovist overlap areas. In the cases where a false door was present this was also the case. It can be therefore concluded that these features were not located at the points where people would be most likely to interact or go to, to get a maximal overview. The same occurs at houses in Amarna where the false doors were located in the main space away from the areas with the highest interaction values. (e.g. the house of Vizir Nakht (house K 50.1, Ricke 1967, 38) and house M 47.4 (Borchardt 1980)).

El-Ashmunein, house j.10–k.10 (Third Intermediate Period, Fig. 9)

At El-Ashmunein (Hermopolis Magna) a structure was excavated by Spencer (1993) that seemed to be domestic in character. The wall thickness varies from 30 cm to 100 cm around the central staircase; it may well have had an upper storey (perhaps housing the more private quarters). The positioning of the doors and the staircase made immediate view into the staircase impossible, concealing it from outside view. The first room, 3.i, contained pottery (including Phoenician ware) and probably was the main access to the building. It is clear in the isovist area analysis (Fig. 10) that this was the room with the highest values, again located at the transition from the first to the second rooms; this first room was kept under observation. It gave access to a large

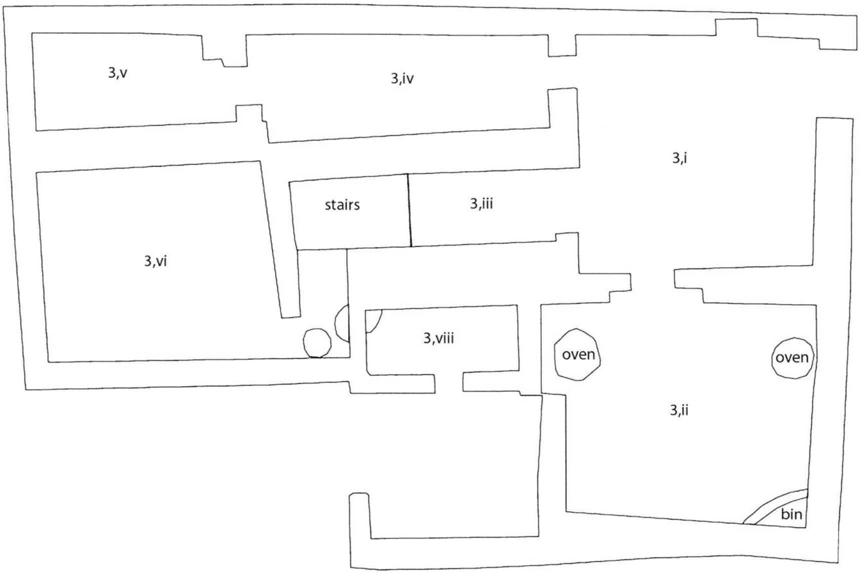

Figure 9. *Schematic representation of the house at El-Ashmunein square j10–k.10 with the most important features and room numbering (after the original by Spencer 1993).*

Figure 10. *Graph showing the results for the isovist area analysis at the El-Ashmunein structure. Note that only spaces connected to the rest of the system will be included in the analysis (space 3,vi has no direct (visible) connection).*

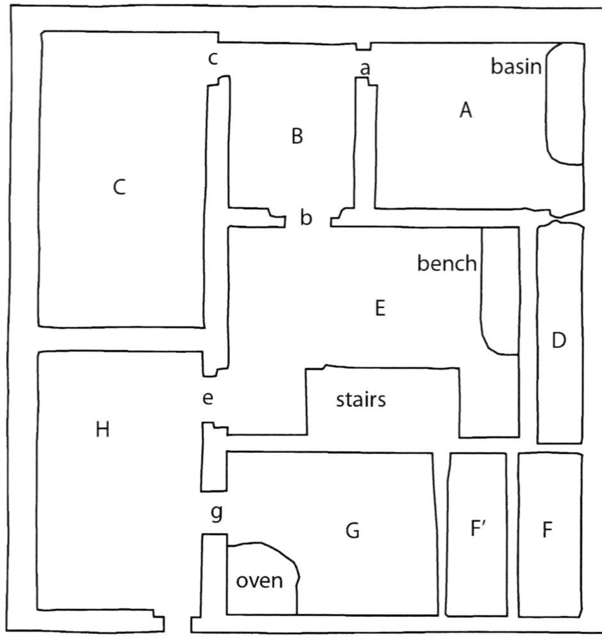

Figure 11. *Schematic representation of the structure at Medinet Ghoran Kom A (after the original by Jouguet 1901) with the most important features and the room and doorway designations.*

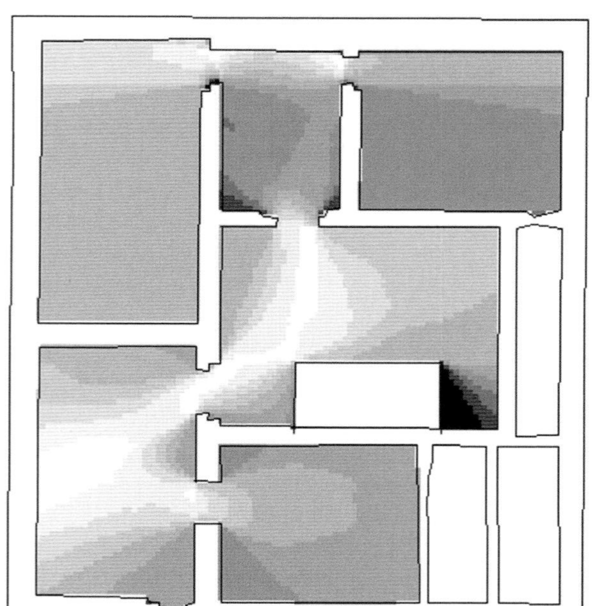

Figure 12. *Graph showing the results for the isovist area analysis at the Medinet Ghoran Kom A structure. Note that only spaces connected to the rest of the system will be included in the analysis (spaces D, F and F' have no (visible) connection).*

room in the south with cooking features (ovens and a hearth) and a burned floor, many figurines, and pottery. Room 3.i also gave access to a corridor-like room (which could be closed by a door) giving access to the inner parts of the building. Of these, room 3.iv might have been a storage space (due to the large amount of complete vessels here) while room 3.v and 3.vi (presumably accessed from room 3.v) were rather clean in finds; room 3.vi did contain some beads and some pottery. The isovist area analysis value in these rooms was relatively low supporting the view that they might have been more private. Additional rooms on the outside might have functioned as some sort of court/animal pens (considering the width of the door of room 3.viii).

Medinet Ghoran (Fayum), Kom A (3rd–1st century BC, Fig. 11)
The structure consists of a number of rooms with different features and a staircase and is similar to some of the Amarna houses classified by Ricke as 'Intermediary Houses' (Ricke 1967, 6 ff.). Space H formed the entrance to the building and might have been a court which gave access to two rooms to the east. The first (most southern) room contained considerable ash deposits that seem to be related to the oven in the southwest corner of the room. The other room (E) was probably also a court. In the east corner was a bench-like feature of about 86 centimeters high. A staircase running up to the southeast was possibly connected to room D and is an indication of a higher level or a roof.

Via an elaborate door from E the rooms A, B and C were accessible. Room B had a small cistern or tub in its west corner. Entering room C one would pass another cistern-like feature as well as a mud brick platform in the north corner. This room, with its view onto the court was one of the innermost rooms of the structure and therefore must have had a more private function (see also below). The same applies to room A in which there was also a cistern or tub in the east corner. This was preserved up to a height of 50 cm and its function is not clear (Jouguet 1901, 394). It was not clear to the excavator whether the "silo-space" D might have been accessible from A.

It is not unthinkable that the spaces H and E had a more public function, were probably unroofed and easy to access (see below), while the rooms A, B and C were only accessible via the well-executed bottleneck-doorway b. Finds from the structure have not been properly recorded to a specific context. Besides the pottery, they included mostly wooden objects such as door handles, furniture parts such as chair-legs, round wooden objects, a wooden cup and some wooden figurines.

If the results from the isovist area analysis are analysed (Fig. 12) it is clear that the areas with the highest values are located in the entrance room H, from H into G, from door e to b, and from door c to a. These are the points where people were likely to meet and which were relatively easy to keep under observation. The largest concentration is in room H, possibly this is an indication that one would receive guests here (similar results were revealed for the Amarna house loggias). Another point is that the concentration in room E stops at door b. This is partly achieved by the positioning of the staircase opposite it, creating a point easy to control at door e. The features which hint at a sanitary installation, and the reduced visibility, might indicate that rooms A, B and C were the more private quarters.

Results

The structures discussed above are but a small part of the complete dataset, which, for obvious reasons, cannot be given fully here.

Main space

What is generally apparent is that there is one space occupying the centre part of the building (e.g. El-Amarna (Borchardt 1980 and Peet 1923), Memphis (Jeffreys 2006), Medinet Ghoran (Jouguet 1901), Soknopaiu Nesos (Boak 1935), Tell ed-Dab'a (Bietak 1991, 1996), Buhen (Emery 1979) and Elephantine (Kaiser 1980; 1988; 1990; 1993)). This space often contained a number of the most prominent features, e.g. querns, ovens, bins, columns, benches and false doors, making it a space that can be ascribed a number of different activities or functions. Its central position often also facilitated connection to other rooms (Figs. 13 and 14). This main space often has a relatively high isovist overlap area (Figs. 12 and 15), indicating that it was a space containing points at which most of the rest of the structure would be visible. This area therefore functioned as an important node, be it for control or interaction of traffic through the structure. The phenomenon of this main space, and its accompanying isovist area values corroborate Helck's view (Helck 1975, 1059) that among others the Amarna Standard House (ASH, see also Fig. 13) can be divided up into three parts: 1) '*Öffentlich zugänglicher Bereich*'; 2) '*Hausgemeinschaftlicher Bereich*'; 3) '*Privatbereich*'. This phenomenon also seems to hold true for structures at, among others, Memphis (Jeffreys 2006), El-Ashmunein (Spencer 1993), Tuna el-Gebel (Nur ed-Din 1996), Malqata (Endo 1995), Dakhla (Wuttmann 1996) and Elephantine (Kaiser 1980; 1988; 1990; 1993).

The transition from the front part (perhaps comparable to Helck's '*Öffentlich zugänglicher Bereich*') to this main space often also showed a high value (Fig. 12 and 15) and this point might be interpreted as the real 'access' to the building. Regardless of what size the buildings were, this feature (especially visible in Amarna and Malqata) ensured that no real direct control over the more private spaces would take place from this front part of the structure. A good illustration of this can be found in some of the Amarna Standard Houses; the so called 'porter's room' (see among others Borchardt 1980, 25) (Fig. 16). There usually is a second entrance to the side of the building, after entering which, one passes a small room. The excavators contend that this was a space where a person was housed who was meant to control traffic in and out of the structure via this entrance, making the small room a type of 'office'. It seems that the household space proper started after this passage from the front to the main part. This possible control aspect seems to support the general view (Helck 1975, 1059) that the first space was a space where visitors would be received and entertained (perhaps comparable to the English parlour). The central or main space often gives access to a number of smaller rooms (sometimes also larger) which were more segregated (i.e. a less integral part of the structure as a whole) implying that they were of a more private character. These spaces seem always present and they need not always be the topologically deepest rooms (e.g. at Deir el-Medina (Bruyère 1939).

Privacy of the back-rooms

A feature especially visible in the Amarna houses is that the back part (which would fit Helck's '*Privatbereich*' (Helck 1975, 1059)) is relatively secluded. The rooms believed to be the most private are the most difficult to access and to look into. In the case of Amarna one can see that, if one is looking from the main space into the back area, no direct visibility would be possible into the most private spaces, e.g. the room that is generally believed to be the bedroom (with the raised platform) and the room with the sanitary installations (see also Fig. 13). If such an attempt was made, visibility would almost always reach into the small transverse corridor located in front of these private rooms or in a small columned hall. There are of course cases where visibility reaches the interior of these private rooms but this is never directly upon the facilities

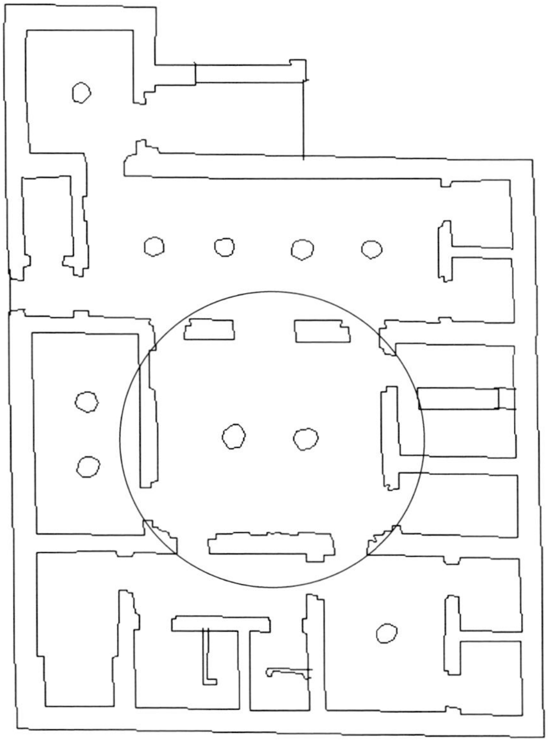

Figure 13. *Schematic plan of the house of the 'Vorsteher' (Q46.1) with the main space marked by the circle (based on the original by Borchardt 1980, 23). The small rooms in the lower centre area, with the small screen walls, are the 'sanitary facilities'.*

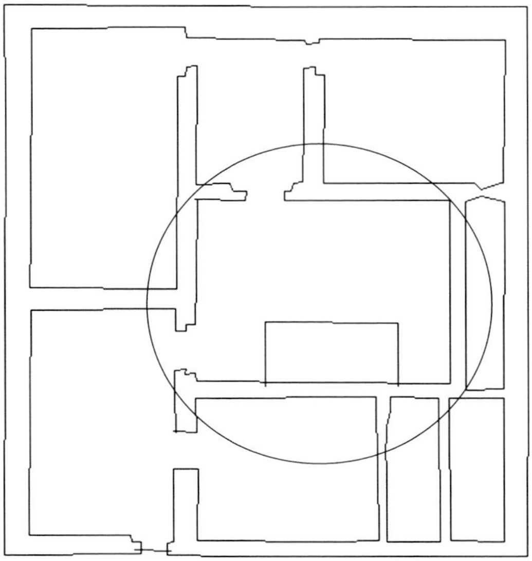

Figure 14. *Schematic plan of the house at Medinet Ghoran Kom A with the main space marked by the circle (based on the original drawing by Jouguet 1901).*

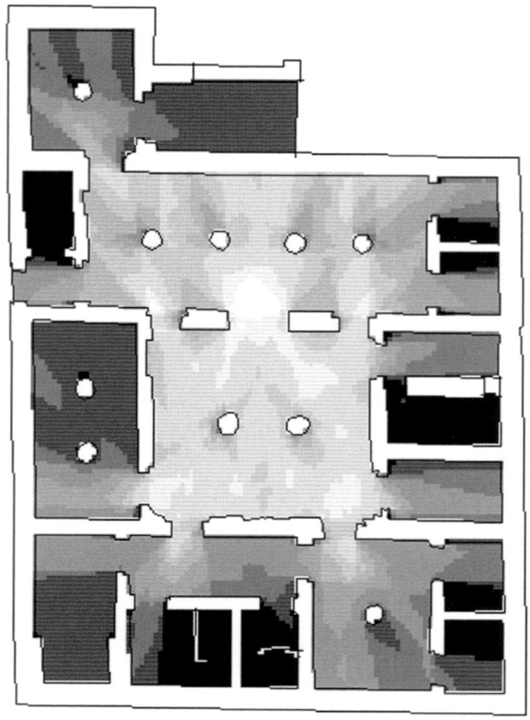

Figure 15. *Graph showing the results of the isovist area analysis for the Amarna Estate House Q46.1 (based on the original plan by Borchardt 1980).*

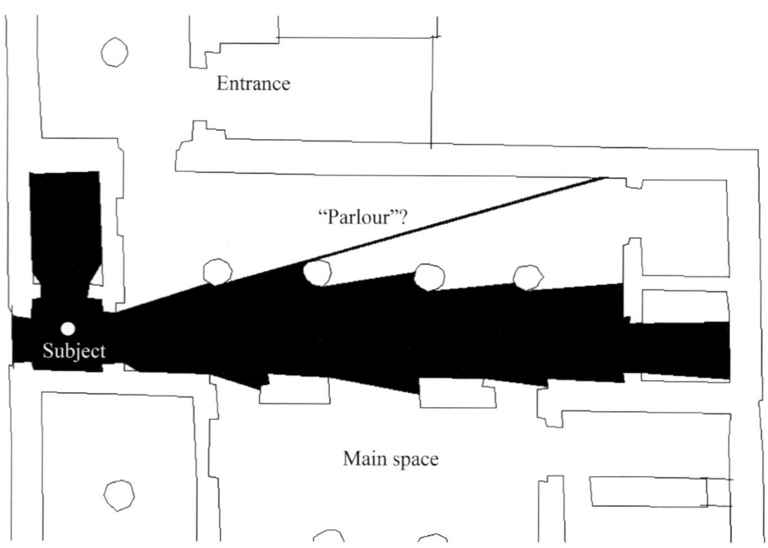

Figure 16. *Schematic overview of part of the Amarna Estate House Q46.1 with the isovist from the "porter's room." From this position one could keep an eye on what was happening at the entrance to the more private parts of the structure (based on the original plan by Borchardt 1980).*

that must have given the rooms their function. We see the same happening in the other locations where the ASH layout is present, i.e. Malqata (Endo 1995) and Aniba (Steindorff 1935; 1937) as well as in Memphis (Jeffreys 2006) and possibly Deir el-Medina (Bruyère 1939).

Prestigious rooms

In some of the structures that were found in the Fayum one sees rooms which are more elaborate than the rest of the spaces. These are the rooms which have stone doorposts or a stone casing on the lower parts of the walls (Gallazzi 2000). This type of room is not (as in the Karnak priests houses of the Third Intermediate Period (Anus 1971)) the first room to be entered, but usually the second room from the main entrance (after the vestibule). What is also apparent is that the entrance to this room is often the one with the highest overlap of isovists. Perhaps the function of this room was to guide the visitors and lead them to enter this prestigious room (again the parlour idea) and not enter the innermost, private parts of the structure. Although Crocker does not mention an elaborate doorway inside the house (Crocker (1985, 52 ff.) is mainly concerned with the entrance to the compound) it would be interesting to include both the stone-cased walls and elaborate doorways in Crocker's list of status symbols.

General trends

Looking at the more general picture it is possible to, firstly, distinguish three trends that are interesting on the regional level. There is a remarkable similarity between some of the structures from the Fayum (Tebtynis (Gallazzi 2000), Soknopaiu Nesos (Boak 1935) and Medinet Ghoran (Jouguet 1901)) and structures from the central Delta regions (Memphis (Jeffreys 2006), Tell el-Rub'a (Mendes) (Wilson 1982), Tell Tebilla (Mumford 2002), Tell Muqdam (Redmount 1997) and Tell Fara'in (Buto) (Hartung 2003)). The square houses (perhaps comparable to Arnold's '*Turmhäuser'*, Arnold 1989, 75 ff and 2003, 38 and 50) with their thick walls and multiple storeys are a phenomenon that might imply scarcity of building space or perhaps a more simple reason such as better ventilation or temperature regulation. In later periods we see this type of house emerging in southern Egypt (Arnold 2003).

The second observation is the geographical spread of the house layouts that are well-known from Amarna. These occur also in Luxor (east and west bank) and in some of the fortress sites in Lower Nubia (Steindorff 1935; 1937; Blackman 1937; Fairman 1938). From this analysis it is apparent that this type of building was not exclusive to Amarna, nor was it invented there. There was a set of conventions already in existence; at least in the time of Amenohotep III, perhaps even earlier.

Lastly, examining the general chronological overview of domestic architecture, Egyptian houses of the New Kingdom appear to be relatively homogenous. As far as can be determined from the available data there might very well have been a set of conventions (at least in the 18th and 19th Dynasties) that were followed by people living at different locations in Egypt (e.g. the 'Amarna Standard House'). This results in the conclusion that house building was a planned event following these conventions or traditional/practical/status values. During the Third Intermediate and Late Periods it is clear that the overall picture reveals a confused house building canon. Some structures follow the traditional or conventional plans as we know them from the New Kingdom, while others reveal experimentation (perhaps with these very same traditions and conventions in mind) with building conventions that ultimately led to the structures that seem to be dominant during the Ptolemaic period. In the Ptolemaic Period elongated rectangular houses (comparable in layout to the Deir el-Medina houses) appear side by side with the square-houses (the prime example of this is of course Soknopaiu Nesos in the Fayum). On the basis of what is known now, it could be argued that the square-house was gaining ground at the end of the Late Period and had its heyday during the Ptolemaic period and after, firmly establishing the vertical house structure in Egypt.

Conclusion

With the investigation of this set of sites, hopefully a small contribution is made to the unravelling of the characteristics of ancient Egyptian domestic architecture. Prior work on the subject has often been focused on the sites of El-Amarna and Deir el-Medina. Aspects like household (Kemp 1989; Tietze 1985), economy (Tietze 1986), status (Crocker 1985) and architecture (Spence 2004) have been subject to thorough scrutiny.

At the end of this investigation four results can be highlighted. First, after examination of a set of sites yielding domestic structures, it can be concluded that there are traces of similarity through time and across regions (Fig. 1). House-building conventions were not phenomena confined to specific places or sites. Exchange of ideas or perhaps transmission via a central institution, or perhaps by way of tradition, may very well have taken place. The phenomenon of the distribution of the so called tower-houses (e.g. Memphis, Mendes, Tell Tebilla, Athribis, Sa el-Hagar and the Fayum sites) as well as the apparently wide distribution of the ASH layout (e.g. Malqata, Aniba and Sesebi) underline this. Still, at the moment, it is very difficult to rigorously prove such phenomena.

Second, the comparative approach used resulted in some interesting points and it should be seriously considered for a follow up investigation once more data is available. The preparation for this approach resulted in a corpus of sites and literature which can be used for future work. Third, the application of Space Syntax Analysis and the Depthmap computer program show promising results. Because only a limited amount of different analyses were used in its application for this investigation one realises that much more can be done with it once its full potential is understood. As a tool SSA and Depthmap might be useful in further unravelling and especially making more visible the characteristics of the Egyptian house and the use of its space. Finally, the investigation of old as well as new material should automatically entail publication of the results in order to make the information available to others.

University of Leiden

Bibliography

Anus, P. and Sa'ad, R. (1971) Habitations de prêtres dans le temple d'Amon de Karnak, *Kemi XXI*.

Arnold, F. (1989) A study of Egyptian domestic buildings, *Varia Egyptiaca* 5, 75–93.

Arnold, F. (2003) *Elephantine XXX. Die Nachnutzung des Chnumtempelbezirks. Wohnbebauung desSpätantike und des Frühmittelalters*, Mainz am Rhein, Von Zabern.

Benedikt, M. L. (1979) To take hold of space: isovist and isovist fields, *Environment and planning B: planning and design*, 647–665.

Bietak, M. (1991) *Tell el-Dab'a V. Ein Friedhofbezirk der mittleren Bronzezeitkultur mit Totentempel und Siedlungsschichten, Teil I*, Wien, Verlag der Österreichischen Akademie der Wissenschaften.

Bietak, M. (1996) *Haus und Palast im alten Ägypten, Internationales Symposium 8. bis 11. April 1992 in Kairo*, Wien, Verlag der Österreichischen Akademie der Wissenschaften.

Blackman, A. M. (1937) Preliminary report on the excavations at Sesebi, Northern province, Anglo-Egyptian Sudan, 1936–37, *Journal of Egyptian Archaeology* 23, 145–151.

Boak, A. E. R. (1935) *Soknopaiou Nesos. The University of Michigan excavations at Dimê in 1931–32*, Ann Arbor, University of Michigan Press.

Borchardt, L. and Ricke, H. (1980) *Die Wohnhäuser in Tell el-Amarna*, Berlin, Mann.

Bruyère, B. (1939) *Rapport sur les fouilles de Deir el Médineh (1934–1935). Trosieme partie: Le village, les décharges publiques, la station de repos du col de la Vallée des Rois*, Le Caire, Impr. de l'Institut Français d'Archéologie Orientale.

Černý, J. (2001) A community of workmen at Thebes in the Ramesside Period in *Bibliothèque d'étude*, 50 (2nd edition).

Crocker, P. T. (1985) Status symbols in the architecture of el-'Amarna, *Journal of Egyptian Archaeology* 71, 52–65.

Demarée, R. J. (2006) A house is not a home, *Aegyptiaca Helvetica* 19, 57–66.

Emery, W. B., Smith, H. S. and Millard, A. (1979) *The fortress of Buhen. The archaeological report*, London, Egypt Exploration Society.

Endo, T. (1995) Amarna-type houses at the Malqata palace-city, *Journal of the Society for the Study of Egyptian Antiquities* 25, 23–37.

Fairman, H. W. (1938) Preliminary report on the excavations at Sesebi (Sudla) and 'Amarah West, Anglo-Egyptian Sudan, 1937–8, *Journal of Egyptian Archaeology* 24, 151–156.

Frankfort, H. and Pendlebury, J. D. S. (1933) *The City of Akhenaten, Part II: the north suburb and the desert altars, volume I*, London, Egypt Exploration Society.

Gallazzi, C. and Hadji-Minaglou, G. (2000) *Tebtynis I. La reprise des fouilles et le quartier de la chapelle d'Isis-Thermouthis*, Le Caire, Institut Français d'Archéologie Orientale.

Hamza, M. and Kemp, B. (2000) Report on a large house at Amarna, discovered near the village of el-Hagg Qandil, *Journal of Egyptian Archaeology* 86, 161–165.

Hartung, U., Ballet, P., Béguin, F., Bourriau, J., French, P., Herbich, T., Kopp, P., Lecuyot, G. and Schmitt, A. (2003) Tell el-Fara'in – Buto. 8. Vorbericht, *Mitteilungen des Deutschen Archäologisches Institut Abteilung Kairo 59*, 199–267.

Helck, W. (1975) *Lexikon der Ägyptologie, Band I*, Wiesbaden, Harrassowitz.

Hillier, B. and J. Hanson (1984) *The social logic of space*, Cambridge, Cambridge University Press.

Jeffreys, D. G. (2006) *Kom Rabia: the New Kingdom settlement (levels II–V)*, with contributions by B. Driskell and N.J. Preston, London, Egypt Exploration Society.

Jouguet, P., 1901: Fouilles de Fayoum. Rapport sur les fouilles de Médinet-Madi et Médinet-Ghoran, *Bulletin de Correspondance Hellenistique XXV*.

Kaiser, W. (1980) Stadt und Tempel von Elephantine: Achter Grabungsbericht, *Mitteilungen des Deutschen Archäologisches Institut Abteilung Kairo* 36, 245–291.

Kaiser, W. (1988) Stadt und Tempel von Elephantine: 15./16. Grabungsbericht, *Mitteilungen des Deutschen Archäologisches Institut Abteilung Kairo* 44, 135–182.

Kaiser, W. (1990) Stadt und Tempel von Elephantine: 17./18. Grabungsbericht, *Mitteilungen des Deutschen Archäologisches Institut Abteilung Kairo* 46, 185–250.

Kaiser, W. (1993) Stadt und Tempel von Elephantine: 19./20 Grabungsbericht, *Mitteilungen des Deutschen Archäologisches Institut Abteilung Kairo* 49, 133–187.

Kemp, B. J. (1977) The city of el-Amarna as a source for the study of urban society in ancient Egypt, *World Archaeology* 9, 123–139.

Kemp, B. J. (1986) *Amarna Reports III*, London, Egypt Exploration Society.

Kemp, B. J. (1989) *Ancient Egypt, anatomy of a civilisation*, London, Routledge.

Kent, S. (1990) *Domestic architecture and the use of space. An interdisciplinary cross-cultural study*, Cambridge, Cambridge University Press.

Koltsida, A. (2007) *Social aspects of ancient Egyptian domestic architecture*, Oxford, Archaeopress.

Lesko, L. H. (1994) *Pharaoh's workers. The villagers of Deir el-Medina*, Ithaca, Cornell University Press.

Menu, B. (1998) Recherches sur l'histoire juridique, économique et sociale de l'ancienne Égypte II, *Bibliothèque d'étude 122.*

Mumford, G. (2002) Reconstructing the ancient settlement at Tell Tebilla, *Bulletin of the American Research Center in Egypt, number 182*, 18–23 (accessed via www.deltasinai.com).

Nur ed-Din, A. e.-H. and Kessler, D. (1996) Das Priesterhaus am Ibiotapheion von Tuna el-Gebel. Vorberichte uber die Grabungen in Tuna 1989–1994 (I), *Mitteilungen des Deutschen Archäologisches Institut Abteilung Kairo* 52, 263–293.

O'Connor, D. (1998) The elite houses of Kahun, in J. Phillips: *Ancient Egypt, the Aegean and the Near East. Studies in honour of Martha Roads Bell*, San Antonio.

Peet, T. E. and Woolley, C. L. (1923) *The city of Akhenaten I*, London, Egypt Exploration Society.

Pendlebury, J. D. S. (1951) *The City of Akhenaten, Part III: the central city and the official quarters, volume II*, London, Egypt Exploration Society.

Petrie, W. M. F. (1909) *Memphis I*, London, Egypt Exploration Society.

Redmount, C. A. and Friedman, R. F. (1997) Tales of a Delta site: The 1995 field season at Tell el-Muqdam, *Journal of the American Research Center in Egypt XXXIV*, 57–83.

Ricke, H. (1967) *Der Grundriss des Amarna-Wohnhauses*, Leipzig, Hinrichs.

Roik, E. (1988) *Das altägyptische Wohnhaus und seine Darstellung im Flachbild*, Frankfurt am Main, Lang.

Soukiassian, G., Wuttmann, M. and Pantalacci, L. (2002) *Le palais des gouverneurs de l'époque de Pépy II. Les sanctuaires de ka et leurs dépendences. Balat IV*, Le Caire, Institut Français d'Archéologie Orientale.

Spence, K. (2004) The three-dimensional form of the Amarna house, *Journal of Egyptian Archaeology* 90, 123–152.

Spencer, A. J. (1993) *Excavations at el-Ashmunein, III the town*, London, British Museum Publications.

Steindorff, G. (1935) *Aniba I*, Le Caire, Service des antiquités de l'Égypte.

Steindorff, G. (1937) *Aniba II*, Le Caire, Service des antiquités de l'Égypte.

Tietze, C. (1985) Amarna, Analyse seiner Wohnhäuser und soziale Struktur der Stadtbewohner, *Zeitschrift für Ägyptische Sprache* 112 48–84.

Tietze, C. (1986) Amarna Teil II, Analyse der okonomischen Beziehungen der Stadtbewohner *Zeitschrift für Ägyptische Sprache* 113, 55–78.

Toivari-Viitala, J. (2003) O.DeM 764: A note concerning property rights, *Göttinger Miszellen 195.*

Turner, A. (2001) Depthmap; A program to perform visibility graph analysis, *Proceedings of the 3rd International Space Syntax Symposium, Atlanta*, 31.1–31.9.

Turner, A. (2004) *Depthmap 4. A researcher's handbook*, London.

Van Nes, A. (2004) *Introduction to configurative methods in urban studies*, Delft (Update version in preparation 2008).

Van Nes, A. (2009) Measuring the degree of street vitality in excavated towns, *Proceedings of the 7th International Space Syntax Symposium, 120* (http://www.sss7.org/Proceedings_list.html).

Welsby, D. (2001) Excavations within the pharaonic and kushite site at Kawa and in its hinterland, *Sudan and Nubia, The Sudan Archaeological Research Society (SARS) Bulletin 5*, 64–70.

Welsby, D. (2002) The Kushite town and cemetery at Kawa, *Sudan and Nubia, The Sudan Archaeological Research Society (SARS) Bulletin 6*, 32–37.

Wilson, K. L. (1982) Cities of the Delta, part II. Mendes. Preliminary report on the 1979 and 1980 seasons, *American Research Center in Egypt Reports 5*, Malibu, Undena Publications.

Wuttman, M. (1996) Premier rapport préliminaire des travaux sur le site de 'Ayn Manawir (oasis de Kharga), *Bulletin de l'Institut Français Archéologique Orientale 36*, 385–451.

Counting the Dead – Some Remarks on The Haker-Festival

Zsuzsanna Végh

Introduction

The Haker-Festival formed part of the Mysteries of Abydos in the Middle and New Kingdom, practised until the 18th Dynasty (Griffith 1977, 929), and at the same time it was a festival of the dead. There have been many studies of the content and sequence of the Osirian Festival in the Middle Kingdom (and also in the Late Period), but so far no one has made a detailed study of the Haker-Festival. In addition to summarizing previous interpretations, the purpose of this paper is to examine the main questions: how can the very diverse sources be brought within a unified framework; based on the written sources, how is it possible to fit the festival into the sequence of the Mysteries and to reconstruct what kind of ritual was celebrated on this occasion? Finally, some possible approaches to the solution of these problems will be suggested.

Fitting the Haker into the course of the Mysteries

The course of the Mysteries

For the sake of this discussion, it is worth outlining the main events of the Mysteries. Attempts to reconstruct the course of the Mysteries of Abydos in the Middle Kingdom have been made by Schäfer (1905 49–86), Anthes (1974, 15–49) and more recently by Lavier (1988, 289–295). It has also been studied, although not in the same detail, by other scholars (Kamal 1939, 272–283; Helck 1952, 72–85; Lichtheim 1988, 100; Assmann 2001, 310–318).

These reconstructions are based mainly on the private feast lists, on the autobiographies from the Middle and New Kingdom, and on the so-called Abydos-formula. The reconstructions are rather varied. There is general agreement that the first event of the festival is the First Procession (*prt tpt*), also designated as the Procession of Upuaut (*prt Wpw3wt*). Anthes suggests that this act could have been a kind of preparation for the later events: it served to transport the statue of Osiris from the temple to a lake of unknown location (Anthes 1974, 26). The following event, the Great Procession (*prt ꜥ3t*) was the first phase of the god Osiris's funerary procession leading to his tomb in Poker. The second phase of the procession was the event known from the feast list as 'God's sailing to Poker' (*ḏ3t nṯr r Pḳr*). However Kamal (1939, 274) and Lichtheim (1988, 100) suggest that the latter should be interpreted as a part of the Great Procession.

The place known as Poker should be identified with the cemetery of the early kings in Umm el-Qaab: it has been proved that in the Middle Kingdom the tomb of Djer was already considered as the tomb of Osiris (Leahy 1989, 55–56). The statue of Osiris spent a night in Poker. This statue is supposed to be a non-anthropomorphic statue in the style of the so-called

Abydos-fetish (Schäfer 1905, 72). Eaton proposed that, at least in the Ramesside Period, this object served as a head for a body made of corn (2004, 417, 423–424). The feast *sḏrt Pḳr* – also known from the feast list – should refer to the night in Poker and the *grḥ n sḏrt* is also to be identified with it (Lichtheim 1988, 80, 100; Lavier 1988, 291). On that night the god was rejuvenated, publically justified, and the kingship of his son (the role played by the king) was legitimised through carrying out the necessary rituals in relation to his father. However, while it is not clear which rituals were celebrated during the night, it is probable that a new gold – or at least a gilded – statue was made on that occasion in the House of Gold (Lavier 1988, 291). Afterwards the god was returned to Abydos.

References to the Haker can be found in all kinds of sources: in the autobiographies, in the 12th Dynasty version of the Abydos-formula and in the private feast lists. First I would like to analyse these texts, focusing on how the Haker can be fitted in the course of the Mysteries. There are also allusions to the Haker in the Book of the Dead. Based on these, the reconstruction of the celebrated rituals might be possible: these will be discussed it in the second part of the article.

Was the Haker celebrated during the night spent in Poker?

As mentioned above, the Haker appears in the 12th Dynasty version of the Abydos-formula. This formula is composed of a group of Osirian afterlife wishes which ask for participation in the cult and procession of Osiris in Abydos (Lichtheim 1988, 55–58, 129–134).
One of these requests is as follows:

> *sḏm.f hnw m r n tꜣ-wr hꜣkr / grḥ n sḏrt / sḏryt nt ḥr šn.*

The first part of the sentence can be translated as follows: 'May he hear jubilation from the mouth of Ta-wer (Thinite nome) at the Haker-feast' (Lichtheim 1988, 86) or 'May he hear jubilation at the gate of This (Thinite nome)' (Griffith 1977, 930).

The interpretation of the second part of the sentence is more problematical. The Haker is mentioned here in connection with the feast *grḥ n sḏrt* and *sḏryt nt ḥr šn,* which are usually understood to be references to the same event (see for example Helck 1952, 78; Griffith 1977, 929) and regarded as equivalents of the feast *sḏrt Pḳr*. The Haker is identified with them (Helck 1952, 78–79; Otto 1966, 40; Assmann 2001, 312) or designated as part of the act (Lichtheim 1988, 100). Apart from the fact that the Haker was celebrated during the night of Poker, the interpretations by these scholars differ widely: the major difference is the way in which they translate the words *sḏrt* and *sḏryt*. According to the dictionary of Hannig (Hannig 2006, 2411–2412), the word *sḏr* could be translated as 'die Nacht verbringen, die Nacht zubringen, schlafen, liegen' (to spend the night, to sleep, to lie). Thus, earlier, the words *sḏrt* and *sḏryt* were translated beyond any doubt as 'repose, sleeping'. More recently, however, in this particular context, the translation 'vigil' has been preferred by scholars.

The night of the Repose

The traditional translation, as mentioned, was 'the night of the Repose' (Moret 1909, 6, n.6; Kamal 1939, 279; Helck 1952, 78–79; Otto 1966, 40). Firstly, Moret connected it with the sleeping of the *sem*-priest (1909, 6, n.6). Helck goes further, stating in his article presenting his approach to the origin of the Mysteries, that the antecedents of the Mysteries may be traced back to the burial ceremony of the kings in the Early Dynastic Period. According to this theory, every event of the festival should refer back to a ritual celebrated during the burial. The ritual of the 'night of the Repose / Sleeping (Nacht des Schlafens) ' and the 'sleeping of the battling Horus (streitbarer Horus)' performed the same function in the course of the Mysteries as the sleeping of the *sem*-priest in the Opening of the Mouth ritual during the burial ceremony (1952, 78). Helck's argument is that *ḥr šn* – a name which is translated as the 'streitbarer Horus' – should be regarded as the 'loving son' of Osiris, a point to which we will return. The sleeping of the loving son, presumably next to his father's (on this occasion, Osiris') statue could refer to only one act: the aforementioned sleeping of the *sem* who acts during the burial ceremony as the loving son of the deceased. He interprets this ritual on the basis of the obscure words which are spoken when the *sem* wakes up: that the *sem* was wandering in his dream in the nether world searching for his father's soul.

It is generally accepted, that the name of the festival derives from the first words of a festival hymn, its original form being *h3j.k r.j,* meaning 'Come down to me' (for further discussion, see: Goodwin 1873, 15; Kamal 1939, 279; Griffith 1977, 930). According to Helck's interpretation, the meaning "Come down to me" is a call addressed by the son to his father's soul during the night of Haker, when the heir/royal successor brings back the personality of his father from the Netherworld. This act should have taken place in the House of Gold, which Helck placed in the Osiris-temple in Abydos, so the Haker should have been celebrated after coming back from Poker. This theory was accepted by Otto (1966, 40) and by Kubisch (2003, 277). However, later it was demonstrated that in the case of the mysteries there should be a place called the 'House of Gold' also in Poker (Anthes 1974, 32, 35). Because of that, Gilliam (2005, 56–58), while accepting the association with the sleeping of the *sem*, identifies the Haker with the night in Poker. It should also be noted that this explanation of the sleeping of the *sem*-priest is rejected by Fischer-Elfert (1997,65, n. 150; contra: Neureiter 2005, 313–330).

The night of the Vigil

The translation of the word *sḏrt / sḏryt* as 'vigil' (Nachtwache) was first recommended by Spiegel (1973, 147), and accepted by Lichtheim (1988, 88, 100) and – at least in connection with Hor Shen – Assmann (2001, 311, 355). Lichtheim (1988, 100) and Lavier (1988, 291) identified the Haker with the night in Poker. Assmann proved that already in the Middle Kingdom, during the night before the burial, 'the night of the justification' ('Nacht der Rechtfertigung'), there was a vigil in the form of Stundenwache in the embalming hall (1986, 104). He states that the night of Haker and the *Nṯryt*-night (the night before the Procession of the Henu-barque by the Festival of Sokar) have the same function in the festivals at Abydos and Memphis as the last night in the embalming hall, during which various rituals were celebrated to prepare the god for his procession (2001, 311, 355). This night in the embalming hall is spent in mourning and with lamentation, so the words 'Come down to me' could be the beginning of the lamentation (Assmann *et al.* 2005, 475).

On Louvre C 166 (dated to the reign of Senwosret I) we encounter the following enumeration: 'Sailing to Poker, Haker, *r grḥ n sḏrt*' followed by a date: I *3ḫt* 20 (cited by Spalinger 1996, 44, n. 63). This suggests that these festivals were celebrated on the same day, and if these are enumerated in chronological order, then the Haker was celebrated after the god's statue was carried to Poker, supporting the above hypothesis. Before showing how problematic the hypothesis is in spite of this, it is worth summarising what is known about the god named Hor Shen.

'The battling Horus'

As we mentioned above, Helck translated the name *ḥr šn* as 'Streitbarer Horus' referring to the Pyramid Texts (PT 220 § 195e, PT 221 § 198d). He explained the nature of this god as the mythical aspect of the new king who comes to power after his father's death (Helck 1952, 74). This is accepted by later scholars (Spiegel 1973, 147; 'Horus-the-fighter': Lichtheim 1988, 79, 88; 'the battling Horus': Griffith 1977, 929–930). In the Lexikon de Ägyptischen Götter und Götterbezeichnungen (LGG) however, there is no suggestion of what the name of the god Hor Shen could mean in connection with the Haker (Leitz *et al.* 2002, 292b).

Earlier the name was explained as 'Horus, lying smitten by enchantment' (Goodwin 1873, 15; Kamal 1939, 279) or it was regarded not as a god but as the name of an area, the place of the First Procession (Dakin 1938, 191 n.6). This misinterpretation goes back to the fact that Hor Shen was also a geographical name. We encounter the ephitet of Upuaut as the 'Lord of Hor Shen' in the tombs of El-Hagarsa dated to the 6th Dynasty (the tomb of Sobeknofer: Petrie 1908, 17, Pl. XIII, see also Kanawati *et al.* 1993, 28, 30; and the tomb of An-Ankhi: Kanawati *et al.* 1993, 46) and from two stelae found in Abydos also dated to the 6th Dynasty (Borchardt 1964, 55–56, no. 1575; 86, no. 1615). Gauthier (1928, 139) suggested that it was the name of the necropolis of Athribis. It was assumed by Gomaà (1977, 929) and suggested in the LGG (Leitz *et al.* 2002, 292c) that the place of el-Hagarsa should be identified with Hor Shen, but this hypothesis has not been satisfactorily proven. What seems certain is that it should be located in the 8th nome of Upper Egypt, probably close to Abydos (Zibelius 1978, 231).

Helck (1952, 74, n.8) showed that the 'canal' (Gardiner N 36) or 'desert, foreign land' (Gardiner N 25) determinative is often used in the writing of the name of the god Hor Shen. He suggests that the reason for this could be that the original meaning of the name of the god 'Hor Shen' was already obscure in the Middle Kingdom. Zibelius concluded that this writing could be an intentional play on the fact that in the Mysteries Upuaut acts as the loving son, as 'Hor Shen' (see below), while also being the lord of a place called Hor Shen (1978, 232).

This topic needs further investigation; the most important fact is the mentioned connection between Hor Shen and Upuaut, which was first realized by Helck (1952, 74). He drew attention to the sources, which connected the two gods together, notably to the Cairo stela CG 20516 (dated to the reign of Senwosret I; Lange and Schäfer 1908, 108–111), where we encounter the following sentence:

> 'May he see the beauty of Upuaut in the First Procession when he goes forth as Hor Shen' [cf. stela in the Ashmolean Museum (No. E 3921), translated by Dakin (1938, 191) as following: 'seeing the beauty of Upuaut in the First Procession in Shen-Hor'].

This sentence leads us to another question: if Hor Shen is connected with the First Procession, which does not lead to Poker, why should we identify the *sḏryt nt ḥr šn* with the night spent in Poker?

Was the Haker-Festival celebrated during the First Procession?

The two stelae mentioned above are not the only examples in which the Haker is connected with Upuaut and with the Procession of Upuaut. In a Cairo stelae: CG 20539 (dated to the reign of Senwosret I; Lange and Schäfer 1908, 150–158) we encounter the following phrase:

> *jr.n.j h3kr n nb.f prt Wpw3wt*

The translation by Kamal is as follows: 'I celebrated the Haker of its master (i.e. Osiris), the festival of Upuaut'. I would prefer the translation of this formula to be 'I celebrated the Haker for its master (lord)' (cf. Piankoff and Clère 1934, 161). The same sentence appears in another stela, CG 20538 (dated to the reign of Senwosret III; Lange and Schäfer 1908, 145–150), but here the word *prt* is in the plural. According to these sources Griffith (1977, 930) and Graefe (1986, 863) designate the Haker as a festival connected to the First Procession.

Was the Haker-Festival the first event of the Mysteries?

Apart from the above-mentioned sources, the Haker-Festival is also known from the private feast lists. It usually appears before the First Procession and is typically mentioned together with the Thoth-Festival and the Wag-Festival. These two mortuary festivals are also known from earlier periods and other places across Egypt, but in Abydos they are connected with the Mysteries (for more about fitting the Wag-Festival into the course of the Mysteries, see Winter 1951, 15–50).

On one of the stelae of Upuaut-aa (Munich GL. WAF 35; the earlier Leiden V 4 also belonged to this individual, see: Spalinger 1996, 44–45), dated to the time of Amenemhet II, they are enumerated as follows: Wag-Festival, Thoth-Festival, Haker-Festival, First Procession, and Great Procession. Spiegel, after analysing the text of the Louvre C 35 (dated to the reign of Senwosret I or Amenemhat II: Lichtheim 1988, 199, n.1), pointed out that the sequence of the feasts mentioned in it refers to the sequence of the feast on the Munich stela. By comparing this sequence and the date of the Great Procession ~(I *3ḫt* 22) known from the Festival-Calendar from Medinet Habu, he found that it was the correct order of the festivals. This is also supported by the fact that the Thoth-Festival was celebrated on I *3ḫt* 19, thus the Haker would have been celebrated on I *3ḫt* 20 and the First Procession on I *3ḫt* 21 (Spiegel 1973, 150–151). We have already encountered the date I *3ḫt* 20 on the Louvre C 166 in connection with the 'Night of the Vigil' above (concerning this date, see also Leitz 1994, 44).

Supposedly, Spiegel's argument was the basis of Altenmüller's conclusion that the Haker should be understood as the first act of the Mysteries (1977, 181–182) but we have seen that on the basis of the Abydos-formula, this cannot be correct. Nevertheless, from the time of Senwosret I there is a stela of the master sculptor Shen who was, as suggested by Spalinger, involved in the making of at least one of the Upuaut-aa stelae (Spalinger 1996, 45). On this stela we encounter the Haker in plural between the *prt Mn* (in plural) and the *sḏrt Pḳr*. These two feasts were also mentioned on the Upuaut stela discussed above but there the feast was recorded side by side, and the *prt Mn* was in the singular. The position of the Haker next to the *sḏrt Pḳr* could either be the result of an attempt to present a calendrical arrangement or of the strong association between the two feasts. The intention of the calendrical arrangement was noted by Spalinger (1996, 45).

Perhaps the reason why the feast *prt Mn* – Procession of Min – appears in the plural, is that it is not only the annual feast of Min but also the name of the 30th day of the lunar month (Bleeker 1956, 70; Parker 1950, 12). This question must be left without further commentary. Considering the Haker festival itself, the cited feast list is not the only reference which mentions the Haker in the plural. We also encounter the Haker in the plural in the BD 145 (at least in the tomb of Senmut: Dorman, 1991, Pl. 69 and by Lepsius: 1842, Pl. LXIII, 54), and in the 21st Dynasty version of the BD 148 in the following context:

> 'Use it on the day(s) of the new crescent-feast, the 6th day feast, the Wag-feast, the feast of Thoth, the birth of Osiris, and the feasts of Sokar and on the nights of the Haker-feasts' (Allen 1974, 140).

What could be the reason for the Haker-Festival appearing in the plural?

The inconsistency of the sources and the fact that the Haker appears also in the plural could be explained if we assume that the Haker was celebrated more than once in the course of the Mysteries. However, if this is the case, we must answer the question: what is the reason for this? The character of the ceremony, as assigned by Spiegel, could be a good explanation. On Louvre C 35 we encounter the phrase 'Seeing his beauty ... at the great portal of Haker, whence he goes forth to his feasts of eternity'. The same phrase was reconstructed on the Louvre C 15, which is dated to the 11th Dynasty (Spiegel 1973, 145–147) and could be the earliest stela mentioning the Haker.

According to Spiegel, the sentence cited above means that the Haker was a kind of 'initial ceremony' to the main events: to the First Procession and to the Great Procession ('... charakterisiert diese Zeremonie eine Art Auftakt zu den Hauptfesten des Ersten Auszuges und des Grossen Auszuges': Spiegel 1973, 151). While Spiegel uses this statement as part of the argument for the hypothetical chronological order described above (Haker, First Procession, Great Procession), the proposal of the Haker as an 'initial' ceremony seems to be correct; that is to say, a ceremony which serves to prepare the god to go outside the temple to begin his procession, which could have been celebrated more than once over the course of the Mysteries. Müller (1937, 85) pointed out that, among other things, the hnw-gesture was the gesture executed by the priests and the nobles when the king appeared – perhaps the wish included in the Abydos-formula refers to the joy over the appearance of the god in the great portal of Haker.

In the following the passages from the Book of the Dead are analysed in order to discover more about the character of the Haker.

References to the Haker in the Book of the Dead

The longest allusion to the Haker is in Chapter 18 of the Book of the Dead:

> 'Oh Thot, who didst vindicate (*smꜣʿ ḫrw*) Osiris against his enemies, vindicate N. in the great Council (*ḏꜣḏꜣt*) that is in Abydos on this night of the *hꜣkr*-feast (at) the counting of the dead, at the reckoning of the Blessed, when dancing took place in Tjeni (*grḥ pwy n hꜣkr / m ṯnw mtw / m sjpt ꜣḫw / m ḫpr jhb m ṯn* '). As to the Great Council which is in Abydos: they are Osiris, Isis and Wepwawet'. (cf. Allen 1974, 33).

In the BD 18–20 the deceased appears before ten different divine courts, in different places and in each time invokes Thoth to justify (*smꜣʿ ḫrw*) himself against his enemies. In his invocations, the deceased mentions various events, regarded as the mythical precedent of the justification of either Horus or Osiris against their enemies. After that the members of the great Court are listed and also some kind of interpretation of the occasion may be given (not in our case).

As we have seen, the Haker is one such mythical precedent, therefore it is understood also in the course of the Mysteries as the occasion of the triumphant accession to the throne by Horus, having been justified before a court against his enemy, Seth (Assmann & Bommas 2002, 79–80).

Explanations for the meaning of the phrase 'counting of the dead' and the reference to the Haker in the BD 145–146.

The antecendents of the BD Chapters 18–20 are the Coffin Text Spells 337–339 (Allen 1974, 227). The phrase 'counting of the dead and reckoning of the Blessed' in the Spells 338–339 appeared in connection with the justifiation of the dead before the court of Abydos. The

Haker-festival appears already in the CT in connection with the phrase 'counting of the dead' – although only on the Theban examples, and only on the coffin B5C (numbered by de Buck) which bears the Spell 339:

> *grḥ pfy jrjt h3kr m jwnw(t) ḥsb mtw 3ḫw* (CT IV 336e [338] T2Be)
> The night of celebrating the Haker in On and counting the dead and spirits.
>
> *grḥ pfy h3kr m ṯnwt mtw m jp 3ḫw* (Coffin of Imeni, see Loprieno 2007, 79, Fig. 113)
> The night of the Haker-feast, counting the deads and reckoning the glorified ones.
>
> *hrw pfy h3kr m š m ṯnwt mtw jp jwtj-sw* (CT IV 338g [339] B5C)
> The day of the Haker-festival in the pool of numbering of the dead and reckoning of him, who has nothing.

The semantic field of the words *ḥsb, jp, ṯnw, sjp* used in this phrase was studied one by one by Zandee (Zandee 1960, 35, 269, 278, 282; see also Grieshammer 1970, 30, 48–51, Assmann *et al.* 2008, 191–192, 453). As can be seen, the phrase *ḥsb mtw 3ḫw* (T2Be) is also encountered, which suggests that the same action was executed with the *mtw* and *3ḫw*. Thus these words seem to be used as synonyms in this context. To sum up briefly, based on the above-mentioned studies; they all may be translated also as counting, assigning, making examination, judging. The word *sjp* may also refer to the execution of the judgement, and, moreover, to damnation (Hornung 1968, 10–11). The phrases *ḥsb ḳdw, jp jbw* are references to the psychostasie; but the original meaning of the epithet of Anubis – who counts the hearts – is to count the hearts of the dead enemies. With this act he not only registers them but also gains power over them (Sethe 1935, 34).

The phrase was interpreted differently by the scholars. However there is one general agreement: the term *mtw* should be interpreted as a term for the punished sinners in the realm of the dead (Zandee 1960, 199; Grieshammer 1970, 68). Griffith suggests that because of the 'association of Haker with the militant side of the Mysteries at Abydos' it may refer to counting the dead enemies, and the glorified ones can be understood as the dead who had championed Osiris (1977, 930) (cf. the aformentioned meaning of the epithet of Anubis).

According to Anthes the phrase can be interpreted as an action known from the escatological literature: the separation of the sheep from the rams ('wohl im Sinne der Scheidung der Böcke von den Schafen in der christlichen Eschatologie' Anthes 1969, 37 n. 46). In the article that he quotes as a reference to this statement (Anthes, 1969, 35) he examines the meaning of the word *jrw* and *tnw* in connection with the cattle tax and with references from the CT (CT II. 203.b, 204 c., 151e) , where the *ṯnwt* of Isis is mentioned as a hostile act against the dead person, and he shows that this metaphor goes back to the 'cattle count'. It suggests that the phrase 'counting the dead' may be interpreted in the same way. We encounter a certain *ṯnwt*-feast on the stela of Upuaut-aa and Shen, listed after the feast *sḏrt Pḳr*. This feast is translated by Faulkner (1952, 5) as the Feast of Numbering. It might be connected to the cattle counting in a certain way, which was recently interpreted by Nolan as a royal ritual (2003, 80), but because of the lack of sources it is impossible to prove.

Grieshammer (1970, 50) interpreted the phrase as the process of judging who will belong to the damned ones and who will be a blessed spirit. Assmann and Bommas (2002, 79–80) connect this phrase with the judgement of the dead, with the 'allgemeine Totengericht'. Before going into further details, it is worth examining the other references in the Book of the Dead.

The Haker appears in the invocation by Horus to the 14th Portal (*sbḫt*) of the Netherworld in the BD 145–146. The latter is the abbreviated version of the former (Allen 1960, 247). The reference to the Haker in the BD 145 has been ignored by scholars so far, although it could help to understand the character of the festival. This chapter includes the following sentence:

> 'Lady of Wrath, Dancing on Red Blood, for whom the *h3kr*-festival is celebrated with braziers (*m* *ʿḫw*), on the day of hearing wrongs (*hrw m sḏm jww*) is thy name' (Allen 1960, 240, 243). [Note, that instead of the phrase *m ʿḫw* could appear in the other versions *r ʿḫm* 'at the quenching', or *m šmm* 'with heat' and can be also omitted (Allen 1960, 243) The phrase *m ʿḫw* occurs in the version on the tomb of Senmut (Dorman 1991, PL. 69)]

The texts of the BD 145 and 146 appear first in the 18th Dynasty. They have no precursors in the Coffin Texts (cf. Allen 1974, 235), although Spell 336 could be regarded as a kind of antitype (Barthelemess 1992, 176). In the full version (extant from the New Kingdom only in the tomb of Senmut) the deceased should pass the 21 portals of the Netherworld in order to reach the Field of Rushes. In order to pass, the deceased should prove his purity at each portal, and he should also prove that he knows the name of the portal and the watchkeeper of the portal.

The phrase '*hrw m sḏm jww*' appears twice in this spell: in connection with the 14th Portal as seen above – and it was also mentioned by the invocation of the 11th Portal:

> 'She Who Cuts Repeatedly, who burns rebel, chief of all portals, to whom jubilation (hnw) is made on the day of hearing wrong, is thy name' (Allen 1974, 131).

To the phrase 'day of hearing wrongs' a parallel is found on a stela dated to the 11th Dynasty:

> 'May his ka be with him, his offerings before him, may his voice be found true at the reckoning of the surplus (*ḥsbt ʿ3w*). Tell your fault (*ḏd.k jw.k*) and it all shall be removed for you from all you have told (...)' (stela of the Troop Commander Intef, Ny Carlsberg Glyptothek Inv. 963, translated by Lichtheim 1988, 62–63).

The connection between the phrase *ḏd.k jw.k* and *hrw n sḏm jww* was also noted by Clère (1931, 445). Clère (1931, 426–447) analysed the meaning of the phrase '*ḥsbt ʿ3w*' which seems to be the occasion when the fault should be told. He concluded that this could be an allusion to the process when, during the judgement of the dead, the heart was weighed on a balance before the divine court (see also Zandee 1960, 269; Willems 1988, 148). Zandee (1960, 269–270) discussed the occurences of the same phrase in the Coffin Texts and approved the suggestion of Clère. This association does not mean necessarily that the phrase 'counting of the dead and reckoning of the glorified ones' should be interpreted as the same allusion and not as an allusion to another aspect of the feast, but makes such an interpretation probable.

Reconstruction of the celebrated rituals

The question must now be asked, whether the references in the BD 18 and 145–146 could be interpreted as some kind of allusion as to how the feast was celebrated. It should be noted that the conclusion about the nature and frequency of the Haker was based mainly on Middle Kingdom sources and the celebration of the Haker in the 18th Dynasty may have been different. On the one hand there are also references in the Book of the Dead where the Haker appears in the plural as seen above. On the other hand, as will be seen, on analysing the references it was found that these may be in correlation with our hypothesis about the initial nature of the Haker.

Based on these observations we assume that there were no major differences in the way the Haker was celebrated in the Middle Kingdom and in the 18th Dynasty.

First, concentrating on the phrase 'when dancing (*jhb*) took place in Tjen (Thinis)', the word *jhb* was generally translated as 'dance' which led to various interpretations (Kees 1956,] 242; Griffith 1977, 930; Helck 1952, 79). However this word is convincingly explained by Brunner-Traut (1938, 80–81) as a word for recitation of a festival hymn. Originally it may mean singing a joyous song accompanied by movement (a kind of dance), and refers to the similar action that is described by the word *hnw*. Relating to the sentence in the BD, Brunner-Traut suggests also the translation 'recitation of a festival hymn' rather than a dance. This seems acceptable, because in this case it may refer to the wish in the Abydos-formula. The jubilation may express, as mentioned above, the joy over the appearance of the god; in the Pyramid Texts it also could be connected to the joy over the vindication (*smꜣꜥ-ḫrw*) of the dead pharaoh (see the discussion of Anthes 1954, 28–29, 31).

The phrase 'counting the dead' is also explained as an allusion to the following: During the Mysteries on the night of the Haker, the dwellers of the necropolis are summoned before the judges in the netherworld, and those who lived according to the Osirian moral would have been declared blessed spirits (Lavier 1988, 291). Although this is also a possible interpretation, in the CT Spell 338 four of the nine events listed in parallel with the night of the Haker, counting the dead and reckoning the glorified ones have direct allusion to the Osiris-myth: on that night of making war and of felling the rebels, on that night of confirming the heritage of Horus in the matter of his father, on that night of Isis making mourning for her brother Osiris, on that night when Horus was vindicated against his enemies. Three others are references to certain feasts (Evening Meal in Letopolis, erecting the djed-pillars, ploughing up the earth). These are in the BD 18 also connected to a certain part of the Osiris-myth. Considering these passages we suggest an interpretation of the phrase counting the dead not as a concrete allusion to what would happen to the dwellers of the necropolis but rather as a kind of mythological reference.

Now it is relevant here to closer examine the passage from the BD 145–146. In connection with the *ḥsbt ꜥꜣw* Willems ascertained that a ceremonial passage of the divine tribunal was included in the burial rituals (1988, 148), the time before the mummy was carried out from the embalming hall (1988,146). If we accept the association between the Haker and the *ḥsbt ꜥꜣw* ritual, and assume that the function of the Haker was similar to the function of the *ḥsbt ꜥꜣw* ritual, than it may be concluded that the Haker may have been celebrated just before the god was carried out of the temple. This idea could fit our hypothesis regarding the initial nature of the ceremony of the Haker.

The rite *ḥsbt ꜥꜣw* may have included a kind of ritual slaughter, which symbolises the destroying of the enemy (Seth) (1988, 149–150). Ritual slaughter is mentioned in the BD 18 in connection with other feasts, which are designated also as mythical precedents of the justification of Horus or Osiris: the *ḫbs-tꜣ* ritual is explained in the text as the slaughter of Seth and his fellows in their form as goats. Slaughter is also depicted elsewhere in the ritual 'raising the djed' (van der Vliet, 409); ritual slaughter and burning known in connection with the Evening Meal (for example see the analysis by Ritner 1990, 30–31, Wainwright 1932, 159–172). The mention of the braziers (*ꜥḫw*) in connection with the Haker could also refer to a similar ritual (cf. for example Eyre 2002, 107–109), although the phrases in the later variations (*m šmm, r ꜥḫm*) may suggest a different explanation.

Conclusion

This hypothesis is that the reason for the contradiction of the sources could be the fact that the Haker was celebrated more than once. It may have been a kind of initial ceremony: the hidden part of it included the ritual destruction of the enemies of Osiris, which was then followed by the public part of the ceremony. The public part contained the triumphant appearance of the god accompanied by jubilation, perhaps celebrated by the priests (cf. the lines 26–29 of the Neferhotep stela and the interpretation of the text: Anthes, 1974, 20, 28–29). It was celebrated at the beginning of the processions, and also at the end of the night spent in Poker, before the procession leading back to Abydos.

It should be noted that this hypothesis does not explain everything. It seems to be difficult to fit into this concept the traditional explanation for the name of the festival ('Come down to me!'). Investigating the references to the Haker in the late funerary literature (see for example. Herbin 1994, 99, 235) may also result in interesting conclusions. But for now I hope that I have managed to outline the main problems concerning the reconstruction of the festival and to show at least a possible approach to how the character of the festival could be described.

Eötvös Loránd University, Budapest

Bibliography

Allen, T. G. (1960) *The Egyptian Book of the Dead: Documents in the Oriental Institute Museum at the University of Chicago,* Chicago, Oriental Institute Publications, University Of Chicago Press.

Allen, T. G. (1974) *The Book of the Dead or Going Forth By Day. Ideas of the ancient Egyptians Concerning the Hereafter as Expressed In Their Own Terms, Studies In Ancient Oriental Civilization No. 37,* Chicago, University Of Chicago Press.

Altenmüller, H. (1977) 'Feste', in Helck, W. and Otto, E. (eds), *Lexikon der Ägyptologie II*, cols.171–191.

Anthes, R. (1954) 'The Original Meaning of *mꜣꜥ ḫrw*', *Journal of Near Eastern Studies* 13, 21–50.

Anthes, R. (1969) 'Die nominalbildungen jrwt "Zeremonien" und jrw "Benehmen" und "Abrechnung"', *Mitteilungen des Deutschen Archäologischen Instituts Abteilung Kairo* 24, 26–37.

Anthes, R. (1974) 'Die Berichte des Neferhotep und des Ichernofret über das Osirisfest in Abydos', in Müller, W. (ed.), *Festschrift zur 150 Jahrigen Bestehen des Berliner Ägyptischen Museum, Mitteilungen aus der Ägyptischen Sammlung 8,* Berlin, Akademie Verlag, 15–49.

Assmann, J. (1986) 'Stundenwache', in Helck, W. and Otto, E (eds), *Lexikon der Ägyptologie* V, cols.104–106.

Assmann, J. (2001) *Tod und Jenseits im Alten Ägypten*, Munich, Verlag C.H. Beck.

Assmann, J. and Bommas, M. (2002) *Altägyptische Totenliturgie I: Totenliturgien in den Sargtexten des Mittleren Reiches,* Heidelberg, Universitätverlag C. Winter.

Assmann, J., Bommas, M. and Kucharek, A. (2005) *Altägyptische Totenliturgie II: Totenliturgien und Totensprüche in Grabinschriften des Neuen Reiches*. Heidelberg, Universitätverlag Winter.

Assmann, J., Bommas, M. and Kucharek, A. (2008) *Altägyptische Totenliturgie III: Osirisliturgien in Papyri der Spätzeit*, Heidelberg, Universitätverlag Winter.

Barthelemess, P. (1992) *Der Übergang ins Jenseits in den thebanischen Beamtengräbern der Ramessidenzeit, Studien zur Archäologie und Geschichte Altägyptens 2*, Heidelberg, Heidelberges Orientalverlag.

de Buck, A. (1951–1961) *The Egyptian Coffin Texts,* Chicago, University of Chicago Press (volumes II, IV).

Bleeker, C. J. (1956) *Die Geburt eines Gottes. Eine Studie über den Ägyptischen Gott Min und sein Fest,* Leiden, E.J. Brill.

Borchardt, L. (1964) *Denkmäler des Alten Reiches (außer den Statuen) im Museum von Kairo*, CG Nr. 1295–1808, Teil *II*: Text und Tafel zur Nr. 1542–1808, Cairo-Berlin.

Brunner-Traut, E. (1938) *Der Tanz im Alten Ägypten nach bildichen und inschriftlichen Zeugnissen, Ägyptologische Forschungen 6*, Glückstadt.

Clère, J. J. (1931) Un passage de la stèle du général Intef (Glyptothèque Ny Carlsberg, Coppenhague), *Bulletin de l'Institut Français d'Archéologie Orientale* 30, 425–447.

Dakin, A. N. (1938) The Stela of the Sculptor Sirē' at Oxford, *Journal of Egyptian Archeology* 24, 190–197.

Dorman, P. F. (1991) The Tombs of Senenmut: *The Architecture and Decoration of Tombs 71 and 353, Publications of the Metropolitan Museum of Art Egyptian Expedition 24*, New York, Metropolitan Museum of Art.

Eaton, K. (2004) *The Ritual Functions of Processional Equipments in the Temple of Seti I at Abydos,* New York, Ph.D. Dissertation, UMI Dissertation Services, New York University.

Eyre, C. (2002) *The Cannibal Hymn: A Cultural and Literary Study*, Liverpool, Liverpool University Press.

Faulkner, R. (1952) 'The Stela of the Master-Sculptor Shen', *Journal of Egyptian Archeology* 38, 3–5.

Fischer-Elfert, H.-W. (1997) *Die Vision von der Statue im Stein. Studien zum altägyptischen Mundöffnungsritual,* Heidelberg, Universitätverlag C. Winter.

Gauthier, H. (1928) 'Dictionnaire des noms géographiques contenus dans les textes hiéroglyphiques Tome V', *Société* royale de géographie d'Egypte, Le Caire.

Gilliam, R. (2005) *Performance and Drama in Ancient Egypt*, London, Duckworth Egyptology.

Gomaà, F. (1977) 'El-Hagarsa', in Helck, W. and Otto, E. (eds), *Lexikon der Ägyptologie II*, col. 929.

Goodwin, C. W. (1873) 'Notes from unpublished papyri', *Zeitschrift für Ägyptische Sprache und Altertumskunde* 9, 15–16.

Graefe, E (1986) 'Upuaut', in Helck, W. and Otto, E. (eds), *Lexikon der Ägyptologie* V, cols. 862–864.

Griffith, J. G. (1977) 'Haker', in Helck, W. and Otto, E. (eds), *Lexikon der Ägyptologie* II, cols. 929–931.

Grieshammer, R. (1970) 'Das Jenseitsgericht in den Sargtexten', *Ägyptologische Abhandlungen* 20, Wiesbaden, Otto Harrassowitz.

Hannig, R. (2006) *Ägyptisches Wörterbuch II. Mittleres Reich und Zweite Zwischenzeit*, Lexica-Hannig 5, Mainz am Rhein, Verlag Philippe von Zabern.

Helck, W. (1952) 'Herkunft des Abydenischen Osirisrituals', *Archiv Orientální 20*, 72–85.

Herbin, F. R. (1994) *Le Livre de parcourir l'Éternité, Orientalia Lovaniensia Analecta* 58, Leuven, Uitgeverij Peeters.

Hornung, E. (1968) *Altägyptische Höllenvorstellungen, Abhandlungen der Sächsischen Akademie der Wissenschaften zu Leipzig*, 59 / 3, Berlin, Akademie Verlag.

Kamal, M. (1939) 'The Stela of *sḥtp-jb-r*ᶜ in the Egyptian Museum', *Annales du Service des Antiquités de l'Égypte* 38, 265–283.

Kees, H. (1956) *Totenglauben und Jenseitsvorstellungen der alten Ägypter - Grundlagen und Entwicklung bis zum Ende des Mittleren Reiches*, Berlin, Akademie Verlag.

Kanawati, N., Charoubim, N., McFarlane, A., Thompson, E. and Victor, N. (1993) *The tombs of el-Hagarsa,* Volume I, Sydney, The Australian Centre of Egyptology, Report 4.

Kubisch, S. (2003) 'Wer wurde eingeweiht in die Geheimnisse des heiligen Platzes?', *Mitteilungen des Deutschen Archäologischen Instituts Abteilung Kairo* 59, 269–282.

Lange, H. O. and Schäfer, H. (1908) *Grab- und Denksteine des Mittleren Reichs,* Theil II: Text zu No. 20400–20780, Berlin.

Lavier, M-C. (1988) Les Mystères d'Osiris à Abydos d'après le stèles du Moyen Empire et du Nouvel Empire, in Schoske, S. (ed), *Akten des Vierten Intenationalen Ägyptologenkongressus, München, 1985*, SAK Beihefte 3, Hamburg, Helmut Buske Verlag, 289–295.

Leahy, A. (1989) 'A Protective Measure at Abydos', *Journal of Egyptian Archeology* 75, 41–60.

Leitz, C. (1994) *Tagewählerei. Das Buch ḥ3t nḥḥ pḥ.wy dt*, Wiesbaden, Harrassowitz Verlag.

Leitz, C. (ed.) (2002) *Lexikon de Ägyptischen Götter und Götterbezeichnungen Band V, Orientalia Lovaniensia Annalecta 114*, Leuven, Uitgeverij Peeters.

Lepsius, R. (1842) *Das Todtenbuch der Ägypter nach dem hieroglyphischen Papyrus in Turin*, Leipzig, G.Wigand.

Lichtheim, M. (1988) *Ancient Egyptian Autobiographies Chiefly of the Middle Kingdom: a Study and an Anthology,* Freiburg, Orbis Biblicus et Orientalis 84, Universitätverlag.

Loprieno, A. (2007) 'Text für das Jenseits: Die Inschriften der Särge des Imeni und der Geheset', in Polz, D. (ed.), *Für das Ewigkeit geschaffen. Die Särge des Imeni und der Geheset*, Mainz am Rhein, Verlag Philipp von Zabern.

Moret, A. (1909) *Catalogue du Musée Guimet. Galerie Égyptienne: Stèles, Bas reliefs, Monuments divers*, Annales du Museum Guimet 32, Paris, Ernest Leroux.

Müller, H.-W. (1937) 'Darstellungen von Gebärden auf Denkmälern des Alten Reiches', *Mitteilungen des Deutschen Institut für Ägyptische Altertumskunde in Kairo* 7, 57–118.

Neureiter, S. (2005) 'Schamanismus im Alten Ägypten', *Studien zur Altägyptischen Kultur 33*, 281–330.

Nolan, J. S. (2003) 'The Original Lunar Calendar and Cattle Counts in Old Kingdom Egypt', in Bickel, S. and Loprieno, A. (eds) *Basel Egyptology Prize: Junior Research in Egyptian History, Archaeology, and Philology*, 75–97, Basel, Schwabe & Co. AG.

Otto, E. (1966) *Osiris und Amun: Kult und heilige Stätten*, München, Himmer Verlag.

Parker, R. A. (1950) *The Calendars of Ancient Egypt, Studies In Ancient Oriental Civilization No. 26*, Chicago, University Of Chicago Press.

Piankoff, A. and Clère, J. J. (1934) 'A Letter to the Dead on a Bowl in the Louvre', *Journal of Egyptian Archeology* 20, 157–169.

Petrie, W. M. F. (1908) *Athribis*, London, British School of Archaeology in Egypt 14.

Ritner, R. K. (1990) 'O. Gardiner 363: A Spell Against Night Terror', *Journal of the American Research Center in Egypt* 27, 25–41.

Schäfer, H. (1905) *Die Mysterien des Osiris in Abydos unter König Sesostris III nach dem Denkstein des Oberschatzmeisters I-cher-nofret im Berliner Museum, Untersuchungen zur Geschichte und Altertumskunde Aegyptens Band IV*, Leipzig, J.C. Hinrich, 47–88.

Sethe, K. (1935) *Übersetzung und Kommentar zu den altägyptischen Pyramidentexten*, Glückstadt.

Spalinger, A. (1996) *The Private Feat Lists of Ancient Egypt*, Wiesbaden, Harrassowitz Verlag.

Spiegel, J. (1973) *Die Götter von Abydos. Studien zum ägyptischen Synkretismus, Veröffentlichungen der Sonderforschungsbereiches Orientalistik and der Georg-August-Universtität Göttingen, IV. Reihe: Ägypten, Band I*, Wiesbaden, Otto Harrassowitz.

van der Vliet, J. (1988) 'Raising the Djed: A Rite' Schoske, S (ed.), *Akten des Vierten Intenationalen Ägyptologenkongressus, München, 1985*, SAK Beihefte 3, Hamburg, Helmut Buske Verlag, 405–411.

Wainwright, G. A. (1932) 'Letopolis', *Journal of Egyptian Archeology* 18, 159–175.

Willems, H. (1988) *Chest of Life. A Study of the Typology and Conceptual Development of Middle Kingdom Standard Class Coffins*, Leiden, Ex oriente lux.

Winter, E. (1951) *Das ägyptische Wag-Fest*, Wien, Unpublished Ph.D. Dissertation, Universität Wien.

Zandee, J. (1960) *Death as Enemy according to the Egyptian Conceptions*, Leiden, E.J. Brill.

Zibelius, K. (1978) *Ägyptische Siedlungen nach Texten des Alten Reiches, Beihefte zum Tübingen Atlas des Vorderen Orients, Reihe B (Geistgewissenschaften)*, No. 19, Dr. Wiesbaden, Ludwig Reichert Verlag.

The Images of Fortifications in the Sety I Battle Reliefs: Comparing Art and Archaeology

Nicholas E. Wernick

The study of warfare in ancient Egypt is a dynamic field in which new finds add to our current body of evidence. However, one must be consciously aware that we must constantly revaluate older theories for purposes of cohesion. An examination of ancient Egyptian warfare can start at many different aspects but each has their inherent pitfalls. For instance, if we were to examine weaponry, we must always keep in mind that the majority of weapon artefacts come from burial contexts and, in most cases, do not show signs of use. Furthermore, if we were to examine human remains from the period in question, we also must be aware that these examples may be murder victims or persons that were killed within a complex socio-religious context. Fortifications hold a certain appeal as a starting point because they can rely on both artistic depictions and archaeological remains. However, the study of fortifications is not without its own inherent shortcomings. This can be seen in the comments from William Hamblin (2005, 10–11). Hamblin claims that using 'martial art' as a starting point for ancient Near Eastern warfare examinations, has three main issues:

> ***Idealization:*** Keeping in mind that art is selectively recreated, not objectively captured, we should try to avoid using these martial scenes as our sole source for our interpretations as it may show certain personages and actions as being eternally victorious and the outcome being a 'foregone conclusion' (Gaballa 1967, 316).
>
> ***Conceptualization:*** Martial scenes may not actually depict an action that has taken place but may be presented as a kind of offering to either the deities the designers believed in or to directly communicate with an audience that would view the scene.
>
> ***Anachronism:*** The composition of the scenes may include archaizing features and may mislead one in their interpretations. This is best exemplified by a modern comparison of military units employing the use of swords and shields in their crests but actually using such sophisticated devices as night-vision goggles, artillery, and machine guns to achieve their aims.

The war scenes that are most often focused upon by researchers come from the 19th Dynasty (1295–1186 BC). During this period, we encounter scenes that are more episodic and lively in their compositions. The features of the characters in these scenes, the sense of motion, the raw fortitude portrayed in the battles connects us emotionally to this period in time. It is thought that it is possible to trace the pattern of political conflict through this period of time based simply on these scenes, none more so than the scenes from Sety I (1294–1279 BCE) located on the exterior of the northern wall of the Hypostyle Hall at Karnak Temple (Murnane 1985, 53). These scenes portray Sety I as he campaigned throughout his reign, performing a *reconquista* to reassert Egypt's control over foreign holdings in the Levant. Interestingly, the scenes contain a total of thirteen fortresses. Can they be used to reconstruct what ancient Egyptian fortifications looked like? We could classify these fortress-images as being hieroglyphic 'ideograms', images that acted as a kind of symbol for communication rather than a depiction that can communicate the facts about ancient fortifications in the Late Bronze Age (the 'LBA', 1600–1200 BC). However, when compared with archaeological sites we can tell that some of the images do portray information that can provide at least clues to how ancient fortifications were planned. Of course we must always keep Hamblin's points in mind when looking at these images of forts. However, to classify that no information at all can be obtained is to ignore the facts that some things in the scenes do relate to the archaeological record.

Layout of the Sety Scenes

The scenes of Sety I's campaigns are divided into three registers on the North side of the East wall of the Hypostyle hallway at Karnak. The registers are divided by a doorway in the centre that separates the registers into six entities. Each scene is displayed with an orientation towards the doorway in that the battle itself takes place at the furthest end from the doorway while the return to Egypt and the presentation of prisoners to Amun-re and other deities are placed closest to the doorway; the "distance-to-doorway" principle (Figs. 1 & 2). Although there has been a lot of dispute about the sequence in which the scenes should be read (Broadhurst 1989, 229), this paper shall try to focus on the images of fortresses contained within them.

The Shasu campaign (bottom left register)

The depiction of Sety I's first campaign into the North Sinai and southern Palestine is located on the bottom left register. The route across the North Sinai was an artery for trade goods and armies in the ancient world and represented a strategic area to control. The strongholds that Sety I marches past in this relief are thought to represent a series of Egyptian-held fortresses that would supply Egyptian armies and control traffic on the road. At first glance, these small fortresses appear to be a copy of one another but that is an over-simplification. Every image of each fort appears to have a different composition and different proportions.

It should be noted that at the time of Gardiner's publication, he was concerned about the poor condition of this particular section of the reliefs (Gardiner 1920, 101–2). They have not fared much better in modern times. However, the University of Chicago completed an epigraphic survey in 1986 to record the Sety I reliefs and this remains the basis for our artistic analysis (Chicago Ep. S. 1986).

The names of these fortresses, Gardiner discovered, can be weighed against a passage in Papyrus Anastasi I (Gardiner 1920; Cavillier 2001, 23). In this section of the papyrus, various locations are sequentially laid out according to a topographical plan. It is this section that deals directly with the route across the North Sinai that we turn our attention to because it lists the particular names for twelve fortresses. On the Karnak relief there is a total of twenty names, each describing bodies of water or a fortified outpost. Despite Gardiner's reservations regarding accuracy, he thought it possible to determine the relative geographic positions of the fortresses based on the reliefs. He does claim that the fortresses do fall into geographic order in Papyrus Anastasi I. That is, the papyrus starts at the "Ways of Horus" fortress, the nearest fort located in the Delta, and proceeds to list fortresses along the North Sinai route as far as Gaza, which marks the start of Canaan (Gardiner 1920, 103). Correlating the names in the Papyrus Anastasi I with the reliefs, then, it is possible to attempt to determine alternate names for these fortresses and so forth.

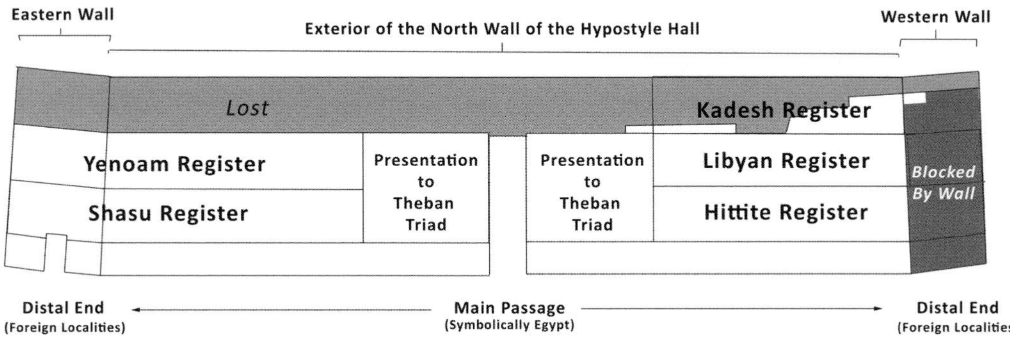

Figure 1. Layout of the Battle Scenes of Sety I at Karnak.

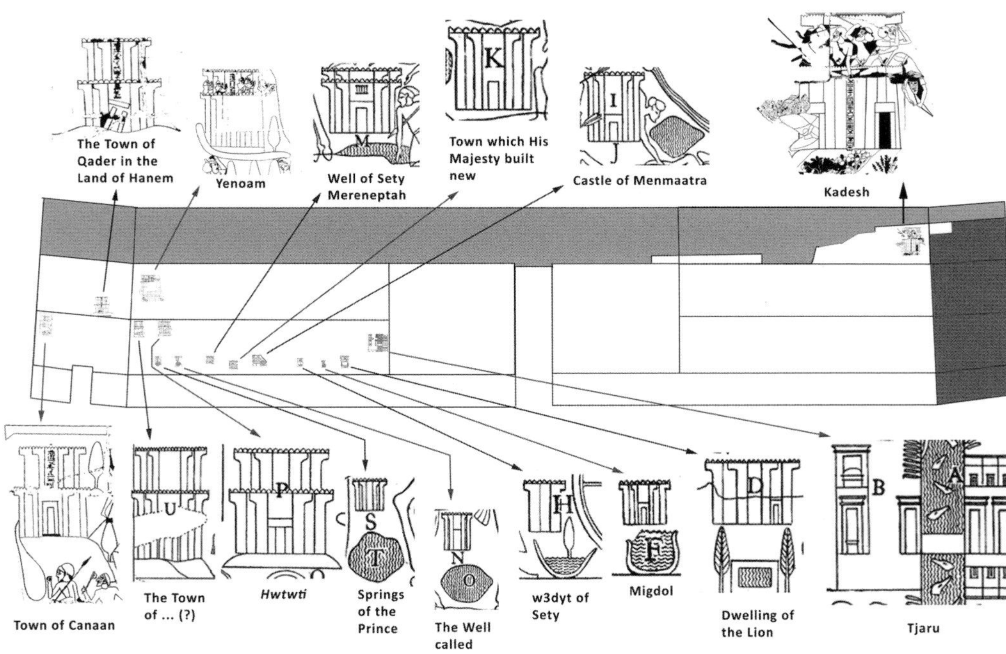

Figure 2. Layout of Fortifications within the Sety I Battle Scenes.

If we are to accept the distance-to-doorway principle, the fortress closest to Egypt is indicated by its placement closest to the doorway of the Hypostyle Hall. In this scene, Sety I returns from his campaign leading three lines of prisoners, who are identified as *Retenu* in the presentation scene (Gaballa 1967, 321). The fortress appears to have been a structure that had a water body dividing it (the canal's name is written in hieroglyphs, dubbing it "The Dividing Waters") (Fig. 2). On either side of the water there are two gates (making four in all). One gate faces the exterior while another internal gate gives access to a causeway across the water (Chicago

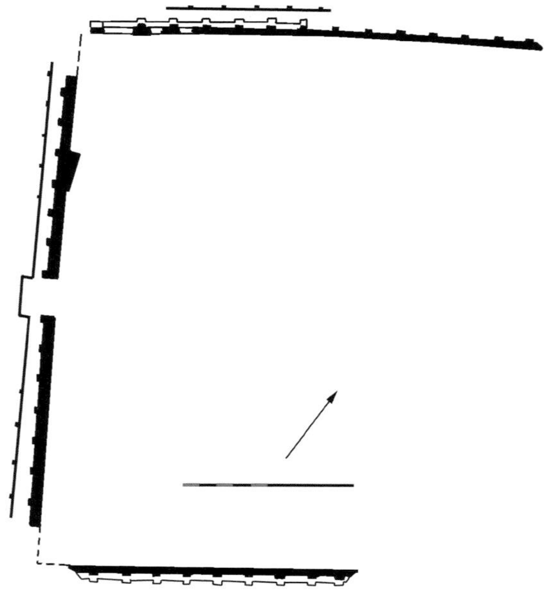

Figure 3. *Outline of the walls of Tell Heboua (redrawn from Maksoud and Vabelle 2005, fig. 1).*

Ep. S. 1986, 26). The eastern side of the fortress has a gate with a rectangular aperture with a defined cornice above it, like all of the gates in this fortress. Above the exterior, Delta-side gate, there is another level that also has a cornice on it; a single, rounded merlon in its opening. The position and angle of orientation seems to indicate that this was a tower above the doorway. It is interesting that these gateways are so characteristic of the Amarna period representations of gate-portals. The identity inscription of the fortress is located on the furthest side (presumably the start of the Sinai), between the two gates. It reads, "The fortress of Tjaru". Looking at this fortress, it is very interesting that it does deviate from the typical image of the fortress in this relief. Given that supply lines will always be stronger at the source, it may be a fortified enclosure of a settled population rather than a frontier fortress.

The fortress of Tjaru has been equated with the site of Tell Heboua, located in the region of Qantara (Fig. 3) (Morris 2005; Maksoud and Vabelle 2005; Hoffmeier 2003). What makes the site very promising for the correlation with the Sety I reliefs is that the site was situated on the edge of a paleo-lagoon. There are satellite settlements on the other side of the water inlet (Heboua II, III and IV). Tell Heboua I, which has been the main focus of the archaeological investigation so far, has a massive mud-brick enclosure wall. Given that the site is very large, covering at least 120,000 sq. meters (Maksoud 1998, 111), this site could be dubbed a "fortified city". Its representation in the Sety reliefs, as being separate from a 'typical fortress' along the Ways of Horus, has led us to perceive it as more a base for a city than an outpost on the frontier. Interestingly, this site also possessed an 'outwork wall'. It was only 1.2 m in thickness which stands in contrast to the 'main wall' which was 4–5 m in thickness. This is where the image of Tjaru differs from the Sety I reliefs as this secondary wall is not depicted. The wall is not flat and continuous but has a series of projections at regular intervals. This is another item that was not depicted in the Sety reliefs. Of the gateways, only one gateway has been found so far at Tell Heboua I. This gateway is placed between two buttresses and was situated on the western side of the fortress. This is the side at which one would arrive at the fortress if coming from the direction of the Nile (Morris 2005, 59). Unfortunately, the gateway is not preserved to a height that allows detection of a tower with a rounded merlon but the gateway does not appear to have been corniced, as in the reliefs. In keeping with perceptions that this fortress would have supplied Levant-bound armies, Maksoud claims that the granaries here could have stored 178.35 metric tons of grain (Maksoud 1998, 119–20).

Going back to the first register of the Sety I reliefs and moving left, we come to our next fortress. It is worth mentioning that only the top half of this installation is still preserved today and we must use Gardiner's drawings to reconstruct its composition. The identity of this fortress is written as "The Dwelling of the Lion". This image appears to be quite stout with the top border capped by semi-circular merlons. There are four vertical sections that flare out at a right angle and then continue vertically. These vertical sections appear as an upside-down "L" shape (for the remainder of this paper, they will be referred to as "piers"). This shape suggests that they represent an overhang that allowed the defenders to rain arrows and stones upon attackers (functioning as *machicouli*) (Wright 1985, i, 177; Yadin 1963, 20). The rectangular gateway is positioned off to the western side between two piers. Reconstructed from previous drawings, a manicured rectangular pool is shown outside (situated below the fort) that was flanked on either side by trees. The overall image of the fortress and the pool is that this was an area still relatively close to Egypt and that could experience some of the benefits of civilization. Furthermore, as we progress in the Shasu register, the shapes of these external pools become much more rugged and wild. Perhaps, alluding to the distance-to-doorway principle, the area beyond Egypt proper was less ordered than in their world-view.

Tentatively identified by James Hoffmeier as being the fortress corresponding to the second fort of the reliefs, "Dwelling of the Lion", is the site of Tell el Borg (Hoffmeier 2006, 257). The remains of two fortresses were found at Tell el Borg between 2000 and 2004. Hoffmeier speculates that the initial fortress was constructed in the time of Thutmose III or Amenhotep III and used until the Amarna period when it was dismantled. A new installation was built, possibly under Horemheb or Sety I (Hoffmeier 2006, 262). The site is located 2–3 km west of the paleo-lagoon mentioned earlier. One feature in Field VIII that survives from the early fortress is a moat or fosse. The moat's outer dimensions are 120 meters long and 80 meters wide (it ends abruptly). Hoffmeier claims that, for some reason, this moat was never completed and probably never served a functional feature for the defence of the fortress (2006, 261). Another fosse was discovered, dating to the 19th dynasty, but it appears that it never completely surrounded the fortress. Perhaps this is the reason why a fosse is not depicted in the Sety reliefs. It was not an integral feature of the fortress and thus did not need to be communicated to the viewer. The 19th Dynasty fortress was square and measured roughly 70 meters on each side (covering 4900 sq. m.) (It should be mentioned that half of the 19th dynasty fortress was destroyed by the modern canal). It is thus possible to suggest an explanation for the existence of the four tower-piers in the depiction of fortresses. The Egyptian artist uses these piers to represent the four corners of the square installation, as if it were 'unfolded'. Interestingly, Field IV yielded a cistern that had three steps down to it – it appears that this depression continued in use for the secondary building of the fortress of the 19th dynasty. Hoffmeier speculates that this was an installation where water could be collected within the fortress. Could this be another deviation from the scenes with a prominent water body outside the fortress? The gateway is 13.5 m wide based on the distance between the fort's walls, which are 3.8m wide, and was directly accessed. However, the gateway does have two parallel walls that extend for 11m and end in a square foundation, made from local caliche stone, that measure 1 m sq. Therefore, the image of the fortress's gateway is in keeping with the archaeological evidence as being rectangular and being displayed 'head-on', avoiding trying to display these projections from the gateway.

The remaining archaeological sites that can be equated with being a 'frontier fortress' cannot be directly correlated to a particular depiction of a fort in the Shasu Campaign. (Preliminary reports of Tell Abyad do indicate a Ramesside residence but further work must be carried out before a correlation to the third fortress can be claimed (Leclère and Valbelle 2008, 32)). Therefore, the rest of the Egyptian fortresses in this register need examining in order to recognize their composition and how they differ from one another. The next fortress is located between the back hooves of the horses and Sety's chariot. Unfortunately, this fortress is totally lost now and so Gardiner's reconstruction has to be relied upon (Gardiner 1920: pl. XI). The fortress appears to have the four towers but the rectangular gate is positioned at the front this time. A water body lies outside this fortress, shaped in a steep 'U', and represents a 'profile-view' of the pool/cistern. Curiously, the water body shape stands in contrast to the previous fort's "bird's eye view". The merlons of this fortress are semi-circular. The next fortress is now totally destroyed, thus earlier scholars' observations have to be relied upon. This fort was located between the chariot's wheel and the attendant following the king. The merlons are clearly rounded but there are only two tower piers with no gate displayed. (Given that all other fortresses possess four tower piers and a distinct gateway, I speculate that this is an error of previous observations that has been solidified in Gardiner's article). The associated pool of water is a similar 'U' shape to that of the previous fort, being in 'profile view', but the sides do not curve up so sharply and there appears to be a tree growing out of the middle of the pool itself. It is interesting that the bodies of water from this point on in the relief appear less formed and more natural, communicating a sense of ruggedness and the wildness of the terrain. Perhaps this tacitly indicates the level of control, as we started with a rectangular pool at the "Dwelling of the Lion" and slowly become less and less formed in these two following examples and would fit in with the distance-to-doorway interpretation.

The next three fortresses encountered are amongst a battle scene in which Sety I triumphs over a Bedouin host. Gardiner suggests that this battle is evidence that the area around the fortresses, and maybe even the forts themselves, were dominated by Bedouin tribes during the Amarna period. Therefore, Sety had to secure this area before he could launch campaigns into Syria and Palestine (Gardiner 1920, 100). It is interesting that none of Sety's opponents appear to have any weapons or armour on them. The three fortresses displayed have the 'typical features'; a rectangular gateway, four tower piers, rounded merlons and an exterior water source. However, the last fortress in this "Bedouin battle" has two additional interesting features. There is a second tier of defences that may suggest another fortified enclosure on the inside of this fortress. The increase in defences may have been a response to this fortress' position in relation to Egypt, being relatively far away. Gardiner's reconstruction displays an odd-shaped body of water below this fort but the new publication by the University of Chicago does not display any zigzag markings. The wall has probably deteriorated so badly today that it is difficult to determine. Above the gate is the other interesting feature that appears to be a window. The remaining two fortresses, located in the next scene (the 'Tribute Scene'), are positioned below Sety's horses and have the 'typical' fortress features.

The sites that could correspond to this group of remaining fortresses do have features that correspond to the images of forts in the Shasu Campaign. The Sinai excavations in the 1970's by Elizer D. Oren revealed that the sites of Bir el-'Abd and Haruba A-289 are thought to be frontier fortresses operating in the early 19th Dynasty (Oren 2006; 1987). Although, Bir el-'Abd was badly deteriorated, it is clear that it is a square fortified structure with 3 metre thick walls (40 × 40 m, covering 1600 sq. m). In addition, there was a rectangular depression, located 200 meters outside the fortress. This is most likely the water cistern represented in the reliefs. Moving east, at Haruba A-295 there is also a square structure (50 × 50 m, covering 2500 sq. m.) but no discernable water cistern has been associated with it (Fig. 4). Interestingly, the walls of this fortress are flat and continuous and thus show a marked difference in their construction from the buttresses of Tell Heboua I. One could surmise that, given the small size of the fortress's layout, the walls did not require buttresses for stability. Could it be then speculated that the buttresses on the fortress of Tjaru are more representative of a structural feature than a defensive one? At this point, this remains unclear. The final archaeological site to be looked at in our examination of the 'Ways of Horus' fortresses comes from the site of Deir el Balah (Fig. 5). The site is located in southern Canaan and it has been asserted that it represents a 19th Dynasty Egyptian outpost (Dothan 1987; 1993). From Stratum 7, there is a rectangular structure with 2.4 m thick walls

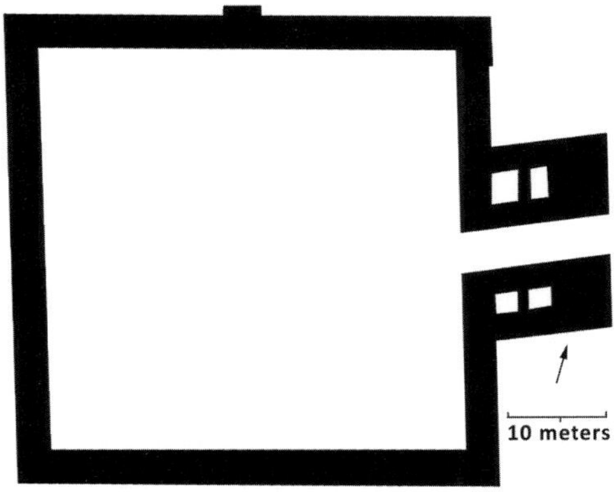

Figure 4. *Outline of Haruba (redrawn from Oren 1987, fig. 6).*

Figure 5. *Outline of Deir el Balah (redrawn after Dothan 1993, 343).*

(20 × 20 m, covering 400 sq. m). At each of the corners, the walls slightly protrude (approximately 0.5 m away from the main wall). This has a direct correlation with the tower piers in the reliefs and shows a construction difference in layout from Haruba A-289. Furthermore, there appears to be no gate in the design of this structure. If this is the case, the Sety scenes do not reflect this marked difference in access. A recent article by Killebrew *et al.* (2006) has conclusively proved that the square depression that was thought to be an external water source (Dothan 1993, 344; Oren 1987, 83) was actually a potter's quarry.

Levantine Fortifications in the Sety I Reliefs

There are six fortified centres which can be classified as "Levantine" in the Sety reliefs. The compositions of these do not deviate significantly from the Egyptian fort depictions that have been looked at (rectangular gates, 4 tower piers and rounded merlons). However there are marked differences in the inclusion of some features that do separate them from 'Ways of Horus'. G. R. H. Wright, with regard to physical remains in the Levant, states that, "Ethnics abound in the biblical record (Syria-Palestinian textual evidence), but as yet no firm associations have been made between them and the styles of building remains" (Wright 1985: i, 2). This is the case with the depictions of fortifications in Egyptian art. The artists depicting the Egyptian forts in North Sinai did not make much distinction between the architecture of their forts and those in the Levant. Therefore, in order to display a fortified centre's ethnicity, an artist sought to portray its people in such a way that they could not be mistaken for Egyptians, via their "strange" clothing and hairstyles. To reinforce this point, an identity inscription drove the point home that this was a foreign entity that Egypt now controlled.

Archaeologically, the cultural transition from the Middle Bronze Age (2300–1550 BC) (MBA) to the Late Bronze Age (1550–1200 BC) (LBA) has a remarkable continuity in Palestine in both cultural remains and architecture. To avoid trying to correlate the Sety I Levantine fort images with a suspected site identification (such a study would go far beyond the scope of this paper) the focus will be more of a 'survey view' of Levantine sites that have features in common and are markedly different from the fortified centres in the Sety I reliefs.

Above the Shasu campaign scenes, is the 'Tribute Scene' in which Sety I receives tribute from a set of Levantine rulers/mayors. There are two fortresses depicted here. The secondary enclosure wall, which appears only once in the 'Ways of Horus' fortresses, is very prominent and displays a full set of tower piers. It is tempting to draw a parallel of this enclosure to represent an inner citadel rather than assume that the initial wall represents an example of an outworked wall with the secondary wall image being the main wall. At Megiddo there is an inner citadel that is situated well inside the surrounding main wall (Wright's 'curtain wall'). Furthermore, both of the fortresses are located on a mound or a 'tell' which is most common at Levantine sites in the LBA. Most of the cities in the LB period were located on the debris of settlements which created a mound. This "tell" was sometimes plastered and had internal brick walls built in it to secure the slope. Ramparts first appeared in the MB IIA period (Kempinski 1992b, 129) and continued in use for the LB period.

The escarpment, or slope of a tell, was constructed with internal core walls of brick and stone to strengthen the entire structure. At Hazor, the internal core wall was c. 8–10 meters thick and c. 10 meters high. A similar core wall was also found in the excavations of Tell Dan's rampart (6.5m thick) (Kaplan 1975, 7). The use of crushed limestone (*huwwar*) and reinforced matting in this construction also show an effort to solidify the slope by alternating with earthen layers within the glacis. Hazor's ramparts are most impressive as they are very well preserved. The western rampart is 15m high and 60m wide. Additionally, excavations at Akko (Accho/Acco) have yielded one of the largest ramparts in Syria-Palestine, measuring approximately 20m high with the length of the escarpment being 50m. Built on firm kurkar soil (a local, loosely cemented sandstone), the rampart is composed of layers of crushed kurkar, sand, and beaten earth mixed with pottery sherds (Dothan 1973, 257–8). This particular rampart is dated to the MB IIB period and so would have been present in the LB period at the site. The argument could be made that the inclusion of a rampart on the Sety I scenes communicates an idea to the viewer that this was a foreign entity and thus would serve as a 'cultural marker' in the art (a 'cultural marker' being an idea that is symbolic in composition but also reflects that reality of Levantine fortification systems). None of the 'Ways of Horus' fortifications have these tells.

Going back to the Shasu campaign register at Karnak, the next foreign city is displayed on the Eastern Approach Wall that is located on the distal end of the bottom register. Unlike the Bedouin scene, these figures are clearly armed (Spalinger 1979, 30; Yadin 1963, 230). A close look into the topography surrounding the fort implies an undulating terrain as figures take long strides to climb it. One soldier even tries to help one up from the pharaoh's "killing zone". Once again, the overall sense to the viewer is to communicate the ruggedness of the terrain in the Levant. A strange oval globule is depicted at the extreme left under the fort. One end stretches behind the left outer walls (Chicago Ep. S. 1986, 5). If this does represent a fosse of a Levantine city, one could draw a similarity with an external fosse, 15 m in depth and 60 m in width, that has been found outside the western ramparts at Hazor (although this fosse has not been subject to intensive investigations yet) (Burke 2008, 57). The depiction of the fortress shows a prominent second enclosure and a rampart.

The viewer of these Levantine fortress depictions will also note that throughout the Karnak Sety I scenes, there are sets of tower piers common with the 'Ways of Horus' fortress depictions. One cannot stress enough the fact that Levantine wall construction was markedly different in its construction and layout (Burke 2008, 60–1). The walls of Levantine sites are not flat and continuous but are jogged and indented (Fig. 6 and 7) (Wright 1985: i, 178–9). These "salient and recessed" walls have an average variance of 50cm. They could be constructed in trapezoidal sections that would have been very strong compared to the flat and continuous walls. An important factor in their introduction is that this architectural trait facilitated the enclosure of the ovoid pattern of the tells, making the construction of the curtain wall more adaptable to individual sites and thus not conforming to an overall square plan as in the sites that are along the 'Ways of Horus' (Fig. 8). Examples of this type of wall construction and layout can be seen at Megiddo (Strata XVII–XII), Lachish (Levels VII and VI) as well as numerous other sites throughout the Levant. The exterior of a Levantine fortification wall would have been reflected in dramatic, vertical shadows as the sun moved through the sky. The artists of the Sety I scenes, for whatever motivation, did not attempt to capture the salient and recessed wall but opted to show tower piers and allude to a square construction.

On the middle register of the left side of the doorway, is an image of a fortress that displays four tower piers on both the outer and inner enclosures with rounded merlons at the top. Figures are on the battlements offering pleas to the pharaoh while the figure at the forefront holds a brazier. The middle of the inner enclosure has an identity inscription that reads, "The town of Yenoam" (Chicago Ep. S. 1986, 36). The lack of a rampart for the foundation is very interesting. Instead the city has a thin globule that hooks upwards on the left hand side. There are numerous trees below the lowest margin with Palestinians hiding from the slaughter. It is unclear from

Figure 6. *Salient and recessed wall from Stratum XII, Megiddo (redrawn after Kempinski 1992a, fig. 2).*

Figure 7. *Northern Gate and Coty Wall at Megiddo, Stratum VIII (redrawn after Baumgarten 1992, 148).*

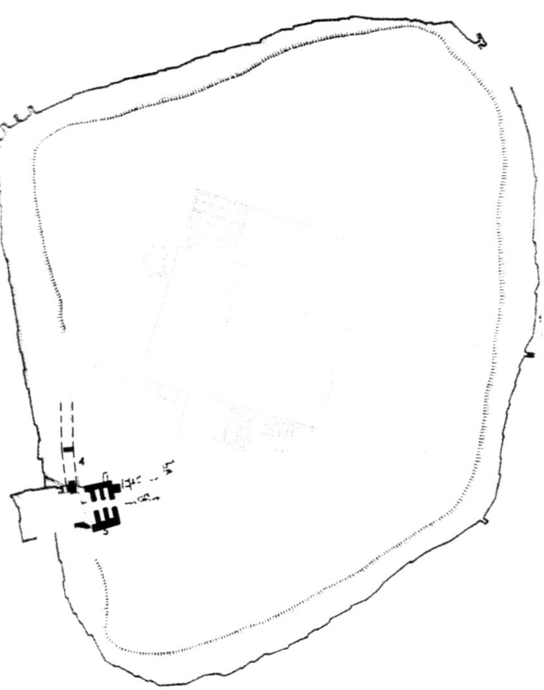

Figure 8. *Map of Tel Lachish: Illustrating the curtain wall being built in segments (redrawn after Ussishkin 1985, fig. 1).*

this depiction if the artist's intent was to portray this forest just to introduce cowardly figures or if he was making an actual observation of the city's surroundings.

Moving to the furthest end on the middle register of the Eastern approach wall there is a notable fortress beneath Sety's horses where the king receives tribute in the form of vassals felling trees (presumably the cedars of the Lebanon area). The identity inscription in the middle reads, "The town of Qader in the land of Hanem" (Chicago Ep. S. 1986, 33). The fortress is rather small with an inner and outer enclosure that conforms to other examples (four piers on each inner and outer enclosure). However, the gateway is unquestionably depicted as destroyed in the relief. The lintel and the doorposts of the passage are disconnected from one another and orientated diagonally slightly to the right (Hoffmeier 2006, 158). There is no rampart base but the base of the scene is an undulating line and so retains that communicative aspect that this is a hilly terrain (the distance-to-doorway assertion is maintained by this).

Gateways at Levantine sites, such as the destroyed one in the 'town of Qader', appear to be the most evolved defensive architectural entity in that they display a development throughout each phase of Palestinian archaeology. The wooden doors of these gateways have not been preserved but we do know from the door sockets at Ras Shamra (ancient Ugarit) that there were two sets of doors at either end (Wright 1985: i, 51). Most Levantine fortifications in the reliefs reveal that their gateways were directly accessed. That is, one was able to walk in a straight line into the city, but there are a few examples of bent-axis designs (such as at Stratum XIII–XII at Megiddo, Tel Poleg and Tell el Farah). The bent axis designs are most interesting for this study because the Egyptian artist could not have portrayed them in a two-dimensional plane (Fig. 9). Instead, the artist would have had to rely on displaying a directly-accessed gateway to communicate to their audience that there was another entry. Such is the case with the presence of two distinct gateways in the 'Kadesh Battle Scene' on the uppermost register, distal end, of the right side of the doorway.

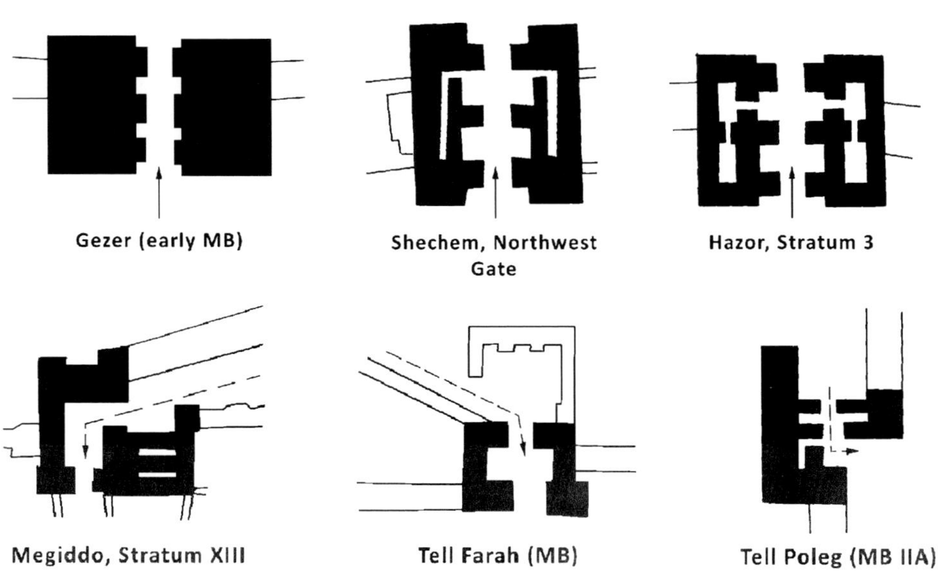

Figure 9. *Examples of Three 'Teethed' Gateways (above) and Bent Axis Gateways (below).*

The work at one site in particular has yielded evidence for the appearance of the portals of the city gate and whether the gateways depicted in the scenes of Sety I correlate with them. The gate area at Tell Dan was found buried in a later rampart and is dated to the MB IIA–B (Biran 1981, 104–5; Herzog 1997, 323). The opening and the inner chamber were roofed with distinct mud-brick arches (Mazar 1992, 207). Although it would be foolish to assume that all gateways in Syria-Palestine were constructed in this way, this type of construction was probably not an isolated anomaly. The representation of the 'town of Qader', as we have seen, shows its broken gateway as rectangular. This is something we must consider as a deviation from the artistic relief (Burke 2008, 72). Could it be that the Egyptian artists were trying to depict a rectangular door outside an arched portal? Given that the actual remains of a gate have not been found, we cannot tell if the door was also of the arched design or if it was rectangular. It may be that the doors of these gateways were of a rectangular design and are therefore properly portrayed by Egyptian artists. We should also consider the possibility that this arched gateway may have been replaced by a rectangular version for the LB period.

Summary

Looking at the art of the Sety I scenes at Karnak and comparing it to the archaeological material does communicate some information about fortifications in the 19th Dynasty. However, there are certain features that were not accurately depicted. The differences in wall construction, the use of bent-axis gateways and possibility of arched gateway portals stand in contrast to the depiction of Levantine centres being displayed in the Sety I reliefs. In addition, this study shows that the scenes of fortresses are depicted as being distinct from one another. The differences lie in the details and we can no longer consider the image of a fortress in the scenes as a 'hieroglyphic ideogram'. Perhaps the motivation for the inclusion of these different details alludes to the fact that no fortified centre, in the Levant or in Egypt, was a 'carbon copy' of another. Only further excavation will reveal how diverse the sites actually were in trying to address the question of how to protect their people from others who would do them harm.

School of Archaeology, Classics and Egyptology
University of Liverpool

Bibliography

Baumgarten, J. J. (1992) 'Urbanization in the Late Bronze Age' in Kempinski, A and Reich, R (eds), *The Architecture of Ancient Israel: From the Prehistoric to the Persian Periods*, Jerusalem, Israel Exploration Society, 143–50.

Biran, A. (1981) 'Tel Dan', *Israel Exploration Journal* 31, 103–5.

Broadhurst, C. (1989) 'An Artistic Interpretation of Sety I's War Reliefs', *The Journal of Egyptian Archaeology* 75, 229–234.

Burke, A. A. (2008) *Walled up to Heaven*. Indiana, Eisenbrauns.

Cavillier, G. (2001) 'The Ancient Military Road between Egypt and Palestine Reconsidered: A Reassessment', *Göttinger Miszellen* 185, 23–33.

Dothan, T. (1987) 'The Impact of Egypt on Canaan during the 18th and 19th Dynasties in the Light of the

Excavations at Deir el-Balah' in Rainey, A. F. (ed.), *Egypt, Israel, Sinai: Archaeological and Historical Relationships in the Biblical Period*, Tel Aviv, Tel Aviv University, 121–35.

Dothan, M. (1973) 'Accho in Israel' in *Israel Exploration Journal* 23, 257–8.

Dothan, T. (1993) 'Deir el Balah' in *The New Encyclopedia of Archaeological Excavations in the Holy Land* Volume 1, New York, Simon and Schuster, 343–47.

Gaballa, G. A. (1967) *Narrative in Egyptian Art*, 2 Volumes, Liverpool, Unpublished Ph.D. Thesis, University of Liverpool.

Gardiner, A. H. (1920) 'The Ancient Military Road between Egypt and Palestine', *The Journal of Egyptian Archaeology VI*, 99–116.

Herzog, Z. (1997) 'Fortifications' in Meyers, E. M. (ed.), *The Oxford Encyclopedia of Archaeology in the Near East,* Volume 2, New York and London, Oxford University Press, 319–26.

Hamblin, W. (2005) *Warfare in the ancient Near East to c. 1600 BC*, New York, Routledge.

Hoffmeier, J. K. (2006) 'Recent Excavations on the 'Ways of Horus': The 2005 and 2006 Seasons at Tell El-Borg', *Annales du Service des Antiquitiés de L'Égypte* 80, 257–279.

Hoffmeier, J. K. and El-Maksoud, M. A. (2003) 'A New Military Site on the "Ways of Horus": Tell El-Borg 1999–2001: A Preliminary Report' in *Journal of Egyptian Archaeology* 89, 169–197.

Kaplan, J. (1975) 'Further Aspects of the Middle Bronze Age II Fortifications in Palestine', *Zeitschrift des deutschen Palästina – Vereins* 91, 1–17.

Kempinski, A. (1992a) 'Urbanization and Town Plans in the Middle Bronze Age II' in Kempinski, A .and Reich, R. (eds), *The Architecture of Ancient Israel: From the Prehistoric to the Persian Periods* Jerusalem, Israel Exploration Society, 121–6.

Kempinski, A. (1992b) 'Middle and Late Bronze Age Fortifications' in Kempinski, A. and Reich, R. (eds), *The Architecture of Ancient Israel: From the Prehistoric to the Persian Periods*, Jerusalem, Israel Exploration Society, 127–42.

Killebrew, A. E., Goldberg, P. and Rosen, A. M. (2006) 'Deir el Balah: A Geological, Archaeological, and Historical Reassessment of an Egyptianizing 13th and 12th Century B.C.E. Center', *The Bulletin of the American Schools of Oriental Research* 343, 97–119.

Leclère, F. and Valbelle, D. (2008) 'Tell Abyad: a royal Ramesside residence', *Egyptian Archaeology* 32, 29–32.

El-Maksoud, M. A. (1998) *Tell Heboua (1981–1991): Enquête archéologique sur la deuxième période intermédiaire et le nouvel Empire à l'extrémité orientale du Delta*, Paris, Ministère des Affaires Étrangères.

El-Maksoud, M. A. and Valbelle, D. (2005) 'Tell Héboua-Tjarou. L'Apport de l'Épigraphie', *Revue d'Égyptologie* 56, 1–44.

Mazar, A. (1992) *Archaeology of the Land of the Bible 10,000–586 B.C.E.,* New York and London, Doubleday.

Morris, E. F. (2005) *The Architecture of Imperialism: Military Bases and the Evolution of Foreign Policy in Egypt's New Kingdom.* Leiden, Brill.

Murnane, W. J. (1985) *The Road to Kadesh: A Historical Interpretation of the Battle Reliefs of King Sety I at Karnak.* Chicago, The University of Chicago.

Oren, E. D. (1987) 'The 'Ways of Horus' in North Sinai' in Rainey, A. F. (ed.), *Egypt, Israel, Sinai: Archaeological and Historical Relationships in the Biblical Period*, Tel Aviv, Tel Aviv University, 69–119.

Oren, E. D. (1993) 'North Sinai' in *The New Encyclopaedia of Archaeological Excavations in the Holy Land*, Volume 4. New York, Simon & Schuster, 1386–1391.

Oren, E. D. (2006) 'The Establishment of Egyptian Imperial Administration on the 'Ways of Horus': An Archaeological Perspective from North Sinai' in *Timelines: Studies in Honour of Manfred Bietak* Volume 2, Leuven, Peeters, 279–292.

Spalinger, A. J. (1979) 'The Northern Wars of Seti I: An Integrative Study', *Journal of the American Research Center in Egypt* 16, 29–47.

University of Chicago (Epigraphic Survey). (1986) *The Battle Reliefs of King Sety I, Reliefs and Inscriptions at Karnak, Volume 4,* Chicago, The Oriental Institute of the University of Chicago.

Ussishkin, D. (1985) 'Level VII and VI at Tel Lachish and the End of the Late Bronze Age in Canaan' in Tubb, J. N. (ed.), *Palestine in the Bronze and Iron Ages: Papers in Honour of Olga Tufnell*, London, Institute of Archaeology, 213–230.

Wright, G. R. H. (1985) *Ancient Building in South Syria and Palestine*, *Handbuch der Orientalistik, Lieferung 3*, 2 Volumes, Brill, Leiden.

Yadin, Y. (1963) *The Art of Warfare in Biblical Lands in the Light of Archaeological Discovery*, London, Weidenfeld and Nicolson.

The word *wnḫ.wj:* its writings, determinatives, meaning and use in the Old Kingdom

Maha Yehia

Introduction

The word *wnḫ.wj* "two strips of cloth" which were presented to the deceased as an offering, bore many determinatives 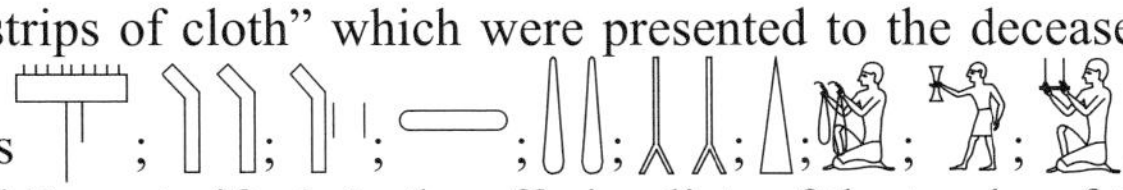, and is translated in (Wb I 324, 3) as 'Zwei Zeugstreifen'. In the offering lists of the tombs of the Old Kingdom, the word *wnḫ.wj* appeared first as a kind of cloth, eventually occupying twelfth place in the list, a position it retained until the end of the Old Kingdom. The earliest mention of *wnḫ.wj* within the offering list dates to the second half of the 4th Dynasty. The meaning of the word is problematic and has variously been translated as "two strips of cloth" (Wb I 324) "two napkins" (Jequier 1921, 120) "two bandages" (Murray 1937, 20). Murray has suggested that it may have been used as a bandage during the mummification of the deceased, or pieces of cloth presented to the tomb owner in order to clothe him on completion of his toilet. (Murray 1937, 20). The determinatives and writings of *wnḫ.wj* varied according to the text, place, and the period.

This short study examines the numerous offering lists in 140 tombs of the Old Kingdom. It describes the word itself, its writings and determinatives, in an attempt to solve the ambiguity of the *wnḫ.wj,* and to discover the significance and use of these two strips, which were always presented in the offering lists from the second half of the 4th Dynasty to the end of the Old Kingdom.

The writing of wnḫ.wj

In the 3rd Dynasty, the term *idmj* was always used in the offering lists (Barta 1963, table 2; 3) but there is no evidence of the word *wnḫ.wj* in any early lists. The earliest mention of *wnḫ.wj* is dated to the beginning of the 4th Dynasty in an unknown tomb at Saqqara (Drenkhahn 1989, Fig. 7). It then appears in the second half of the 4th Dynasty in the tombs of *Dbḥn* at Giza (Hassan 1943, Fig. 122, pl. L), *Ms s3* (Borchardt 1937, 103) and *Mṯn* (Lepsius, *1842–1845,* II, 6) at Saqqara, and was widespread in most of the offering lists until the end of the Old Kingdom (Hassan 1948, pls. XXV; XXXIII; XLI; LVII; LXV; LXXIII; CXV; CXXIII).

During the 4th, 5th and 6th Dynasties the word had various writings: ,  (PM 1974, 694 ; Capart 1906, pl. II ; Säve-Söderbergh 1994, pl.43; PM 1934, 191; Hassan 1948, pl. LXXXIX; Davies 1901, pl. XXVI) and 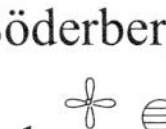(PM III 1974, 673,

694; Hassan 1948, pl CXV; CXXIII; Borchardt 1964, pl. 74). The predominant writing in the 5th and 6th Dynasties was: (Table 1, group A), especially in tombs at Giza and Saqqara, with different determinatives, including the form without determinative (Table 1 group B).

During the 6th Dynasty the writing of *wnḫ.wj* became characteristic when the sign was replaced by , and appeared as , and its variant (Table 2 group C). It appears first in the tomb of *Dw3 Rˁ.w* of the 5th Dynasty at Dahshur (Borchardt 1937, I, 50, pl. 12) and continues in the 6th Dynasty in Saqqara, Sheik Said, El-Qasr Wa-es-Saiyad, in the tombs of *Ḥnn.t* (Hassan 1948, pl. LXXXIX; Davies 1901, pl. XXVI), *Pn.w* (PM III², 1974 681; Hassan 1948, pl. CVI), *Mḥj*(PM III², 1974 681; Hassan 1948, pl. CVI); Jequier 1935, Fig. 81), *Bjw* (PM III² 1974, 677; Hassan 1948, pl. CXV), *Sb3k.w* (PM III² 1974, 681; Hassan 1948, pl. CXV; Jequier 1935, Fig. 87), *T3wj* (PM V, 121–122; Säve-Söderbergh 1994, pl. 43), *Šj* (PM III² 1974, 682; Hassan, 1948, pl. CXXIII), *Nfr k3 Rˁ nḫt* (PM III² 1974, 680; Jequier 1935, 138). This substitution may be related to suppression of the human and animal signs in the Pyramid Texts (PT), and occurred in those lists which were inscribed upon the walls of burial chambers or on sarcophagi. During the reign of Pepi II, this form was widespread at Saqqara but not at Giza.

In the tomb of *T3wj, wnḫ.wj* is written on the northern wall with , while was written on the southern wall. The writing occurs in the tomb of *Šdw* (Petrie 1898 pl. XX), and is written in the tomb of *K3j pw Rˁ* (Hassan 1948, pl. XLIX). Perhaps the sign here is incorrectly substituted for the sign (Table 2 Group D).

The determinatives

The determinatives of *wnḫ.wj* in the Old Kingdom are very interesting as they reveal the variety of forms:
The royal offering lists include the following types: , (PT 57e).

The private offering lists include the following types: , , , , , , , ,
The predominant determinative is the sign S 28, (Table 3, group A) "Cloth with fringe", which was used throughout the Old Kingdom.

By the 5th Dynasty the determinative appeared in the tomb of *Ptḥ ḥtp* (Hassan 1948, pl. LVII; Davies 1900, pl. XXX), and continued to appear in tombs dating to the reign of Pepi I at Giza and Saqqara. The sign also occurred in the tombs of *Ḳ3r* (Hassan, 1948, pl. LXXXI) at Giza, and *3nḫ mrj Rˁ* (Altenmüller 1998 Fig. 31, pl. 68, 90) at Saqqara dating to the 6th Dynasty. The sign (Table 3, group B) and its variant which are both used as a determinative for this word occurred only in the tombs of the 5th and 6th Dynasty. The sign (Table 3, group C) appeared once in the 4th Dynasty in the tomb of *Mṯn* (Lepsius 1842–1845, II, 6), and the tomb of *M3 nfr* (Lepsius 1842–1845, II, 68). It occured in most of the tombs of Akhmim from the 6th Dynasty, and continued to the end of the Old Kingdom. The sign (Table 4, group D) S 27, "Cloth with two fringes", used as determinative in the word *mnḫt* "cloth", also occurred as a determinative for *wnḫ.wj* in the 5th Dynasty and also remained in use until the end of the Old Kingdom. In the tomb of Princess *Jdw.t* (PM III[2] 1974, 617–619; Hassan, 1948, pl. LXXIII) the word *wnḫ.wj* is written in the chapel as but in the burial chamber as , where both figures of the chick and the man are eliminated.

The sign (Table 4, group E) M 44 occurred in the tombs of the 6th and 8th Dynasty. The sign (Table 4, group F) appeared in the Mastaba of *K3.w nsw* (Hassan 1936, Fig. 86, pl. 25) of the 4th –5th Dynasty at Giza, then continued to be used also in the tombs of *3ḫ.t htp* (PM III[2] 1974, 634–637; Ziegler 1993, 164–165) at Saqqara and *N ḫft-k3j* (Hassan 1948, pl. LXXXIX) in Deshasha dating to the 5th and 6th Dynasty. It then spread to the tombs dating to the end of the 6th Dynasty, for example in the tombs of *Ḥb sd nfr k3 Rᶜ* (Jequier 1940, Fig. 59), *Sb3k.w* (PM 1974 III[2], 681; Hassan 1948, pl. CXV; Jequier 1935, Fig. 87), *Bjw* (PM 1974, 677; Hassan 1948, pl. CXV) and *Nfr k3 Rᶜ nḫt* (PM 1974, 680; Jequier 1935, 138) at Saqqara.

The sign (Table 4, group F) V 38 was used as a determinative in *wt* "wrapping", and also as a determinative for *wnḫ.wj* by the middle of 6th Dynasty in the tomb of *B3wj*, *B3.f Min* (Kanawati 1980–1992, IV, Fig. 30) and *ḥntj* (Kanawati 1980–1992, IV, Fig. 31) at Akhmim. It continued to occur at Saqqara to the end of the 6th Dynasty in the tombs of *Sn.t* (PM 1974, 681; Hassan 1948, pl. CVI) and *Mḫj* (PM 1974, 681; Hassan, 1948, pl. CVI).

The sign N 18 as a determinative, found in the word *d3jw* "linen or bale of cloth", occurred as a determinative in *wnḫ.wj* first, in the tombs of *Mṯn* and *M3 nfr* of the 4th Dynasty at Saqqara, then spread in the 6th Dynasty at Akhmim in the tombs of *Ḥtp.t* (Kanawati 1980–1992, IV, pl. 12; Fig. 30) and *Jpj* (PM 1962 V, 23 ; Kanawati 1980–1992, VII pl. 13; Fig. 41) in dual form .

The sign U 12, "pitchfork," a determinative in *sḏb* "obstacle", *ᶜbj* "collect" and *ᶜbt* "pitchfork", was also used as a determinative in *wnḫ.wj,* in the tombs of *N-k3-ᶜnḫ* (Petrie and Murray 1952, pl. III), *Mn.w nfr* Hassan 1948, pl. LXV), *Ṯ3wt.j* (Säve-Söderbergh 1994, pl. 43) and *Jdw.t* (PM III[2], 617–619; Macramallah 1935, pl. XVI.

Some determinatives are unfamiliar, such as , V 33, and "bag" variants act as determinatives in *ᶜrf* "pack, envelop" and *šsr* "fine linen". This sign is depicted in the tomb of *Tj* (Hassan 1948, pl. XLI) of the 5th Dynasty. The sign occurs once in the tomb of *Jḥy* (Hassan 1948, pl. LXXXIXI), as does the sign which was also depicted in the tomb of *Šdw* (Petrie 1898, pl. XX) of the 5th Dynasty at Deshasheh. Sometimes the word was written without any pictorial determinative, terminating in only the stroke determinative referring to the number of items presented, i.e. two pieces.

In the tomb of *K3j* (Junker, 1938, 99) the sign is used. The sign is used in Cairo No. 1503 (Hassan 1948, pl. LXV; Borchardt 1937, 207) but this may be an erroneous rendering of the sign . Sometimes the determinative occurs in offering scenes, for example a man holding the *wnḫ.wj* and offering them to the deceased. Such determinatives are attested in the tombs of *Sꜥnḫ wj ptḥ; Jdw; S3bw; Ptḥ ḥtp; Nj m3ꜥt rꜥ; ꜥnḫ n.s* (Hassan, 1948, pls. LXXIII; XCVIII; LVII; CXXXIV).

The presentation of the wnḫ.wj in scenes

After discussing the textual evidence for the word *wnḫ.wj,* an analysis of the scenes and the many representations on the chapel walls may help to define its uses. *wnḫ.wj* were sometimes depicted as two narrow strips of cloth , wider at the lower end, bent over at an angle near the upper end, the latter being sometimes trimmed with a fringe. Their shape may be due to the fact that the upper part is grasped by the priest, and thus is somewhat gathered together.

The earliest word recognized to be read as *wnḫw* dates to the beginning of the 4th Dynasty at Saqqara, where *wnḫw* is represented as single strip held in the hand of the offering bearer, who holds an unguent jar in the other hand (Drenkhahn, 1989, 29, Fig. 5). In the tombs of high officials of the Old Kingdom the deceased can be either seated, as in the tomb of *K3w nswt* (Hassan 1936, Fig. 86) (Fig. 1), or standing, as *3ḫt ḥtp* (Hassan, 1932, Fig. 139) (Fig. 2); (Hassan 1932, Fig. 142) (Fig. 3) and *K3 m nfr.t* (Hassan 1932, 107) (Fig. 4). In Figure 4, the donor is shown putting his left leg forward, wearing a wig, necklace, kilt with triangular projection, and a leopard skin suspended from his left shoulder. In all these tombs the *wnḫ.wj* are presented by the *ḥm k3* priests who sometimes also carry a box of unguents and a strip of *wnḫw* (Drenkhahn, 1989, 29, Fig. 5), (Hassan, 1932, Fig. 139) (Fig. 2) or two pieces of linen (Hassan 1936, Fig.

Figure 1 (above). *Presentation of wnḫ.wj in the offering scenes of K3w nsw (Hassan 1936, fig. 86).*

Figure 2 (right). *Presentation of the wnḫ.wj in the tomb of 3ḫt ḥtp (Hassan, 1932, fig. 139).*

Figure 3. *Presentation of wnḫ.wj in the tomb of ȝḫt htp (Hassan 1932, fig. 142).*

Figure 4. *Presentation of wnḫ.wj in the tomb of Kȝ m nfr.t (Hassan 1936, 107).*

Figure 5. *Presentation of wnḫ.wj in the tomb of Rʿ wr II (Junker 1938 Fig. 46).*

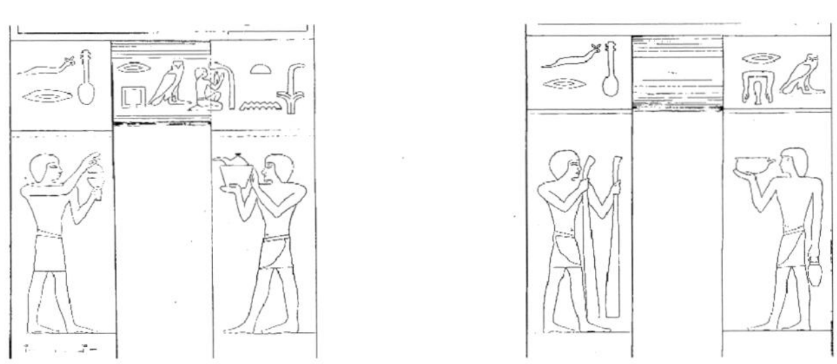

Figure 6. *Presentation of wnḫ.wj in the tomb of Nfr (Junker 1940, Fig. 7).*

86) (Fig. 1), (Hassan 1936, 107) (Fig. 4) and *K3gmnj* (Harpur 2006, pl. 38) (Fig. 6) At other times the priests hold an incense jar in one hand and a strip of *wnḫw* in the other (Hassan, 1932, Fig. 139) (Fig. 2).

In the tomb of *Rᶜ wr* II, the *wnḫ.wj* are presented together with incense in the first register, while in the second register is the presentation of the food offerings (Junker 1938, fig. 46) (Fig. 5). On the false door of *Nfr* four figures are represented, two on each side. The righthand figures perhaps represent the *ḥm k3* priests, one of whom holds two strips of *wnḫ.wj*, while the other carries a jar and basin. On the left are two further figures, one burning incense and the other carrying a *kbḥw* jar (Junker 1940, fig. 7) (Fig. 6).

In all the scenes under discussion, the presentation of *wnḫ.wj* is carried out by the *ḥm k3* priests, holding either one or two strips of cloth. This may symbolise the presentation of new or clean clothing which formed one of the preliminary ritual acts, and which was always accompanied by other priests pouring libations using the "*ḳbḥw*" vessel and burning incense "*snṯr*", before the presentation of the meal.

Arrangement of items in the offering lists

The chronological order of the word *wnḫ.wj* in the offering lists may help to identify its nature. The offering lists of 140 tombs dating to the Old Kingdom were examined and the word was found to be followed by *snṯr* and *ḳbḥ.w,* and was mostly found in the 12th position, between *w3ḏ.w smd.t* and *snṯr ḫt.*The linen list would seem to represent qualities of cloth differentiated by fineness, colour or material used, while its subdivisions represent the amounts of the material to be supplied. *wnḫ.wj* occurs as dual but not among the detailed linen list.

According to the earliest inscriptions, the first appearance of *wnḫ.wj* in the offering lists, followed by the burning of incense and the libation of cool water, was in the tomb of *Ms s3* (Borchardt 1964, 103). This order became standard during the 5th and 6Ith Dynasties and continued until the end of the Old Kingdom (Hassan 1948, pls. XXV; XXXIII; XLI; LVII; LXV; LXXIII; CXV; CXXIII).

1. '*sṯ*' 'to pour Water on the ground' ; Water for pouring
2. '*snṯr ḫt*' 'Burning incense'
3. '*stj ḥb*' 'Festival perfume'
4. '*ḥknw*-oil' ' Heknu oil'
5. '*sftj*-oil' 'Sefetj oil'
6. '*nḫnm*-oil' 'Nekhenem oil'
7. '*tw3.wt*-oil' 'Twaut oil'
8. '*ḥ3t.t ᶜš* ' 'best Cedar oil'
9. '*ḥ3t.t ṯḥn.w*' 'best Libyan oil'
10. '*wrḥ*' '*Wrḥ* Ointment'
11. '*w3ḏ.w smd.t*' 'Green and black Eye cosmetic'
12. '*wnḫ.wj*' 'Two strips'
13. '*sntr ḫt*' 'Burning Incense'
14. '*kbḥ.w bd ṯ3*-2' 'Libation of Natron, two Pellets' and its variation *kbḥ.w bd šmᶜ ṯ3*-2 'Cool Water and two pellets of Natron of the south'.

The meaning and the use of wnḫ.wj

The *wnḫ.wj* are presumed to be two strips of cloth presented to the deceased, but their purpose is unclear. From their place among the preparatory procedures for the repast, Jequier (Jequier 1921, 120) regards these objects as napkins employed in the course of the toilet of the deceased. Murray translates the *wnḫ.wj* as "two bandages" (Murray 1937, 20), but bandages do not seem to have a place here, for the deceased is already embalmed and bandaged. Moreover it always occurs in a specific arrangement and not in the linen list, which was positioned later in the offering lists. It always took place before the ceremony of presenting food. Allen translates *wnḫ.wj* as 'Sovereign's linen' (Allen 2005, 182). It would be tempting to consider the *wnḫ.wj* as napkins for use during the meal, but the fact that the *wnḫ.wj* always occupies twelfth place and was connected with the action of censing and pouring cool water gives strong evidence that *wnḫ.wj* should be translated as a linen of a certain quality related to the rite of censing and libation.

The *wnḫ.wj* are mentioned in the Pyramid Texts. For example, in PT 57eW 'May you sit opposite Wenis in his divinity, may you part his path at the fore of the *3ḫ.w*, that he may come to stand at the fore of the *3ḫ.w* as Anubis at the fore of the westerners, to the front with Osiris' 'two strips of linen'. This spell occurs before the libation and censing and the spell of food preparation. The same concept occurs on the west walls of the 19th Dynasty tombs of Deir el-Medineh. There we see one, two or three wicks in a cup presented to Osiris or Anubis as the sun sets in the western hills. In this case they take the shape of tapers or of conical pastilles lit at the tip (Davies 1924, 10).

In the reliefs of private tombs depicting the presentation of *wnḫ.wj,* there are elements which may be of some possible importance in ascertaining the use and meaning of the word which previous studies have not taken fully into account. There are several representations in the surviving private lists which show the presentation of the *wnḫ.wj* as part of the offering list. In addition, there are a considerable number of scenes (for more scenes see: Junker, 1940 Fig. 71; 1944, Fig. 69) dealing with the presentation of the meal for the deceased, either royal or noble, in which a priest performs the same act, i.e. presents two strips of cloth. This rite can consist of the following prominent elements:

1. The priest presents two strips of cloth "*wnḫ.wj*" and is accompanied by another priest holding a ewer and basin
2. The priest presents two strips of cloth accompanied by a priest burning incense
3. The priest is accompanied by other priests; one holding incense, one a ewer, and the third holding a basin and a jar.
4. The priest holds a strip of cloth in one hand and an unguent jar in the other, accompanied by two priests, one burning incense, and the other holding a ewer and basin.
5. The priest holds a strip of cloth in one hand and an incense pot in the other.
6. The priest is sometimes accompanied by another priest holding a goose.

In the cult chamber of the tomb of *K3 nj nswt,* (Junker, 1934, Fig. 20) one of the offering bearers presents the *psj wnḫw* as a conical shape  (Fig. 7) which bears a close resemblance to the pyramidal shaped white loaf; hence, we return to the question of the function of the shape.

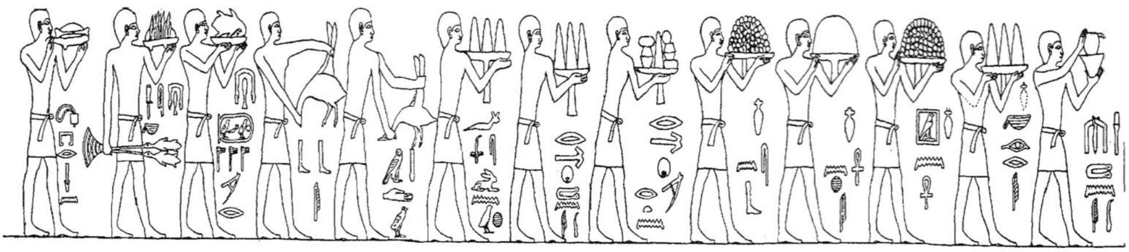

Figure 7. *Presentation of wnḫ.wj conical in shape from the mastaba of Kꜣ nj nsw.t (Junker, 1934, fig. 20).*

Figure 8. *Taper and conical shaped candles from the Ramesside era (Davies 1924, pls VII, 13; 15).*

Figure 9. *Presentation of candles in the temple of Kawa (Macadam 1955, pl. XVc).*

Analysis of this form in conjunction with similar representations in the reliefs of private tombs during the 18th Dynasty and the Ramesside era may prove elucidatory. In these scenes offerings of candles are accompanied by a male figure who censes and makes libations, as indeed were depicted in the Old Kingdom scenes mentioned above (Fig. 7). The candles take the shape of tapers (strips) or cones (Fig. 8), which would imply that these conical objects are themselves a form of candle. The presentation of the conical shape is depicted in tomb 10 from the reign of Ramesses II, namely of *Kꜣsꜥ* and his son *Pnbj*. The presentation of a pair of ritual tapers was generally made by the priest (in tombs Nos.: 39, 40, 54, 90, 93, 176) (Davies 1924, 10) and in the temple of Kawa (Macadam 1955, pl. XVc) (Fig. 9). The purpose of this rite was to afford light to the deceased in the dark necropolis, signifying the emergence of new light after spiritualization. Although they are connected with "making a light" or even "striking a light" the means and process of ignition are never indicated. Even in the New Kingdom scenes the action of lighting of the candle is never seen. Whether this was intended to be done by the deceased at night or at evening festivals, or for some other ritual reason, is not clear.

It seems that the lector priest recited the prescribed formula in front of the deceased. The formula is intended to ensure that demons would recoil or withdraw. He holds a "*wnḫw*" with probably a special fragrance that possesses such properties and this would explain the ritual representations of the priest, holding only one strip of cloth in one hand and a jar of unguent in the other.

Conclusion

The many determinative shape variations of the *wnḫ.wj* from the Old Kingdom (Tables 3 and 4) would imply a similar variety of functions. The determinative  shows the shape of the two pieces of cloth which occurs only for *wnḫ.wj*. In the offering lists, *wnḫ.wj*, is generally shown between incense *snṯr* and the green and black eye make-up, usually with the quantities stated. It remains unclear, however, what kind of candle the *wnḫ.wj* was. The most likely candidate would be a taper made of a strip of folded linen soaked in fat. Evidence is available proving that during the Old Kingdom it was made of a type of linen (Junker 1938, Fig. 28) especially in the Pyramid Texts, in which *wnḫ.wj* was mentioned in reference to *tȝj.t*. – a superior quality of linen soaked in fat in order to infuse it with special fragrance or scent and thereby imbue it with magical powers. It seems that these tapers were fixed upon or beside the offering table. Whether they were placed as lights or as incense burners on the table is not clear, but the frequent presence of both cones and tapers on the offerings table suggest that the taper is to give light, and the cone to give odour. Although these suggestions are tentative explanations, they may serve to shed light on the purpose of these unique elements in the scenes of private tombs of the Old Kingdom.

Tables

Group A: the word written with Complete Epigraphic signs.

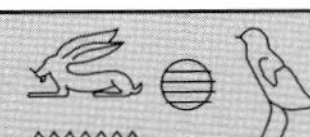

Date and Location	III–IV (Saqqara)	IV (Giza)	IV (Saqqara)	IV–V (Giza)
Private Tombs	-	1	1	2

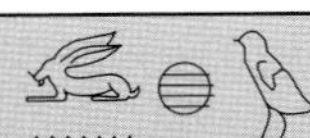

Date and Location	V (Saqqara)	V (Giza)	V–VI (Dahshour)	VI (Saqqara)	VI (Giza)	VI (Akhmim)
Private Tombs	7	9	1	28	12	1
Royal Tombs	(W)					

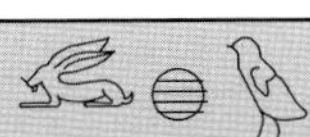

Date and Location	VI (Edfu)	VI (Deshasha)	VI (Meir)	V–VI (Saqqara)	VI (Hagrasa)
Private Tombs	1	1	3	4	1

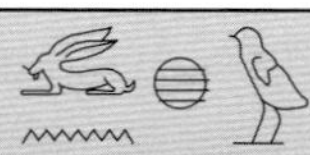

Date and Location	VI (El-Qasr wa-es-saiyad)	VI (Dendara)	End VI (Akhmim)	VI (Sedment)
Private Tombs	1	1	2	1

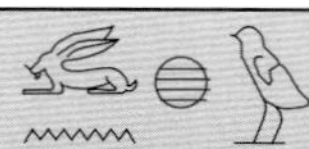

Date and Location	VI (Quseir el Amarna)	VI (El hagrasa)	Old Kingdom (Sheik Said)	VIII (Nag'ed Deir)	VIII (Saqqara)
Private Tombs	1	1	1	1	1

Group B: the word written with all Epigraphic signs but without the sign  *at the end*

Date and Location	III–IV (Saqqara)	IV (Giza)	IV (Saqqara)	IV–V (Giza)
Private Tombs	1	1	1	4

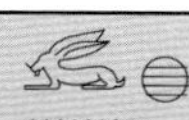

Date and Location	V (Saqqara)	V (Giza)	V–VI (Dahshour)	VI (Saqqara)
Private Tombs	3	7	3	10

Date and Location	VI (Giza)	VI (Akhmim	VI (Sedment)	VI (unknown)	Old Kingdom (Atamna)
Private Tombs	1	7	2	2	1

Group C: the word written with sign  *instead of the sign* *, occurring mostly in the VIth Dynasty at Saqqara:*

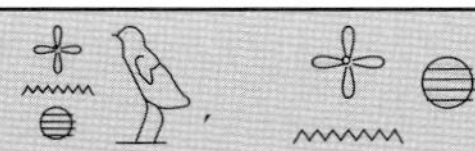

B1 B2

Date and Location	V (Dahshour)	V–VI (Dahshour)	VI (Saqqara)	VI (Giza)	VI (Sheik Said)
Private Tombs	**1**	**1**	**1**	_	**1**

B1 B2

Date and Location	VI pepi II Saqqara	VI pepi II El-Qasr wa-es-saiyad	EndVI Saqqara	EndVI Saqqara
Private Tombs	**3**	**1**	**6**	**2**
Royal Tombs	**Pepi II+ N.t**			

Group D: the word written with the sign  *which is an incorrectly substituted for the sign*  *:*

D1 D2

Date and Location	III–IV (Saqqara)	IV (Giza)	IV (Saqqara)	IV–V (Giza)	V
Private Tombs	-	-	-	-	**1**

D1 **D2**

Date and Location	V Giza	V Saqqara	VI Saqqara	VI Giza	VI Akhmim	VI Sedment
Private Tombs	-	**1**	-	-	-	-

The Determinatives

Group A: 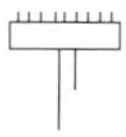

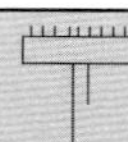

Date and Location	IV–V (Giza)	V (Giza)	V–VI (Dahshour)	VI (Saqqara)	VI Pepi II (Meir)
Private Tombs	3	6	1	9	3
		V (Saqqara)			
Royal Tombs		(W)			

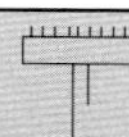

Date and Location	VI (Akhmim)	VI (Heliopolis)	VI (Giza)	VI (Sedment)	Late OK (Atamna)
Private Tombs	1	1	2	1	1
Royal Tombs					

Group B: 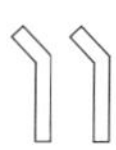

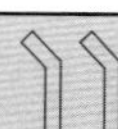

Date and Location	V (Giza)	V–VI (Saqqara)	V (Saqqara)	V–VI (Dahshour)	VI (Giza)
Private Tombs	6	5	6	1	5

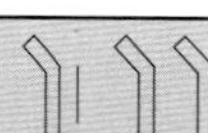

Date and Location	VI (Deshashah)	VI (Sedment)	VI or later (Saqqara)	VI (unkown)
Private tombs	1	2	2	1

Group C

Date and Location	IV (Saqqara)	V–VI (Saqqara)	VI (Akhmim)	End VI or later (Akhmim)
Private Tombs	1	1	4	3

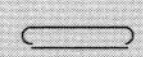		
Date and Location	**VIII (Nag'ed Deir)**	**OK (Akhmim)**
Private Tombs	1	1

Group D  and 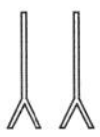

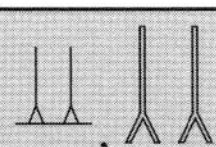				
Date and Location	**IV–V (Giza)**	**V (Saqqara)**	**V (Giza)**	**VI (Edfu)**
Private Tombs	1	1	1	1

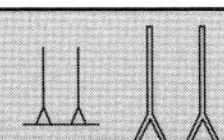				
Date and Location	**VI (Akhmim)**	**VI (El-Qasr wa-es-saiyad)**	**VI–VIII (Saqqara)**	**Old Kingdom (Sheik Said)**
Private Tombs	1	1	1	1

Group E 

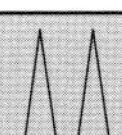				
Date and Location	**VI Saqqara**	**VI Giza**	**End VI Saqqara**	**VIII (Saqqara)**
Private Tombs	4	1	3	1

Group F 

Date and Location	**IV–V Giza**	**V Giza**	**V–VI Saqqara**	**V–VI (Deshasheh)**
Private Tombs	1	1	1	1
Royal Tombs			Pepi II+ N.t	

Date and Location	**VI (Saqqara)**	**End VI (Saqqara)**	**VI (Akhmim)**	**End VI (Saqqara)**
Private Tombs	2	3	2	2

Abbreviations

PM Porter, B. and Moss, R. L. B., *Topographical Bibliography of Ancient Egyptian Hieroglyphic Texts, Reliefs, and paintings, 7 Vols*, Oxford 1927–1952.

Wb Erman, A. and Grapow, H., *Wörterbuch der Ägyptischen Sprache.* Berlin 1982

Bibliography

Allen, J. P. (2005) *The Ancient Egyptian Pyramid Texts*, Society of Biblical Literature 23, Leiden, Brill.

Altenmüller, H. (1998) *Die Wanddarstellungen im Grab des Mehu in Saqqara*, Mainz, von Zabern.

Barta, W. (1963) *Die altägyptische Operliste, von der Frühzeit bis zur griechisch-römischen Epoche.* Münchner ägyptologische, Berlin, Hessling.

Borchardt, L. (1937) *Denkmäler des Alten Reiches (Außer den Statuen), Catalogue Général des Antiquités Égyptiennes du Musée du Caire Nos. 1295–1808*, Teil I, Berlin, Reichsdruckerei.

Borchardt, L. (1964) *Denkmäler des Alten Reiches (Außer den Statuen), Catalogue Général des Antiquités Égyptiennes du Musée du Caire Teil 2 Text und Tafeln zu Nr. 1542–1808*, Cairo, Reichsdruckerei.

Capart, J. (1906) *Chambre funéraire de la Sixième Dynastie, aux Musées Royaux du Cinquentenaire*, Brussells, Vromant.

Davies, N. de G. (1900) *The Mastaba of Ptahhetep and Akhethetep at Saqqareh,. Part I, the Chapel of Ptahhetep and the Hieroglyphs*, London, Egypt Exploration Society.

Davies, N. de G. (1901) *The Rock tomb of Sheik Said*, London, Egypt Exploration Society.

Davies, N. de Garis (1924) 'A peculiar form of New Kingdom Lamp', *Journal of Egyptian archaeology 10.*

Drenkhahn, R. (1989) *Ägyptische Reliefs im Kestner-Museum Hannover*, Hannover, Kestner-Museum.

Harpur, Y. (2006) *Egypt in miniature 1. The Chapel of Kagemini Scene Details*, Oxford Expedition to Egypt.

Hassan, S. (1932) *Excavations at Giza* (1929–1930), I, Cairo, Faculty of Arts of the Egyptian University.

Hassan, S. (1936) *Excavations at Giza* (1930–1931), II, Cairo, Faculty of Arts of the Egyptian University.

Hassan, S. (1943) *Excavations at Giza* (1932–1933), IV, Cairo, Faculty of Arts of the Egyptian University.

Hassan, S. (1948) *Excavations at Giza* (1934–1935), VI^{2}: *the offering-list in the Old Kingdom*, Cairo, Faculty of Arts of the Egyptian University.

Jequier, G. (1921) 'Les Frises d'Objets des sarcophages du Moyen Empire', *Mémoires Institut Français d'Archéologie Orientale du Caire* 47, Le Caire, Impr. de l'Inst. Français d'Archéologie Orientale.

Jequier, G. (1935) 'Tombeaux de particuliers de l'époque de Pepi II', *Annales du Service des Antiquités de l'Égypte 35.* Cairo, Impr. de L'Inst. Français.

Jequier, G. (1940) *Le monument funéraire de Pepi II, 3 vol, Tome III. Les approches du temple. Excav. Saqq.*, Cairo, Inst. Français d'Arch. Orientale.

Junker, H. (1929–1955) *Bericht über die von der Akademie der Wissenschaften in Wien auf gemeinsame Kosten mit Dr. Wilhelm Pelizaeus unternommenen Grabungen auf dem Friedhof des Alten Reiches bei den Pyramiden von Giza.* 12 Bde., Denkschriften / Akademie der Wissenschaften, Philosophisch-Historische 69–75, Wien/Leipzig.

Junker, H. (1934) *GIZA II, Die Mastabas der beginnenden V.Dynastie auf dem Westfriedhof*, Wien und Leipzig, Hölder-Pichler-Tempsky.

Junker, H. (1938) *GIZA III, Die Mastabas der vorgeschrittenen V. Dynastie auf dem Westfriedhof,* Wien und Leipzig, Hölder-Pichler-Tempsky.

Junker, H. (1940) *Giza VI. Die Mastabas des Nfr (Nefer), Kdfjj (Kedfi), Klhjf (Kahjef),* Wien und Leipzig. Holder-Pichler-Tempsky.

Junker, H. (1944) *Giza VII Der Ostabschnitt des Westfriedhofs*, Wien und Leipzig, Holder-Pichler-Tempsky.

Kanawati, N. (1980–1992) *The Rock tombs of El-Hawawish. The cemetery of Akhmim.* 10 Vols., Sydney/West, Macquarie Univ.

Kanawati, N. and Abder-Raziq, M. (1998*)* 'The Teti Cemetery at Saqqara. Vol. III. The Tombs of Neferseshenre and Seankhuiptah', *Australian Centre for Egyptology Reports 11*, Warminster, Australian Centre for Egyptology.

Lepsius, R. (1842–1845) *Denkmäler aus Ägypten und Äthiopien: nach Zeichnungen der von Seiner Majestät dem König von Pressen Friedrich Wilhelm IV. nach diesen Ländern gesendeten und in den Jahren 1842–1845 ausgeführten wissenschaftlichen Expedition/ auf Befehl Seiner Majestät hrsg. Und erläutert von C.R. Lepsius. Abt. 1*–6 in 12 Bd., Berlin.

Macadam, L. F. M. (1955) *The Temple of Kawa II. History and Archaeology of the site*, London, Oxford University excavations in Nubia.

Macramallah, R. (1935) *Le mastaba d'Idout. Fouilles a Saqqarah.* Le Caire, Impr. de l'Institut Français d'Archéologie Orientale.

Murray, M. A. (1937) *Saqqara Mastabas Part II*, London, Quaritch.

Petrie, H. F. and Murray, M.A. (1952) *Seven Memphite Tomb Chapels*, London, Quaritch.

Petrie, W. M. F. (1898) *Deshasheh*, London, Kegan Paul.

Porter, B. and Moss, R. L. *Topographical Bibliography of Ancient Egyptian Hieroglyphic Texts, Reliefs, and Paintings, V. Upper Egypt: sites (Deir Rifa to Aswan, Excluding Thebes and Temples of Abydos, Dendera, Esna, Edfu, Kom Ombo, and Philae)*. Oxford.

Porter, B. and Moss, R. L. (1974–1981) *Topographical Bibliography of Ancient Egyptian Hieroglyphic Texts, Reliefs, and Paintings, III. Memphis. 2 Bde,* Oxford, Griffith Institute, Ashmolean Museums.

Säve-Söderbergh, T. (1994) *The Old Kingdom Cemetery at Hamra Dom (El-Qasr Wa Es-Saiyad*), Stockholm, Royal Academy of Letters History and Antiquities.

Ziegler, C. (1993) *Le Mastaba d'Akhethetep. Une chapelle funéraire de l'Ancien Empire*, Paris, Peeters.